Let me tell you about the very rich.
They are different from you and me.
F. Scott Fitzgerald

BOOKS BY TROY TAYLOR

DEAD MEN SO TELL TALES SERIES
Dead Men Do Tell Tales (2008)
Bloody Chicago (2006)
Bloody Illinois (2008)
Bloody Hollywood (2008)
Without a Trace (2009)
Blood, Guns & Valentines (2010)

HAUNTED ILLINOIS BOOKS
Haunted Illinois (1999 / 2001 / 2004)
Haunted Decatur (1995 / 2009)
More Haunted Decatur (1996)
Ghosts of Millikin (1996 / 2001)
Where the Dead Walk (1997 / 2002)
Dark Harvest (1997)
Haunted Decatur Revisited (2000)
Flickering Images (2001)
Haunted Decatur: 13th Anniversary (2006)
Haunted Alton (2000 / 2003 / 2008)
Haunted Chicago (2003)
The Haunted President (2005 / 2009)
Mysterious Illinois (2005)
Resurrection Mary (2007)
The Possessed (2007)
Weird Chicago (2008)

HAUNTED FIELD GUIDE BOOKS
The Ghost Hunters Guidebook
(1997/ 1999 / 2001/ 2004 / 2007 / 2010)
Confessions of a Ghost Hunter (2002)
Field Guide to Haunted Graveyards (2003)
Ghosts on Film (2005)
So, There I Was (with Len Adams) (2006)
Talking with the Dead (with Rob & Anne
Wlodarski) (2009)

HISTORY & HAUNTINGS SERIES
The Haunting of America (2001 / 2010)
Into the Shadows (2002)
Down in the Darkness (2003)
Out Past the Campfire Light (2004)
Ghosts by Gaslight (2007)

OTHER GHOSTLY TITLES
Spirits of the Civil War (1999)
Season of the Witch (1999/ 2002)
Haunted New Orleans (2000)
Beyond the Grave (2001)
No Rest for the Wicked (2001)
Haunted St. Louis (2002)
The Devil Came to St. Louis (2006)
Houdini: Among the Spirits (2009)
And Hell Followed With It (with Rene Kruse) (2010)

WHITECHAPEL OCCULT LIBRARY
Sex & the Supernatural (2009)

STERLING PUBLICATIONS
Weird U.S. (Co-Author) (2004)
Weird Illinois (2005)
Weird Virginia (Co-Author) (2007)
Weird Indiana (Co-Author) (2008)

BARNES & NOBLE PRESS TITLES
Haunting of America (2006)
Spirits of the Civil War (2007)
Into the Shadows (2007)

HISTORY PRESS TITLES
Wicked Washington (2007)
Murder & Mayhem on Chicago's North Side (2009)
Murder & Mayhem on Chicago's South Side (2009)
Murder & Mayhem on Chicago's West Side (2009)
Murder & Mayhem in Downtown Chicago (2009)
Murder & Mayhem in the Chicago Vice Districts (2009)
Wicked New Orleans (2010)
Haunted New Orleans (2010)
Wicked Northern Illinois (2010)
Wicked Decatur (2011)

STACKPOLE BOOKS TITLES
Haunted Illinois (2008)
True Crime Illinois (2009)
Big Book of Illinois Ghost Stories (2009)
Illinois Monsters (2011)

THE TRUE STORY OF THE RISE & FALL OF THE LEMP EMPIRE

SUICIDE & SPIRITS
BY TROY TAYLOR

- A Whitechapel Press Publication from Dark Haven Entertainment -

This book could not have been written without the kind assistance of
Cheryl Sochotsky and that of Andrew Paulsen and other descendants of
the Lemp Family. Not only has it been an honor to try and set the record
straight about the family, but it's been a pleasure to become your friend,
as well. Thanks for everything!

Original Cover Artwork Designed by

©Copyright 2011 by Michael Schwab & Troy Taylor

Visit M & S Graphics at http://www.manyhorses.com/msgraphics.htm

This Book is Published By:

Whitechapel Press
A Division of Dark Haven Entertainment, Inc.
Chicago, Illinois / 1-888-GHOSTLY
Visit us on the internet at http://www.americanhauntings.org

First Printing -- February 2011
ISBN: 1-892523-73-6

Printed in the United States of America

INTRODUCTION

Along a quiet street on the south side of St. Louis stands a house with a long history in the city. It looks out over a busy highway, the muffled roar of traffic seeming out of place among the old homes and buildings where once was heard the hollow clop of horses' hooves and the rattle of carriage wheels.

Nearby, a cluster of massive red brick structures looms over the neighborhood. The crumbling factory has seen several uses over the years, each further removed from its original incarnation. The complex of buildings once held bustling loading docks, storage areas, offices, and huge round towers filled with thousands of bushels of grain, all designed for the production of beer. Hidden throughout the old brewery are mysterious symbols and decorative shields that once bore the name of the family whose enormous wealth went into constructing these brick walls and stone towers. Most of the signage and symbols have been worn away over the years, destroyed by time and weather. Others have been painted over and cut away, as if someone wanted to forget what the buildings were once used for. However, there is one sign, standing higher than anything else, which cannot be erased; it can be seen from anywhere in the surrounding city. Painted in bold white on the dark red bricks at the highest point of the brewery, it has only four letters but they speak volumes about the history and lore of St. Louis – simply and enigmatically spelling out "Lemp."

The Lemp Brewing Company, and the family that founded it, came to prominence in the middle 1800s as one of the premier brewers of St. Louis. For years, they were a nationally known beer-maker, a fierce rival to Anheuser-Busch and the first brewers of lager beer in the region. Today, the Lemps are largely forgotten, remembered more for the grand and mysterious house in which they once lived than for the beer they brewed.

The Lemp Mansion, as the house is commonly known, is a monument and memorial to decadence, wealth, tragedy and death. Perhaps for this reason, there is a sadness that hangs over the place and an eerie feeling that has remained from its days of horror, disrepair and abandonment. It has since been restored as a restaurant and inn, and yet the sense of sorrow seems to remain. By day, it is a thriving restaurant, filled with people and activity, but at night, after everyone is gone and the doors have been locked tight, something walks the halls of the Lemp Mansion.

Are there ghosts here? Are they the restless spirits of the Lemp family, unable to find rest? Quite possibly, for this unusual clan was as haunted as their house is purported to be. They were once one of the leading families in St. Louis but all that would change and their eccentricities would eventually lead to their ruin.

Come along with me on a journey back in time to the opulent days of St. Louis in the Gilded Age and to the lavish times before Prohibition brought ruin to many of the city's beer barons. Discover the true story of the Lemp family and its rise to power, wealth and extravagance. It's a story that has become legend over the years but one that few people truly know. The story of the Lemp family and their enduring mansion has inspired books, ghost stories and numerous television shows over the years, making them perhaps one of the most documented haunted families in American history. Unfortunately, the story has become a confusing and convoluted mess in the course of the last few decades. There are so many legends, tales, myths, misconceptions and outright lies about the Lemps that it has become hard to separate truth from fiction.

This led me to write the book that you hold in your hands.

Inspired by the countless legends that have been told and re-told, the bad television shows and the phony stories concocted by so-called psychics, I decided to try and present a true and authentic history of the Lemp family. I was assisted in my plan for the book by some of the family's last surviving members and by a collection of never-before-seen photographs, relics and artifacts – many of which you will see in these pages. I have been fascinated (some might say obsessed) with the Lemps for more than two decades and have written about them in several of my previous books. It has not been until now, however, that I can finally relate the story that I have always wanted to tell.

The history of the Lemp family is a true American tragedy, one of triumph over opposition, hard work, perseverance, genius and madness, eccentricity and passion, horror, death and suicide. It was played out against the backdrop of America's changing landscape in the late 1800s and early 1900s. It is also the story of the beer industry in St. Louis, the German immigrant experience, and a riveting look at the lives and deaths of those for whom money truly was no object.

In his 1926 short story *The Rich Boy,* F. Scott Fitzgerald wrote, "Let me tell you about the very rich. They are different from you and me." You will understand exactly what he meant by that as the story of the Lemp family unfolds.

Troy Taylor
Winter 2010-11

1. "Beer Made St. Louis"

A History of Brewing in the City

In 1929, Gerald Holland wrote in the *American Mercury* magazine, "whatever odium may be attached to beer in other parts of the Republic, its status in St. Louis is as firmly grounded as James Eads' span across the Mississippi... beer made St. Louis."

And he was right. There has not been a time in St. Louis' history as a frontier station, fur-trading outpost, hard-living river town and gateway to the West that there has not been beer in the city. Dating back to 1809, when a man named John Coons set up a primitive brewery on the riverfront, and continuing today, St. Louis is a city where beer is king. Over two hundred breweries have existed in and around St. Louis during the past two centuries. Many were small, long-forgotten operations that lasted only a few years while others grew to be national, and international, companies that are still in existence today.

The first known brewery in North America was established in 1612 by Dutch settlers in what is now Manhattan. St. Louis would not see its first beer until many decades later. In the 1700s, the location that would grow into St. Louis was the far western frontier. Located on the western bank of the Mississippi River, it was land that did not yet belong to the United States. It was still a French territory in those days and it soon became a center for the fur trade in the West. Pierre Lacléde, who went on to become a St. Louis pioneer and business leader, established a trading post along the river in 1764. His men built a collection of log cabins and a warehouse for furs, which were traded from the Native Americans. A village grew up around the trading post, three blocks wide and a mile long, and by 1770, it was home to more than five hundred hearty settlers. By 1800, the population had doubled.

In 1803, the Louisiana Purchase transferred ownership of the region from France to the United States, a development that would bring about a period of tremendous growth for the city. It would gain national

attention when Thomas Jefferson tasked Meriwether Lewis, William Clark and their Corps of Discovery to journey from St. Louis into the uncharted West.

Six years later, in 1809, St. Louis was officially incorporated as a town, with boundaries at Franklin, Poplar and Seventh streets. This was also the year when brewing began in the city.

As in most American cities, the origins of brewing in St. Louis were humble, usually beginning with a few small, two- or three-man operations that produced a dozen or so barrels of beer a year that were sold in local taverns. This was the general state of things until the latter part of the 1830s, when a great influx of German settlers began moving into the region. The arrival of the Germans, among them a man named Adam Lemp, changed everything.

The first real brewer in St. Louis was apparently a man named John Coons, who besides making beer also worked as a carpenter and joiner. He came to the city in 1786 and later moved into St. Louis County. His brewery only operated for about two years, but it became known as the first in the city. Coons' beer was available for sale at his brewery and at the local printing office.

The second official brewery, located on the north side of St. Louis, was opened by Jacques Marcellin de St. Vrain and Victor Habb in 1810. The brewery was a small one, offering barrels of beer for $10 each. St. Vrain, a wealthy farmer and landowner, put up the money for the operation while Habb, a brewer by trade, did all the labor. Ahead of their time, they launched an advertising campaign in the local newspaper that started they were taking orders for their brand of table beer. Unfortunately, there was little interest in their dark, bitter-tasting ale and the brewery only lasted for a short time. The buildings burned to the ground in 1812. After that, Habb found employment in the other breweries that followed.

In 1815, Joseph Phillipson started the crude St. Louis Brewery on Main Street at the north end of town. He hired Victor Habb as his brewer. Habb cooled the beer "in a dug-out canoe, which lay in the north side of the building," according to J. Thomas Scharf's 1883 *History of Saint Louis City and County.* Despite these primitive conditions, the brewery produced enough beer to sell locally and to ship to Ste. Genevieve, Missouri, where Phillipson's brother sold it in his store. By 1816, St. Louis had grown to more than three thousand inhabitants. Habb took out a newspaper advertisement stating that he "would be operating a cart through the streets of St. Louis daily to supply the residents with beer and vinegar by retail."

Five years later, Phillipson was still the only brewer in St. Louis but he now had to deal with competition from imported beers, which were beginning to arrive in the city by way of steamboats on the Mississippi River. The brewery struggled and was partially damaged by fire in 1822. Phillipson was forced to sell out to local businessman John Mullanphy, who leased the property to Simon Phillipson, Joseph's brother. The Phillipsons retired from the beer business in 1824. Mullanphy continued operating the brewery, with Matthew Murphy as his brewer, until 1829, when fire destroyed the operation for good.

In late 1826, James C. Lynch began supplying the city with ale and porter at seventy-five cents per dozen bottles and $5.50 a barrel. The operation was a huge success and Lynch continued expanding every year. By 1831, he had more than eight hundred barrels of beer on hand and was starting to do his own bottling. Unfortunately, he was hit with massive debt in 1835 and was forced to sell his brewing facilities to satisfy his creditors.

By 1830, the population of St. Louis had swelled to more than six thousand and the following year, Samuel Wainwright, an immigrant from Yorkshire, England, started the Fulton Brewery. His products were traditional types of English ale. He was followed by the Finney brothers, James and William, who had been in St. Louis since 1818. They operated a grocery business and specialized in importing beer from eastern breweries. In 1834, they started the City Brewery on Cherry Street, remaining in business until 1848.

By the middle 1830s, the first wave of German immigrants began arriving in St. Louis. Soon, breweries and beer gardens began to sprout up all over town, none of them suffering from lack of patronage. New breweries opened as the city's longtime residents began to join the newcomers in their appreciation for beer. One of the new operations belonged to Ezra English, who opened the Saint Louis Brewery on the south side. It operated for fifty years and became one of the first to utilize the natural caves underneath the city for storing beer. Known as English Cave at what is now Benton Park, the subterranean beer garden was a place of ghostly legend, said to carry a curse on those who occupied it. Later on, we'll take a closer look at the mysterious caverns beneath St. Louis and at the unlucky Ezra English and the others who followed in his path, including the ill-fated Lemp family.

The first real German lager beer was produced in St. Louis by Johann Adam Lemp, likely around 1840.

St. Louis in the 1840s, the period of greatest German immigration to the city, and the beginning of beer and brewing heyday in St. Louis.

Lager beer was unlike any other beverage being produced in the city at the time. It was a crisp, clean, sparkling beer that not only tasted better than the bitter, thick ales that were common at the time but it also did not have to be consumed as quickly before it went bad. St. Louis was well suited to this type of beer making, thanks to the natural caves beneath the city. Lager beer could be brewed during the winter months and stored in caves and cellars during the summer drinking season. With no artificial refrigeration at the time, the beer was cooled naturally by the caves' low temperatures, aided by blocks of ice that were cut from the frozen Mississippi River in the winter, hauled to the caves, and packed in straw. By introducing lager beer to the city, Lemp helped to start a revolution in the brewing industry and he is rightly considered the father of modern brewing in St. Louis.

By 1840, the city's population had grown to more than sixteen thousand people, among them scores of newly arrived German immigrants. As the city continued to expand, many more breweries opened in response to the increasing demand for beer. While some of the operations were small, others served as the start of national businesses. But in spite of the multitude of new breweries springing up, it was almost impossible for them to keep up with demand. Lemp began brewing his beer in a twelve-barrel kettle. The resulting brew was met with such acclaim by the local populace that he soon had to build several new buildings to allow for a greatly increased output.

Around 1842, Michael Kuntz began making beer in the area around Eighth and Carr streets. The Lafayette Brewery, as it was called, later moved to Cass Street where it was operated by William Nolker, Theodore Brinckwith and Franz Griesedieck. The latter name would become an important one in St. Louis beer history.

In 1843, Julius Winkelmeyer and Frederick Stifel began the Union Brewery on South Second Street. Four years later, they moved to a new facility on Market Street, using storage caves that extended under the site of what is now the main U.S. Post Office at 1720 Market Street. Unfortunately, both Stifel and his wife died in the cholera epidemic of 1849. Winkelmeyer carried on with the business, eventually developing

Julius Winkelmeyer

it into one of the largest breweries in the U.S.

Joseph Uhrig bought a plot of land on Market Street in 1846 and one year later opened the Camp Springs Brewery, overlooking Chouteau's Pond. The brewery's storage caves were a short distance away, beneath what is now the corner of Jefferson and Washington avenues. A short distance west of the city limits, the caves were a popular gathering place for locals, offering music, theatrical performances and a picnic area. It finally closed in 1891 to make way for the construction of Union Station. The St. Louis Coliseum was built on the site of the brewery caves in the early 1900s.

Samuel Wainwright, who had joined his brother Ellis in the St. Louis brewing industry, took control of the Fulton Brewery after Ellis' death in 1849. In 1857, he purchased half of the former George Busch brewery, which was located on Gratiot Street. In the late 1850s, he and his partner, Charles Fritz, abandoned the production of ale and began brewing lager beer. When Samuel Wainwright died in 1874, his son, also named Ellis, took over as the company's president. Ellis Wainwright served as president of the United States Brewers' Association in 1891 and 1892.

By 1850, St. Louis was home to seventeen operating breweries, which produced about sixty thousand barrels of beer every year. The city's population had now reached more than seventy-seven thousand souls, with German immigrants comprising at least twenty-two thousand of them. It was around this time, and through the middle 1850s, that the American outlook on beer changed dramatically. It was a change that would be felt across the country and especially in St. Louis.

Americans had always had a strange relationship with alcohol production and consumption. The first colonists who carried beer to North America soon abandoned it, but not for religious reasons as one might expect. Even the most pious among them, including the Puritan minister Increase Mather, considered alcohol to be a benign pleasure, as long as drunkenness did not ensue. Mather called it "...a good creature of God, and to be received with thankfulness, but the abuse of drink is from Satan; the wine is from God but the Drunkard is from the Devil." The practical Puritans treated drink as a necessary component of daily life, as long as it was taken in moderation and did not interfere with worship and hard work. While there was no religious objection to moderate imbibing, beer was given up because of the difficulty involved in producing it. Trees had to be cut and burned to clear rocky land that might produce only a meager crop of corn and wheat. Given the amount of labor needed to produce enough food to feed a family, only a fool would waste his time trying to grow hops and barley to make beer. Southern settlers could grow almost anything in their warm and humid climate, but the hot weather quickly turned ale to swill, making beer production impractical. It was easier to plant apple and pear trees, which needed little attention and produced plenty of fruit for fermenting into cider and brandy.

Rum was the colonials' most popular drink. In the late 1600s, Caribbean plantation owners flooded the colonies with molasses and rum, made from waste products of the sugar cane mills. The colonists developed a passion for rum's sweet taste. They drank it straight or mixed with fruit juice or milk, served hot or cold and consumed morning noon and night.

The age of rum came to an end with the start of the American Revolution, when the price of molasses soared. Americans quickly adapted and when the war ended, they moved west over the mountains and began buying up cheap land whose thick soil produced more grain than a family could use. Farmers built crude stills and converted their grain surplus to hard liquor. Soon, whiskey became the alcoholic beverage of choice. Like rum, whiskey warmed the body and eased the mind. Every occasion, from communal barn raisings to family meals, births, funerals and weddings was accompanied by copious amounts of whiskey. Captain Frederick Marryat, an English naval officer, novelist and a contemporary of Charles Dickens, wrote upon visiting America, "They say the English can settle nothing without a meal. I am sure the Americans can fix nothing without a drink. If you meet, you drink; if you part, you drink; if you make an acquaintance you drink. They quarrel in their drink, and they make it up with a drink."

By the early 1800s, more than fourteen thousand distillers were producing some twenty-five million gallons of whiskey every year – about seven or eight gallons for every adult in the country. There were only two hundred or so breweries in the country, all producing English-style ale.

But starting in the 1820s and 1830s, the passion for drink was met with stern opposition from those whose passions ran strongly against it. Hordes of well-meaning crusaders began to try and reform the American character. It was not just alcohol that they sought to ban; they railed against every conceivable national vice, from dueling to spitting in public, masturbation and even some architecture styles. Others campaigned for healthy exercise, well-chewed food (promoted by Horace Fletcher and called "Fletcherizing," each bite of food was supposed to be chewed up to one hundred

The temperance movement -- largely made up of women -- marched on taverns and saloons around the country, using slogans, campaigns and advertising to call attention to the evils of liquor.

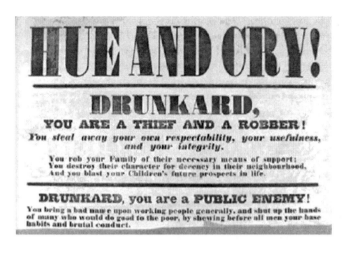

times), cold baths, abolition of slavery, free education, and voting rights for women.

The main thrust of the reform movement, though, was temperance. Not even the reformers who brought about Prohibition could match the passion with which ordinary people waged war on whiskey in the early 1800s. They regarded it as the root of the nation's ills. The temperance campaign began in the 1820s as an army of anti-liquor zealots preached, prayed and sang about the evils of whiskey and rum. They were desperate to convert their fellow Americans to the ways of sobriety and clean living. Alcohol, they claimed, wasted the mind and body, ruined marriages, destroyed families and stripped a man of any ambition. It spawned murder, theft, prostitution and gambling and deprived a poor man's family of food. If allowed to go unchecked, alcohol would ruin the country. By eliminating drink, they believed, they could vanquish all of America's ills.

The temperance movement gained many converts. Between 1820 and 1850, millions of Americans pledged to abstain from drink and that first generation of anti-drink crusaders made the manufacture, sale and consumption of alcohol so disreputable that the stain had never gone away. Respectable people abstained and those who trafficked in alcohol, whether making it, selling it or drinking it, were of questionable character.

Not surprisingly, the embrace of alcohol by Irish and German immigrants clashed with this new American disdain for drink and those who made it. Neal Dow, the mayor of Portland, Maine, was widely quoted as saying that the only people who drank excessively were "working people" like the Irish. Take away alcohol, he said, and the poor would have more money to spend on their basic needs and in the process become good citizens. Dow's words inspired his state's legislators to pass the nation's first Prohibition act. The Maine Law, as it was called, banned the sale, manufacture and consumption of alcohol. The new law in Maine thrilled the temperance movement and terrified brewers and distillers. Between 1850 and 1855, legislators in two territories and eleven of the thirty-one states followed Maine's lead.

But everywhere that Prohibition came into effect, violence erupted as mobs challenged the alcohol bans. In Chicago, riots broke out when temperance candidates filled city hall and a new mayor ordered a ban on Sunday drinking. Designed more as a bias against German immigrants than as a statement against alcohol, Chicago closed the city's "foreign-owned" beer gardens but turned a blind eye to "American" taverns that stayed open in violation of the law. When violators, mostly German, went on trial, mobs stormed the courthouse and fought the police in the streets. The riot ended after shots were fired on both sides, leaving one man killed and scores of others injured.

A few weeks later, violence erupted in Cincinnati on Election Day as a mob attacked German voting stations and destroyed more than one thousand ballots. Germans barricaded the bridge leading to their neighborhood, but their opponents, armed with muskets and a cannon, broke through their defenses. The riots went on for three days, leaving many dead and wounded on both sides. During what came to be known as the August 1855 "Bloody Monday" riots in Louisville, local troublemakers, as well as German and Irish immigrants, roamed the streets with guns and knives, attacking and taking shots at one another. Nineteen men died during the battles over liquor. Violence even broke out in Portland, Maine, where Mayor

Dow claimed Prohibition had eradicated all crime. Rumors spread that Dow had purchased liquor and sold it to the state for medicinal purposes. A mob gathered outside the Portland liquor agency and Dow ordered the local militia to the scene. When the rioters broke into the building, Dow ordered the militia to fire on them, killing one person and wounding seven others.

Incidents like this occurred all over the country, as Prohibition laws unexpectedly created the kind of chaos and disorder they had been designed to eliminate. This turn of events troubled many Americans and by the middle 1850s, many of those who once supported the anti-alcohol movement began to see it as being too radical to really solve the country's drinking problems. But it was not long before America had more important things to worry about – namely issues of slavery and what to do about it. With clashes between abolitionist groups and pro-slavery mobs now stealing the headlines from the temperance movement, the Prohibition crusade collapsed.

While the battle over drink was short-lived, it created an unintended consequence that shaped the next fifty years of the brewing industry. On one hand, the anti-drink zealots were forced to admit that Prohibition created more problems that it solved but on the other hand, it became the sincere belief of many Americans that liquor posed a genuine threat to America's future. The question was how to create a balance between the two?

The answer, it seemed, was simple and could be found with the very people and beverage that had once been accused of degrading America's moral fiber – Germans and their beer. Weary of the temperance movement and the conflict that had been caused because of it, native-born Americans began to embrace lager and the German model of social drinking that allowed them to make a compromise between abstinence and Prohibition.

The violence that had accompanied the short-lived attempt at Prohibition had drawn attention to the German-American lifestyle, to the beer gardens that welcomed entire families at convivial gatherings, and to beer itself. Attempts to demonize the Germans failed when it became apparent that the vast majority of German-Americans worked hard, lived respectably and drank in moderation. They had embraced the American way of life and had prospered while doing so. They built churches, kept orderly homes and many owned their own businesses, all of this in spite of the fact that they drank beer every day.

The *St. Louis Republican* newspaper hammered the point home. Between March and September 1854, it was estimated that St. Louis residents had consumed nearly eighteen million glasses of beer. In spite of this, Germans "contributed the smallest ratio to the sick list and the smallest number of convicts or criminals." It was added, "Germans prosper in health, worldly goods and happiness." Temperance adherents insisted that alcohol led to nothing but crime, vice and decay and yet the Germans were living proof that it was possible to drink and still be respectable citizens.

As the public image of beer began to change, it even made an impression in legal circles. In February 1858, a Brooklyn brewer and beer garden owner named George Staats went on trial on charges of violating the city's Sunday drinking laws. Staats' lawyer came up with a novel defense, claiming that his client was not guilty because lager beer was not intoxicating.

Scientific witnesses took the stand to explain that, with a three-percent alcohol content, lager beer could only make a man drunk if it was consumed in extraordinary quantities. A *New York Times* reporter explained, "If it takes a pail-full of beer to make a person drunk, and the same person could get drunk on an eighth the quantity of rum, then lager is not an intoxicating drink, but may be a wholesome beverage." Many people agreed and witness after witness took the stand to testify to drinking enormous quantities of beer – twenty to ninety pints per day – with no ill effects. The jury debated the case for three hours and returned to declare both Staats and lager beer to be not guilty.

Three months later, an almost identical case came to trial in Manhattan. Physicians took the stand to defend George Maurer against a charge of selling intoxicating liquor on Sunday. One of the doctors

A German-American beer garden of the 1850s

analyzed lager from three different New York breweries and concluded that, when consumed in moderate quantities, lager was not an intoxicating drink. Another stated that he had seen men consume as many as sixty glasses of beer with no evidence of intoxication – a claim that seemed hard to believe. As a testament to its veracity, though, a portly German man took the stand and volunteered that he drank as many as one hundred glasses of beer each day and never got drunk. In fact, he added, in case the jurors doubted his word, he'd finished off twenty-two glasses before coming to court that morning. The jury was unable to reach a verdict and the case was dismissed.

A new taste for German beer was sweeping the country. *Harper's Weekly* declared, "Good lager beer is pronounced by the [scientific] faculty to be a mild tonic, calculated, on the average, to be rather beneficial than injurious to the system."

Americans were rendering their own verdicts on the case for beer – finding it both good and safe. By the late 1850s, beer saloons and beer gardens were lining the streets of American cities both large and small. Men and women danced to German bands, listened to German choral groups, enjoyed opera, dramas and comedians and relaxed with refreshing glasses of fresh lager. The popularity of lager beer made it something that was no longer strictly for German-Americans; it was now being consumed by everyone.

As the beer began to flow, breweries opened everywhere, nearly all of them owned by Germans who hoped that lager would pave their way to wealth. In many cases, it did, and money began to be made in staggering amounts, creating empires for a lucky few.

The latter half of the 1850s and the first half of the 1860s were the start of a boom time for St. Louis brewers. The general acceptance and popularity of lager created a need for more breweries and they began opening across the city.

One of the first major breweries of the 1850s was the Arsenal Brewery, which was started by Guido and Aldelbert Steinkauler and was later purchased by Louis Obert. Located on the corner of Twelfth and Lynch streets, it operated as an independent brewery until Prohibition and opened again as the law was repealed in 1933.

Also in the early 1850s, William Stumpf began making beer at a brewery that would operate under many names over the years, including Stumpf's, Thayer Brewing Company, Anton Griesedieck, Miller Brothers Brewing Company, Consumers Brewing Company, Griesedieck Brothers and the Falstaff Brewing Corporation. The latter incarnations of this brewery played a key role in the story of the Lemp Brewery after Prohibition.

In 1852, George Schneider started a small brewery on the south side of St. Louis, located on the east side of what is now South Broadway. Four years later, he moved to a new location on the west side of

Eighth Street and gave the place a new name, the Bavarian Brewery. In 1857, a severe economic depression hit the country and Schneider, overextended and deep in debt, was unable to secure enough credit to continue his operations. Forced to sell, the brewery was purchased later that year by Phillip Hammer, a local cooper or barrel-maker. Within a week, Hammer entered into a partnership with his brother, Carl, and they changed the name of the company to C. and P. Hammer Company. When a third brother, Adam, joined the company, the brothers formed a partnership with Dominic Urban. The new firm, Hammer & Urban, immediately began expanding the Bavarian Brewery, starting with the construction of a new brick brewhouse.

An advertisement for the Bavarian Brewery, after it was taken over by Eberhard Anheuser. The company's financial problems would lead to the building of a brewing empire.

By 1860, production had increased to 3,200 barrels a year, ranking Hammer & Urban at twenty-ninth among the city's forty breweries. In spite of this, the company was in dire financial straits. The brewery's production capacity far exceeded the demand for its product and the partners were forced into bankruptcy. During the legal proceedings that followed, two of the brewery's creditors took over its operations. E. Anheuser and Company, the new operator, was made up of a partnership between Eberhard Anheuser, a successful candle and soap maker, and William D'Oench, a wholesale medicine supplier. D'Oench became a silent partner in the company and Anheuser assumed control over all of the brewery's operations.

Disaster struck for local beer drinkers in 1854 at the same time that lager's popularity was starting to soar nationwide. It became known as "the year the beer ran out." Between the months of May and September, drinkers in St. Louis managed to literally tap out all of the lager that had been produced in the city. The reasons for the drought were cited as an unusually hot summer, a poor barley crop from the previous year and a dramatic increase in the number of German immigrants arriving in the city. Newspapers widely reported that no beer would be available until late in October, much to the dismay of many St. Louisians.

In response to the shortage, and the increased demand for beer from those who had recently discovered the refreshing beverage, more breweries opened. When Anton Jaeger began building the Gambrinus Brewery on Victor Street, he ran into opposition from the neighborhood until he agreed to build the brewhouse in the Gothic style. That way, if the brewery was not successful, the building could be turned into a church. Incidentally, the company did fail, but it was never turned into a church. Instead, it was taken over by the Anthony & Kuhn Brewing Company.

(Left) The Green Tree Brewery and wagon shed.

(Above) An old label for one of the company's early beers.

In 1855, one of the most successful breweries in the city's history opened on Second Street. The Green Tree Brewery was started by Joseph Schnaider, a German immigrant who had mastered the brewer's art after a three-year apprenticeship at a large brewery near Strasburg. On arriving in St. Louis, he became the foreman of the Philadelphia Brewery and two years later, he opened the Green Tree Brewery. He and his partner, Max Feurebacher, remained at the same location for seven years before Schnaider sold out and opened a new brewery on Chouteau Avenue in the Soulard neighborhood. The new establishment included a beer garden and was known for its good food, fine music and pleasant family atmosphere. After the Civil War, Schnaider formed a light opera company to provide entertainment at the beer garden and compete with the success of the St. Louis Browns. The ball team was luring away many of his customers. The St. Louis Grand Orchestra and the Musical Union Symphony also played at Schnaider's beer garden, as did other popular bands, and it is believed that the site was the basis for the founding of the St. Louis Symphony Orchestra. Schnaider was forty-nine when he died in 1881 and his company collapsed without him. The Chouteau Avenue Brewery buildings and lagering cellars were not destroyed until 1960.

War Comes to St. Louis

The beginning of the Civil War brought momentous changes to St. Louis, including its beer brewing industry. In 1821, Missouri had been admitted to the Union as a state, but only on the condition that it was classified as a "slave state," meaning that it was permissible for slaves to be owned and kept within its borders. This was a result of Henry Clay's "Missouri Compromise," which maintained the balance between free and slave states.

But Missouri was never a typical slave state. In 1860, only three slave states had fewer slaves than Missouri and of those, only Delaware had a smaller percentage of slaves in its total population. Slave ownership was uncommon in Missouri as only one in eight families owned slaves and of those, most owned fewer than five. And if slavery was uncommon in the state of Missouri, it was downright rare in St. Louis. There was little for slaves to do in the city, aside from domestic work, and since St. Louis was home to a huge population of German immigrants, who abhorred slavery as a threat to individual rights, the city became a haven for the state's free blacks.

Because of the city's growth in the decade before the Civil War, there was almost always work to be found, further negating the need for slavery. The commercial and industrial markets both grew dramatically in this period, especially after the arrival of the railroad in 1853. The riverboat era was still in its heyday and thanks to this, St. Louis was really the only urban area in Missouri that was worthy of being called a city. This tended to put the city at odds with the rest of the state, which was primarily made up of farmers and small merchants who owned the vast majority of slaves.

St. Louis also differed from the rest of the state politically. In November 1860, white male Missourians went to the polls to vote for a successor to President James Buchanan. Four candidates appeared on the ballots. Stephen A. Douglas, the famous Democrat from Illinois, received nearly thirty-six percent of Missouri's votes. John Bell, who ran on the Constitutional ticket, was a close second, drawing thirty-five percent of the vote. Another candidate, John C. Breckenridge, was the "Southern Rights" Democrat on the ticket, garnering about nineteen percent of the vote. Coming in last, with ten percent of the votes cast, was Abraham Lincoln, the candidate from the young Republican Party.

But again, things were much different in St. Louis. St. Louis County became only one of two counties in the entire state in which Abraham Lincoln carried the election. Breckenridge, the "slavery candidate," received slightly over two percent of the vote. In all of the slave states combined, Lincoln only received 27,000 votes, but more than 17,000 of these came from the German-Americans of Missouri and more than half of those came from St. Louis.

A few months before the national election, Missourians had elected Claiborne Fox Jackson, from the planter class of central Missouri, as governor. While Jackson claimed to be a "Douglas Democrat," which put him more on the moderate side, his views were more in line with "slavery candidate" Breckenridge. Jackson would soon find himself at odds with the political force in St. Louis, which was beginning to challenge the dominance that the slave-holding elite of Central Missouri had long held over politics in the state. A civil war was coming to America and the state of Missouri was ready to erupt.

Tensions ran high in St. Louis as pro-Union city officials worked to stave off attempts by pro-Confederate state officials to take control of the city and the valuable cache of arms and ammunition at the St. Louis Arsenal. President Lincoln understood that if St. Louis fell to the Confederacy, the Union army would lose control of the Mississippi River, which would be a valuable asset during the war. St. Louis had to be held and that meant keeping a firm grip on the city's wharves, warehouses and rail connections to the eastern United States.

Over the next few months, Union troops struggled to maintain order in a place that was divided by loyalty to opposite sides in the growing conflict. Eventually, federal troops under

Military encampment in St. Louis during the Civil War

the command of Captain Nathaniel Lyon seized the United States Arsenal, a hulking structure filled with weapons and gunpowder, to keep it from falling into Confederate hands. The arsenal was only two blocks away from Eberhard Anheuser's Bavarian Brewery.

The war turned out to be a boom time for the city's beer-makers. St. Louis was filled with troops traveling to and from enemy territory, bringing with them a multitude of prisoners, wounded men, refugees, escaped and freed slaves, camp followers, merchants and assorted others connected to the war. Military clerks went from warehouses to stores, from butchers to bakers, looking for supplies. Bricklayers, blacksmiths, carpenters and stable hands arrived, looking for and finding work. Soldiers guarded the docks, railroads, warehouses and the arsenal, as well as the line of encampments located on the city's western edge.

And every single one of these new arrivals needed beer.

A physician with the army wrote, "I have never seen a city where there is as much drinking of liquor as here. Everybody – almost – drinks. Beer shops and gardens are numerous." The doctor, who was not an admirer of drink, blamed the wet condition of St. Louis on the Germans.

But his disdain for Germans and their beer was not shared by the multitudes. The Civil War in St. Louis became a conflict fought with beer. Military commanders banned all intoxicants – except lager beer – from the camps and it soon became the drink of choice. Supply clerks contracted with brewers to provide the troops with lager, which traveled better and stayed fresh longer than ale. Hundreds of thousands of soldiers forged friendships over tin cups of St. Louis lager, carrying their love for the brew home with them after the war.

Lager even received the approval of the United States Sanitary Commission, a civilian organization that was established to monitor the health of the troops. A USSC doctor who studied camp diets reported that lager drinkers suffered less from diarrhea than those who did not drink beer. Lager beer, he wrote, "regulates the bowels, prevents constipation, and becomes in this way a valuable substitute for vegetables" (a food group in short supply for men on the battlefield). He added that he encouraged all of the troops to drink lager.

This was good news for America's brewers, another one thousand of whom set up operations during the war. But no matter how long they had been in business, all of them paid the price for their success. In the summer of 1862, the U.S. Congress, looking for a way to raise money for the war, began taxing "luxury" items: billiard tables and playing cards, yachts, carriages, liquor and beer. The new legislation levied a tax of one dollar per barrel on beer and required brewers to purchase a federal manufacturer's license, which amounted to $100 annually for those producing more than five hundred barrels and $50 a year for smaller brewers. Over the next three years, the newly formed Internal Revenue Service collected $369 million in taxes, nearly $80 million of that from beer.

The German brewers, ready to affirm their patriotism and loyalty to their adopted country, paid the tax, glumly recognizing that once imposed, the levy would never be rescinded. Less than one month after President Lincoln signed the tax into law, a few dozen Eastern brewers met in New York to talk over the new regulations. The group managed to persuade Congress to lower the rate to sixty cents per barrel. As the war dragged on, though, lawmakers raised the tax back to one dollar. In spite of this, the brewers learned a valuable lesson – it was better to cooperate than to resist and their best interest lay in educating the nation's lawmakers instead of ignoring them. That meeting in New York inspired the nation's first trade and lobby organization, the United States Brewers' Association.

In St. Louis, the end of the war brought a downturn in the brewing business. As the surrender of the Confederacy played out in April 1865, the supply clerks and troops that had once been so thirsty for lager beer mustered out. Refugees began their journeys back to the South and the carpenters, bricklayers and builders packed their tools and headed home. The market for beer in the city was about to take another dramatic turn.

The Story of Anheuser-Busch

The end of the Civil War brought fear to the heart of Eberhard Anheuser, owner of the troubled Bavarian Brewery on the city's south side. Anheuser had ended up with the place as payment for debts that were owed to him and it was never clear why he had held onto it. Already wealthy from soap manufacturing, it was not as if he needed a failed brewery. For whatever reason he took charge of the place and, as luck would have it, he turned it into a lucrative business during the war – despite the poor quality of his beer.

When the war ended, he knew he was in trouble. His partner had sold out in 1864, leaving Anheuser to run the brewery on his own. Anheuser had never claimed to be a master brewer. He knew everything there was to know about making soap, but beer remained a mystery to him. Union troops and thirsty laborers had been willing to drink his beer but the discriminating Germans of St. Louis didn't want any part of it. They didn't have to settle for a mediocre brew when there were a dozen other breweries in the city turning out far superior lager for the same price.

While Anheuser may not have known much about beer, he had become rich by knowing how to run a business. He knew that he needed help right away and he knew where to find it – with his talented and charismatic son-in-law, Adolphus Busch.

Adolphus Busch arrived in St. Louis in 1857 and found his first employment among the commission houses on the levee. Born in Germany in 1839, Busch was the well-educated son of a successful businessman. The second-youngest of twenty-two children, some of them half-siblings, he attended school at the Gymnasium of Mainz, the Academy of Darmstadt and the Collegiate Institute of Brussels. He spoke, in addition to German, fluent French and English and was proficient in Italian and Spanish, as well. Within a couple of years, he began specializing in malts and hops and as a supplier to Eberhard Anheuser, he came to admire Anheuser's blonde, curly-haired daughter, Elisa, known as "Lilly." On March 7, 1861, Adolphus and seventeen-year-old Lilly were married in a double-ring ceremony with Adolphus' brother, Ulrich Busch, Jr., and Lilly's sister, Anna. Legend has it Adolphus was twenty minutes late for the wedding because he had stopped to close a business deal. Despite the inauspicious start to their union, Adolphus and Lilly went on to have fourteen children, nine of whom survived to adulthood. Shortly after the wedding, Ulrich and Anna moved to Chicago, where Ulrich went into the brewery supply business. Adolphus enlisted in the Union Army, where he joined up with one of the regiments from the south side of the city and was sent to fight in southern and western Missouri. When he returned to St. Louis, he went back into the supply business and in 1864 he began working part-time as a salesman for the Bavarian Brewery.

In 1869, he sold his shares of the supply company and used the funds to buy into the Bavarian Brewery. The company was restructured, with Anheuser continuing as president and Busch becoming secretary. Anheuser turned most of his attention back to soap manufacturing and placed the

Elisa "Lilly" Anheuser

Adolphus Busch

management of the brewery into the hands of his capable son-in-law. In five years, Busch increased the production of beer from eight thousand barrels per year to eighteen thousand. Busch also seized upon many of the latest scientific and industrial innovations including pasteurization, which allowed the brewery to package, ship and store beer with a much longer shelf life, and artificial refrigeration, which allowed brewers to store beer in warehouses, making the lagering caves obsolete. Under Busch's guidance, the brewery began bottling its beer in 1872. In 1883, Busch would become a full partner in the company and its name would be changed to the Anheuser-Busch Brewing Association.

In those days, brewing was still a local industry but there was a huge amount of money to be made in St. Louis. Busch was determined to corner the market. Unfortunately, he could not make claim to having the best brew in town; that honor was held by the Lemp family. However, even bad beer, if marketed correctly, could make the brewery a huge amount of money. In those days, the sales strategy for beer revolved around the "beer collector," who bought beer but did not sell it. All brewers had such spending agents, but Busch gathered together an accomplished group of men and soon his beer was selling as well as the Falstaff brand from the Lemp brewery. Every saloon that sold Busch beer was favored by a visit from the collector once each month. He would travel from saloon to saloon, spending an amount proportionate to the saloon's monthly beer purchase. This made the collector an important person with high social standing among men from all walks of life; indeed it was the habit of loafers to follow the beer collector's carriage from saloon to saloon, hoping to be treated to free drinks at each stop. The usual protocol was for the beer collector to buy a man a Busch beer as long as that man turned around and bought two more for himself and his friends.

The collector had other duties besides buying drinks and these required him to be part minor celebrity and part extended family member. He was expected to attend the funerals of saloon owners' family members to ensure there would be plenty of rounds of Busch beer bought at the gathering after the solemn rites were over. For that reason, the German-speaking residents of the Carondelet section of the city called him *der todsaufer* – the dead drinker. He went to weddings, giving the happy couple a handsome gift and delivering a witty toast at the reception. At Christmas, he purchased gifts for the saloon keepers' wives and children. The collectors were in a position to wield considerable influence in local politics, some of them becoming ward committeemen. As long as they kept customers buying Busch beer, they were treated well by the company and by Adolphus himself.

Busch was a consummate salesman who became known for his clever and innovative advertising. He gave away watch fobs, chinaware and other Victorian-era novelties advertising his product. Among the promotional items was a jackknife that doubled as a corkscrew, a useful item since beer at that time was corked rather than capped. On the handle was the E. Anheuser & Co. logo and at one end was a peephole through which could be viewed a portrait of Adolphus Busch. Another popular promotional item was a tray

BUDWEISER GIRL

CUSTER'S LAST FIGHT
ANHEUSER BUSCH BREWING ASSOCIATION.

"Custer's Last Fight" became one of Anheuser-Busch's greatest ads.

(Left) The Original "Budweiser Girl"

embellished with a picture of the Anheuser-Busch Brewery with flags flying proudly from every cupola and tower. Seated in a prominent spot was a *zaftig* young lady with a modest wisp of veil covering her lap, her pulchritude winsomely promoting the virtues of Busch beer.

There were many of these curvaceous women depicted in Busch artwork and they sold a lot of beer, but not nearly as much as a tremendously popular painting of General George Armstrong Custer did. Artwork depicting sailing ships, famous battles, and semi-nude females were *de rigueur* in the all-male atmosphere of saloons of the day. As a form of advertising, breweries often issued a complimentary series of paintings to be used as decoration in the bars that served their beer. One of the most popular was F. Otto Becker's stirring if inaccurate depiction of the Battle of Little Bighorn. The painting was based on the original by Cassily Adams, who drew on his experience as a Union soldier who had been wounded in the Battle of Vicksburg to produce a terrifically action-packed interpretation of the battle with Custer in the center of the melee, swinging a saber at a toppling Indian. Adams painted the epic battle scene on a sixteen-foot by five-foot nine-inch piece of wagon canvas in 1884, eight years after the battle, as part of a traveling exhibition. Busch purchased it, along with the reproduction rights, for $35,000 and made it the centerpiece of an Anheuser-Busch advertising campaign. It was an immediate hit and the picture became so popular that the brewery still receives requests for copies today. The original painting by Adams was sent to Custer's army regiment, the Seventh Cavalry, for display in its mess hall at Fort Riley, Kansas. F. Otto Becker, an artist who worked for the Milwaukee Lithographing Company, was hired in 1889 to make a poster-size reproduction of Adams' painting. It became one of the most popular pieces of artwork in the world. The star-crowned "A" and the eagle of Anheuser-Busch has appeared on hundreds of different kinds of advertising, but to this day, there has never been another ad like "Custer's Last Fight."

Adams' giant painting was later sent to Fort Bliss in Texas, where it was destroyed in a 1946 fire in the officers' mess hall.

During the years that the breweries were running at full stream, there was probably more beer consumed in St. Louis than in any other city of its size in the world. With beer sold at a nickel a glass (which also included the customary free lunch), it was a luxury that was within the reach of almost everyone. And for a time, St. Louis beer was even cheaper than that.

In the late 1890s, an English syndicate came to St. Louis and attempted to corner the local beer market. They succeeded in buying up many of the smaller breweries but William Lemp and Adolphus Busch refused to sell. A beer war ensued and the price for a barrel of beer dropped from $6 to $3. Saloons cut their prices to two glasses for five cents. The affair reached the point of absurdity when one quick-thinking tavern owner offered two glasses of beer and a boat ride on the lake adjoining his establishment for just a nickel. Lemp and Busch weathered the battle and the Englishmen, beaten by the two Germans, withdrew.

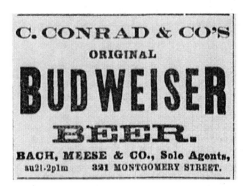

A Budweiser bottle from the 1870s

Because of the constant fighting within the local market, the process of obtaining a saloon became a simple task for any aspiring barkeep with $100 in his pocket. He only needed to hint to some of the brewery collectors of his intentions and then wait for the offers to come in. Busch was usually the first to appear with a generous proposal. The candidate first had to get the approval of the majority of the residents of the neighborhood in which he planned to set up shop. Once he had that, he bought a government license for $25. After that, he had to obtain fixtures, glassware and a city license, which cost around $600. However, if the saloon keeper agreed to become a Busch beer establishment, Busch would take care of all of these costs for him. He would arrange for the rental of the shop, install fixtures and a few choice murals and then instruct the man on how to begin his operation. He charged the new customer $9 for a keg of $6 beer, applying the additional $3 to the amount the man owed him.

Despite all these ingenious plans and clever marketing schemes, Busch was still trailing the Lemps in popularity and sales when the great beer revolution began and it became possible to bottle beer for a longer shelf life. Busch immediately installed bottling facilities at its brewery. Soon, though, it would be a brand of beer that would bring even great acclaim to Busch and his thriving brewery.

In 1876, Budweiser lager beer came on the market, brewed by the Anheuser brewery and bottled by Carl Conrad, a local wine and liquor merchant. It went largely unnoticed at first. According to the story, Conrad was traveling in Europe in the early 1870s and dined in a small Bohemian monastery, where he was served the most wonderful beer he had ever tasted. He offered to buy the recipe from the monks but they gladly gave it to him for free. After returning to America, he asked his friend

Adolphus Busch to make the beer for him. It was dubbed "Budweiser" after the small town of Budweis where Conrad had discovered it. He bottled the beer that Busch made for him and sold it in his shop. Not long after, he ran into financial trouble and borrowed money from Busch to stay afloat. In January 1883, he declared bankruptcy and licensed the Budweiser name, bottling and marketing rights to the Anheuser-Busch brewery. Busch had been his largest creditor and had a $94,000 lien on his property. In January 1891, Busch legally acquired all rights to the Budweiser name and trademark and Conrad, with whom Busch maintained a lifelong friendship, joined Anheuser-Busch as a technician.

Budweiser was different from the other beers being produced because it was brewed with rice rather than corn grits for natural carbonation. It was then subjected to a second fermentation process and aged, as a true lager must be. Despite its higher price, it was soon in such demand that Busch was scarcely able to get enough bottles to its suppliers. So, the brewery invested in glass factories. Busch founded the Adolphus Busch Glass Factory of St. Louis and Belleville, Illinois, and the Streator Glass Company of Streator, Illinois, remaining chief stockholder in both to keep the cost advantage for the brewery.

Now, Busch not only had bottled beer to sell, but he had the best bottled beer in the country. His innovations were disastrous to the small breweries that were left in St. Louis and by 1900, only nineteen of them remained. Brewing had changed from a neighborhood business to one with the potential to reach markets everywhere, which is just what Busch began to do. While his competitors in St. Louis were struggling, he invested deeply and became a "traveling ambassador of beer."

The genial mustachioed Busch was impeccably dressed and portly, as befitted a successful man of his day. While he appeared dignified he wasn't a bit snobbish and had friends from all ranks of society. He loved a good laugh and didn't mind poking fun at himself. He especially enjoyed pulling pranks on his friend and frequent traveling companion, St. Louis restaurant owner Tony Faust.

One time, the two of them were in a restaurant in France. Busch, who spoke French, was teaching his friend how to order a meal. When they finished dining, Faust asked what he should say to ask the waiter for cigars. Bush spoke a phrase in French and Faust repeated it to the waiter, who obligingly brought Faust the check. Busch roared with laughter and his friend realized he'd been had.

Word of Budweiser beer began to spread and Busch began marketing and advertising in every state in the growing nation. The plant in St. Louis began to expand, employing as many as 7,500 men. Each year, Anheuser-Busch produced 1.6 million barrels of beer. Nearly all was consumed in the United States, but even the small amount sent abroad exceeded the entire sales, domestic and foreign, of most of the company's rivals.

Busch continued to expand and bought railroads, a coal mine and several hotels, all to further the cause of his beer. He had agents in every major city and owned property in every state in the union. With Budweiser now the chief product of the brewery, he reduced his sixteen brands to just four: Budweiser, Michelob, Faust and the standard pale beer. At that time, Michelob was the finest beer being made in America and was also the most expensive at twenty-five cents a glass. Like Budweiser, it originated in Bohemia, and it was Adolphus himself who discovered it. He bought a glass of beer one day for the equivalent of a few cents and it struck him as being even better than Budweiser. He returned home and ordered his staff to duplicate it. Michelob was the result, but it cost so much that sales were always low. This brand would not be bottled for many years. The Faust brand was named in honor of Tony Faust. One of Busch's daughters, Anna Louise, later married Faust's son, Edward.

Eberhard Anheuser died in 1880, stunned by the success that his son-in-law had achieved. At the time of his death, only the Lemps could continue to compete with Anheuser-Busch. They had also expanded into national distribution and, like Busch, were using refrigerated railroad cars to ship their acclaimed Falstaff brand across the country. The two companies battled for domination in the market for years but by the middle 1880s, the Lemp Brewing Company had started to fall behind. Anheuser-Busch soon had no true

Adolphus Busch was bitter over what he felt was unfair judging at the 1893 World's Columbian Exposition in Chicago. After a reversal, he lost out to his closest competitor, Pabst in Milwaukee. His anger over the judging caused him not to enter any beers in the competition at the 1904 World's Fair in St. Louis.

rivals in St. Louis – but the same could not be said on a national level.

In the late 1800s, worldwide competition for medals at expositions and fairs was fierce. At the World's Columbian Exposition held in Chicago in 1893, regarded by brewers as the most prestigious competition of the century, the rivalry between Busch and his closest competitor came to a head. At the time, the Pabst Brewery in Milwaukee (operated by Frederick Pabst, a close friend and relative by marriage of William Lemp) was the largest in the United States, with Anheuser-Busch a close second. At one point in the competition, Anheuser-Busch had been awarded six medals for its beer and Pabst had received five. The grand prize was still to be awarded and the judges' scrutiny was intense. A dispute began over the makeup of the panel of judges and the method they were using of awarding points. The brewers, interested only in product quality, were upset that points were to be given for "commercial importance."

Ultimately, Budweiser was given the highest award over Pabst's Blue Ribbon beer but the decision was later reversed based on a chemical analysis that showed Budweiser contained impurities. The award was then given to Pabst. Outraged, the hot-tempered Busch appealed the decision, angering the exposition commissioners so much that they decided that no award would be given at all. After Busch threatened legal action, the commission reversed itself again and gave the award to Budweiser. Pabst complained and, after yet another reversal, he was declared the winner. Enraged, Busch pursued one of the judges across Europe to try and get him to change his mind. In late 1894, the commission announced its refusal to reconsider the decision. Busch sputtered in rage in the newspapers, "Prizes are not given to the goods meriting same but are secured by money and strategy." This statement offers a hint as to why no Anheuser-Busch products were presented for judging during the World's Fair held in St. Louis in 1904.

The controversy over the judging at the Columbian Exposition certainly didn't damage Anheuser-Busch's business. In fact, it helped it and the brewery continued to expand. As Busch made more and more money, he began to spend it quite freely. He maintained his family in luxury and constructed a mansion known as No. 1 Busch Place. It was located in a park-like section of the 142-acre brewery grounds. The spacious rooms were known for their color schemes -- the Rose Room, the Green Room, the Blue Room, etc. On the gleaming parquet floors were dazzling Oriental rugs. Stained glass windows admitted filtered light, and walls, tables and shelves were jammed with a massive array of art objects, as was the fashion of the time. As was fitting for the home of a merchant prince, expensive imported furniture filled every inch of space and frescoed ceilings, antique tapestries and artwork added to the overall majesty of the decor. Murals of plump, scantily clad women appeared to float across the ceiling of the main salon, where the walls were covered with paintings from some of the prominent artists of the day. Busch was one of the first to recognize the talents of American landscape artist William Keith. He was also an admirer of John Singer Sargent and James McNeill Whistler.

Outside, the gardens were equally impressive. There were carvings from Grimm's Fairy Tales placed among the trees and a small army of gardeners kept the flowers and shrubs looking perfect at 1 Busch Place, as well as all the Busch homes.

Anyone of note who visited St. Louis visited with the Busch family, including Enrico Caruso, Theodore Roosevelt, Edward, Prince of Wales, and many others. They often entertained local friends and held grand parties at the house. The exuberant Busch loved children and holidays. Every year, during the first week of December, a brewery watchman dressed as St. Nicholas visited the Busch children, filling their stockings with fruit and treats to start the holiday season. On Christmas Eve, a huge tree on a revolving stand was the center of activity for everyone. Easter brought even more festivity when Busch decided to have an egg hunt for his and his neighbors' children. It turned out to be a huge success and each year brought ever-larger numbers of "neighbor" children until the event was eventually moved to Forest Park.

Busch loved animals, especially horses, as is evidenced by the brewery's enduring reputation for its outstanding Clydesdales. It was in Adolphus' day that teams of the majestic, high-stepping animals first pulled the red and green Busch delivery wagons. Busch worried so much about the care of horses that he could not stand to think of his guests' carriage horses standing outside in bad weather. After the passengers had been

The Anheuser-Busch Brewery

discharged, Busch gave orders for the carriages to be driven into a large rotunda in the carriage house. There the horses were comfortably stabled and the coachmen could relax in a recreation room, where plenty of food and Budweiser beer were kept on hand.

Busch maintained one of the finest stables of riding and carriage horses in the United States. The stable building, located just across the drive from 1 Busch Place, could house up to thirty horses at a time. He also kept a large collection of wheeled conveyances: carriages, coaches, barouches, landaus, shooting wagons and the like. Sets of gold- and silver-mounted harnesses were displayed in glass cases along the stable walls.

In the early 1900s, Busch also became interested in the "horseless carriage" and developed a fascination for motorcars. He commissioned one of the first automobiles in St. Louis, an ornate Pope-Toledo with a specially built wicker body and brass fittings.

The Busch family lived in sumptuous luxury but unlike some of the tycoons of his day who were notoriously tightfisted, Adolphus was gave freely of his fortune. His gifts included large donations to Washington University in St. Louis and to Harvard. He contributed relief funds to the victims of the 1906 San Francisco earthquake and every Groundhog Day, he gave $5,000 to a convent in St. Louis. He also gave freely to charities in Germany, a habit that would come back to haunt the family with the advent of the First World War.

Employees of Anheuser-Busch lived well. Not only did the brewery pay a good wage, every man was entitled to a generous portion of free beer each day, which he was expected to drink. The trips to the keg were seen as an important part of the day's routine, an affirmation of the employees' dedication to their product. It was thought that a man needed a certain amount of beer each day to maintain good work habits and vigorous health. One man was actually thrown out of the brewers' union for failing to drink his daily quota of beer. He took his case to court and it was decided that it wasn't necessary to drink beer in order to do a good day's work. Union members shook their heads in disbelief, but the man was reinstated.

The new century got off to a great start for Anheuser-Busch. In 1901, it finally overtook the annual production levels of Pabst. With preparations being made in St. Louis for the World's Fair in 1904, Busch accepted the position of fair director. Many of the local brewers, led by Busch, came together to create a gigantic entertainment venue -- a replica of the Tyrolean Alps. Located at the end of the "Pike," next to the main entrance, the Alps covered more than six acres of Forest Park and proved to be among the fair's most popular attractions. But behind the scenes there were numerous disputes between the operators of the Alps and the fair's management, including issues of trash pickup, blocking of the service entrance by railroad cars, squabbles over the width of the walkways and the amount of water and electricity used by the attraction. The problems festered all summer, leading to Busch's resignation as the fair's director in November 1904.

After the fair closed down, most of the state and national buildings were sold off or demolished. Busch purchased the Belgium national building and had it moved onto the brewery property, where it was reconstructed for use by the Adolphus Busch Glass Manufacturing Company.

Busch's hard work and generosity led to him being popular with the people of St. Louis, especially the lower and middle classes. In spite of his vast wealth, he encountered coolness from members of the city's upper crust, who refused to accept the brash German as one of their own. But Busch couldn't have cared less. He gathered his own circle of friends around him and managed to stay in the good graces of those who were buying his beer.

By the Buschs' golden wedding anniversary in 1911, most of the daily operations of the brewery had been turned over their son, August. He had become so skilled in running the company's business affairs that Adolphus and Lilly had time to indulge their love of travel. They toured Europe and visited many parts of the U.S., spending considerable time in their houses in Pasadena, California, and Cooperstown, New

York.

Adolphus and Lilly wanted to make sure that each of their eight surviving children had their own home. Their eldest son, Adolphus Busch, Jr., nicknamed "Bulfy," had died of a perforated appendix in 1898. He had been named a corporate director at twenty-one and if he had lived, he might have taken over the company. August and his wife, Alice, received a grand home that had been built at Grant's Farm, southwest of St. Louis, the former home of Ulysses S. Grant; Edmee Reisinger and her husband, Hugo, received a mansion on Fifth Avenue in New York; Clara von Gotard, who was married to Baron Paul von Gotard, was given a mansion in Berlin, Germany; Mrs. J.W. Loeb received a home near Lincoln Park in Chicago; and Mrs. Edward A. Scharrer was given a house in Stuttgart, Germany.

There was a huge celebration in St. Louis to mark the Buschs' anniversary, although Adolphus and Lilly were unable to attend. They were in Pasadena at the time, where Busch was seriously ill. Some thirteen thousand employees and friends celebrated in their absence. The brewery was closed for the day and all five thousand employees had been given the day off with pay. The party took place at the Coliseum, where a fifty-piece band played and employees paraded, sang, danced and waved flags. Lights gleamed on a center fountain that fired off a thirty-foot jet of water and the crowd partied into the night. It was reported that more than forty thousand bottles of beer were consumed, along with 100,000 sandwiches. The Buschs' well-wishers sent them a solid gold card of congratulations. President William Howard Taft sent the couple a $20 gold piece. Former President Theodore Roosevelt one-upped him by giving them a gold loving cup.

By this time, the storm clouds of Prohibition were already starting to gather and Anheuser-Busch, along with other national brewers, began working to separate the various beer-makers from the hard liquor industry in the minds of lawmakers and temperance supporters. They eventually failed at this although they did manage to start producing low-alcohol and non-alcoholic beers. Anheuser-Busch trademarked the Bevo brand, a non-intoxicating malt-based beverage, in 1908.

Unfortunately, Busch's health did not improve. He had suffered from dropsy, as edema was then called, since 1906. In October 1913, he and Lilly traveled to Langenschwalbach, Germany, for a stay at Villa Lilly, one of their two homes on the Rhine. He hoped that the brisk autumn weather would improve his health but it did no good. On October 10, at the age of 74, Busch suffered a heart attack while sitting at his desk. He died peacefully a few hours later. His body was returned to St. Louis and a viewing was held at No. 1 Busch Place.

A final farewell was said to Busch at the house where he had welcomed dignitaries and common people alike. It took twenty-five trucks to haul all of the funeral flowers to the cemetery. A crowd of nearly 25,000 people gathered around the brewery to pay their last respects.

The funeral procession left No. 1 Busch Place and departed for Bellefontaine Cemetery. St. Louis residents solidly lined the route. Mayor

The elaborate Busch mausoleum at Bellefontaine Cemetery in St. Louis

Henry Kiel requested that all business in the city be halted for five minutes during the burial. The Jefferson Hotel and the Planter's House turned off their lights during that interval and all of the city's streetcars were stopped. A committee of Busch employees was granted permission to carry the casket through the brewery and along the route that Adolphus had once walked to work each day. Busch was laid to rest in an ornate mausoleum resembling a miniature cathedral, complete with gargoyles and with its own watering system for plants and bushes.

Charles Nagel, one of the leading citizens of St. Louis, gave the eulogy. He was joined by a number of other honored guests, including congressmen, the presidents of Harvard and the University of Missouri and Baron von Lesner, the personal representative of Kaiser Wilhelm II, who was a longtime friend of Busch. Nagel called Busch "a giant among men. Like a descendant of one of the great and vigorous ancient gods, he rested among us and with his optimism, his far seeing vision, his undaunted courage and his energy, shaped the affairs of men."

After Busch's death, Lilly divided her time between Europe and California, with only occasional stops in St. Louis. The house was seldom used and after her death in 1928, the Busch children divided the contents and it was closed up for good. It was finally demolished to expand the brewery in 1929.

August A. Busch, Sr., who had been running the company for several years, continued the growth and the expansion of the brewery until the outbreak of World War I. By 1917, the United States had entered the conflict, which brought dark times to the family. The two countries to which the Buschs were devoted were now at war. Lilly Busch was actually in Germany when America entered the war and it took former senator Harry Hawes seven and a half months to get her home. The brewery was handicapped by rumors that the Busch family was pro-German. Despite purchases of large amounts of Liberty Bonds by the company and by the family, the malicious stories refused to go away. The Busch family, as well as the scores of Germans living in St. Louis, were kept under close watch but they managed to weather the storm of the war.

And then something worse came along.

By the late 1910s, Anheuser-Busch, like breweries all across America, was confronted by Prohibition. In an effort to combat the growing threat against beer sales and production, Busch filled the newspapers with ads in favor of personal liberty. But all the while, the company prepared for the inevitable. It stepped up production of Bevo, which was being sold all over the world by 1919. One year before, production of real beer had stopped, so there seemed to be little cause for concern about Prohibition. No one realized at the time that the disappearance of real beer would largely destroy the demand for "near-beer" products like Bevo. Just because liquor was illegal, it was certainly not hard to get. The horrible taste

of bootleg hard liquor was usually so bad that it had to be disguised, which brought about the creation of sweet mixed drinks. People who became accustomed to the taste of these syrupy new drinks often lost the taste for the tart flavor of beer, or in this case, near-beer. And with real beer being illegally produced by bootleggers, the good stuff was still easy enough to get. So, why drink non-alcoholic beer when you could get the real thing at the local speakeasy? By 1923, sales of Bevo fell off to almost nothing, causing grave concerns at Anheuser-Busch.

The early years of Prohibition were grim across St. Louis. The Lemp Brewery, the neighbor and chief local competitor of Anheuser-Busch, closed down and sold off its huge plant for a fraction of what it had been worth a few years before. August Busch refused to give up, though. He was determined to find a way to keep the company afloat until the Prohibition laws were repealed. A short time later, Anheuser-Busch began to produce truck bodies and refrigerator cabinets and they went into the yeast business. Their superior product soon gained control of the market and money began trickling back into the coffers again. They also began bottling soft drinks, including Busch Extra-Dry Ginger Ale, and canned malt syrup, which was often used illegally to make home brew by eager customers.

But Busch was not happy just holding the company together. He wanted to make beer and he loathed Prohibition. On his own, he began investigating the corruption and hypocrisy of the law and he made his findings public. He discovered that liquor was sold aboard American flagships and discovered the failures of law enforcement and outright graft within the ranks of the Anti-Saloon League. He pressed for a uniform and effective enforcement of the law as long as it was on the books. On the other hand, he used his attorneys to appeal to Presidents Coolidge and Hoover and to Congress to repeal the law. He insisted that law-abiding businessmen were suffering while lawbreakers flourished, as long as Prohibition was the law of the land. Busch supported just about any politician who stood against Prohibition and finally, President Franklin D. Roosevelt was elected in 1932. Roosevelt said he "wants repeal, and I am confident that the United States of America wants repeal." Prohibition finally came to an end on April 7, 1933.

Under a permit to brew beer in advance of the date for its legal sale, Anheuser-Busch had 250,000 barrels ready and while they planned to resume business quietly, April 7 arrived in St. Louis like a combination of Mardi Gras and New Year's Eve. A jubilant crowd surrounded the brewery as the gates were thrown open and a fleet of trucks rolled out to deliver the first supply of Budweiser to the city's packed taverns. It was a great night in south St. Louis as August Busch had brought the old brewery from "doom to boom."

After Prohibition was repealed, Anheuser-Busch Clydesdales delivered a shipment of Budweiser to President Roosevelt at the White House.

Sadly, August A. Busch would not be around to enjoy the celebration for long. As the company began to enter a new period of growth, Busch's life came to an end. He had suffered from several heart attacks during the hard years and was pained by gout and dropsy. On the night of February 13, 1934, in tremendous agony, he wrote a letter to his family, signed and sealed it, and then turned up the radio before shooting himself.

He was succeeded by Adolphus Busch III, known around the brewery simply as "The Third." He was a retiring man who grappled with the problems the company faced during the Depression and World War II. He died after a short illness on August 29, 1946.

August A. Busch, Jr., or "Gussie" became the fourth Busch to become president of Anheuser-Busch and is remembered today as one of the most popular and outgoing members of the family. He carefully protected the company's reputation and further expanded its image to make it one of the best known (or perhaps *the* best known) brewery in the world today. In 1953, when it was thought that the St. Louis Cardinals might be sold away from St. Louis, Gussie wrote the check that bought the baseball team and turned Sportsman's Park into Busch Stadium.

And while the Busch family and the brewery continue to thrive in St. Louis today, the family has not been without its scandals and troubles over the years, from brushes with the law, death and even kidnappings. But through it all, they have managed to prosper and to build a great legacy in St. Louis.

St. Louis Beer until Prohibition

After recovering from an initial drop in sales following the Civil War, the 1870s became a boom time for St. Louis breweries. In addition to the Anheuser operation, there were fifty other breweries in the city, employing more than seven hundred workers among them. William Lemp's Western Brewery was the largest.

During this time period, the brewers began using names, logos and trademarks for their various lines and began taking advantage of pasteurization. This discovery, which was originally intended to aid the French wine industry, was ever more important to the brewing world. Pasteurization kept beer stable, allowing for it to be bottled and stored for longer periods of time than was ever thought possible. The bottles, hand-sealed with corks, allowed the beer-makers to ship their products to distant markets. When pasteurization was combined with cars that could be loaded with ice at stations along a railroad route, brewers were able to expand production, sales and profits. Both Adolphus Busch and William Lemp took advantage of these innovations and expanded their markets worldwide. Lemp's beer was soon available for purchase in South American ports, and in Calcutta, Yokohama, Hawaii, Shanghai, Australia, London, Paris and Berlin. Anheuser's products could be found in the East and West Indies, Central America, Japan, China, Australia and Africa.

By 1877, the local and national brewing industry was beginning to evolve, with small, poorly managed breweries closing down and the larger ones expanding. In June 1879, the United States Brewers' Association held its nineteenth annual convention in St. Louis. More than one hundred and fifty members attended, coming from eighteen states and the District of Columbia. The official reception and meetings were held at the Germania Club Hall at Gratiot and Eighth streets, and the first evening's entertainment was held at Schnaider's Garden, with local beer lovers joining the brewers for a night of festivities. While in St. Louis, convention attendees toured the larger local breweries and the city itself, traveling in carriages to Lafayette Park, Tower Grove Park, Shaw's Garden, Forest Park and the Fairgrounds Park, where a grand reception was held. On the final evening, the brewers took a steamboat ride to Carondelet and back to the St. Louis riverfront, receiving salutes from the workers at the Lemp and Anheuser breweries as they passed.

By 1880, St. Louis was the third-largest brewing city in the United States, behind only New York and Philadelphia. Within two years, mechanical refrigeration was introduced in the city, an innovation that Anheuser-Busch and the Lemps quickly took advantage of. This new invention allowed them to stop using the underground caves, made year-round production possible, and provided more stable and easily controlled storage temperatures. Over the course of the next decade, no new breweries of any significance opened in the city but those still operating raced against one another to modernize their facilities.

Mechanical methods of bottling, pasteurization, mechanical refrigeration and shipping to the far corners of the globe not only increased the cost of doing business, but raised the initial costs for those who wanted to get into the business. Numerous ownership changes took place among the smaller breweries and the larger ones began dealing with trade labor unions, which pressed for shorter workdays and better wages.

Along with the modernization costs, union issues and increased production came the inevitable price wars. Concerted efforts were made to sustain the existing price structure by the large breweries. In an effort to compete, smaller operations had little choice but to consolidate. In June 1889, eighteen St. Louis-area breweries were merged to form the St. Louis Brewing Association. The only significant breweries to remain independent were Anheuser-Busch, William J. Lemp's Western Brewery and Louis Obert's Arsenal Brewery.

In November of that year, the St. Louis brewing community was stunned when it was announced that an English syndicate had purchased the St. Louis Brewing Association, effectively snapping up most of the breweries in the city. Ellis Wainwright was named to head the American wing of the syndicate, which was seeking American investments during an economic depression in Great Britain. These same investors also set up separate brewing syndicates in twenty-one other cities over the course of the next two years. Foreign investors also attempted to consolidate Anheuser-Busch and the Lemp Brewery with the Pabst, Schlitz and Miller breweries in Wisconsin. This effort was unsuccessful. The local syndicate took immediate steps to become more competitive with the larger breweries, however. The older and less efficient breweries were shut down, production was moved into the newer plants, management was consolidated and bulk purchasing plans were established to help cut the cost of raw ingredients.

Lemp and Anheuser-Busch fought back against the syndicate, expanding their production and enhancing their extensive network of depots and bottling plants across the country. From St. Louis, their beer could be shipped to these locations in bulk, then repackaged and bottled for local distribution. William Lemp had sixty-four depots in Texas and more than two hundred nationwide. Adolphus Busch, in addition to setting up depots around the country, also began to purchase an interest in out-of-town breweries. At different times, he held a position in the Alamo and Lone Star breweries of San Antonio, the Texas Brewing Company in Fort Worth, the American Brewery in Houston and the Shreveport Brewery & Ice Company in Louisiana.

The St. Louis Brewing Association wasn't destined to last. Within a year, its members began to revolt, including the brewing interests of a branch of the Koehler family, which merged to form the new American Brewing Company. A new brewing facility was built on the site of the former Excelsior Brewing Company to be operated by Henry, Hugo and Oscar Koehler. They were the first to leave the association and start a new and independent company but they would not be the last.

In February 1892, the owner of a Baltimore machine shop, William Painter, received a patent on a newly designed bottle closure that would revolutionize the brewing industry. What Painter called a "crown cork" we know as a bottle cap. It led to increased standardization in the packaging industry and ushered in the brewing industry's use of high-speed bottle-filling machines. The new closure soon replaced rubber and ceramic bottle tops. Except for a few minor changes, the design remains the same today.

A handful of other breweries started in St. Louis in the late 1800s and early 1900s. The Columbia Brewing Company was

(Left) The engineering department at the Empire Brewing Company, which started in 1901.
(Right) The Schorr-Kolkschneider Brewing Company, an independent brewery that started in 1902 and continued operating as a brewer -- illegally -- during Prohibition.

started in 1892 at Twentieth and Madison streets. The Union Brewing Company opened a plant in 1898 and Paulus Gast, a longtime St. Louis wine manufacturer, opened the Gast Brewing Company in 1900. In the spring of 1901, the Empire Brewing Company began operating at Sarah Street and Duncan Avenue and in 1902, Jacob Schorr and Henry Kolkschneider, two men who had long been associated with brewing in the city, opened the Schorr-Kolkschneider Brewing Company. It operated as an independent brewery until it was – supposedly – closed down during Prohibition.

In 1904, the city of St. Louis welcomed visitors from all over the world for the Louisiana Purchase Exposition, also called the St. Louis World's Fair. Between opening day on April 30 and the closing ceremony on December 1, more than nineteen million people came to the fair. The local brewers did their part to make it a resounding success. Adolphus Busch served on the board of directors, as did William Lemp, although his suicide on February 13 left his son, William, Jr., to take his place. The local brewers joined forces to create the Tyrolean Alps exhibition that became the largest dining and entertainment venue at the fair.

In June 1907, a second consolidation of the local brewing industry took place. Its coming had been rumored for nearly a year but it finally occurred that summer. Most of the smaller breweries that had started since the 1890s had been unable to expand because of the competitive local and national markets. Taking a cue from the syndicate that had formed in 1889, nine local breweries merged to form the Independent Breweries Company. Members included the American Brewing Company, Central Brewing Company (East St. Louis), Columbia Brewing Company, Consumers Brewing Company, Empire Brewing Company, Gast Brewing Company, Home Brewing Company, National Brewing Company, and the Wagner Brewing Company of Granite City, Illinois. The output of these combined breweries was estimated to be around 650,000 barrels per year and they employed about 1,500 men. Henry Griesedieck, Jr. of the National Brewing Company was elected to serve as IBC president and one representative from each brewery formed the board of directors.

Edward Wagner, who had merged his Wagner Brewing Company into the IBC, became dissatisfied with the arrangement and broke off on his own in 1910. He and his son opened Forest Park Brewing Company on the south side of Forest Park Boulevard. The site would in later years become the cornerstone of the

The Mutual Brewing Company was founded in St. Louis in 1913, the last before Prohibition. It only lasted until 1917, unable to survive the rationing that took place during World War I.

Falstaff Brewing Corporation.

The last new brewery to be built in St. Louis before the advent of Prohibition was the Mutual Brewing Company, which sold its first beer in the city in August 1913. It only survived for four years. In 1917, its assets were sold at public auction.

Dark days were coming for St. Louis brewers. With American involvement in World War I and Prohibition just around the corner, what many have called the golden era of the American brewing industry was just about to end.

Needless to say, anti-Prohibition sentiment was strong in St. Louis. A city that had literally been built by the brewing industry wasn't interested in giving up its beer – and it couldn't afford to, either. One of the ways that the brewers were fighting against the Prohibition movement was to publicize the amount of money that would be lost if the law was passed. St. Louis brewers spent over $1.1 million each year on new buildings and machinery and these expenditures provided jobs. The breweries in St. Louis also employed 9,617 men, whose combined salaries amounted to more than $5 million annually. Without jobs, these men would end up on the breadline. Appealing directly to the government, they also pointed out that they paid over $3 million in taxes each year. Unfortunately, these pleas weren't enough to prevent the law from passing.

In addition to the pressure being felt from the Prohibition movement, the brewers, most of whom were of German ancestry, began facing a wave of anti-German sentiment that was a direct result of the war in Europe. These hard-working men were once celebrated residents of the city, but they now found that many of their former friends and neighbors had turned against them.

In spite of all of the grim happenings in the brewing industry, Joseph "Papa Joe" Griesedieck purchased

the failing Forest Park Brewing Company in 1917. He re-named it the Griesedieck Beverage Company.

On January 16, 1919, the Eighteenth Amendment to the United States Constitution was ratified and, one year later, Prohibition became the law of the land. It became illegal to manufacture and sell all forms of alcoholic products, including wine, hard liquor and beer. Some of the brewers who hoped to weather the new law prepared in advance for the inevitable, making near beer or, as Anheuser-Busch did, turning their manufacturing over to non-alcoholic beverages, ice cream, syrup, and malt products that could be legally manufactured.

But Prohibition sounded the death knell for scores of other breweries, from small operations to legendary empires like the Lemp Brewing Company.

And that, as they say, is another story altogether.

2. "Father of Lager Beer in St. Louis"
The Lemp Story Begins

The history of the Lemp family and its brewing empire began in 1838, when Johann Lemp, who went by his middle name, Adam, established a store that sold household items and groceries at what is now Delmas and Sixth streets, not far from the St. Louis riverfront. Lemp was born on May 25, 1798 in the province of Hessen, now part of central Germany. His father, Wilhelm Christoph Lemp, was a master cooper or barrel-maker who moonlighted as a church caretaker. Adam Lemp learned the brewer's trade as a young man in Eschwege, Germany. He would eventually earn the title of master brewer.

In 1836, Lemp immigrated to America, leaving behind his wife, Justine, and his infant son, William, who had been born on February 21 of that year. After arriving in the United States, Lemp first settled in Cincinnati and then, two years later, moved west to St. Louis. In 1838, he opened a small store at Sixth and Morgan streets. In addition to offering general merchandise for sale, Lemp also began making and selling small quantities of vinegar and beer.

Much to his surprise, his beer became very popular. Thanks to the influx of German immigrants to the city, there was a demand for an authentic German-type beer, a beverage that was in short supply in St. Louis at the time. Sales were so brisk that by 1840, he was able to abandon the grocery business altogether and devote his full time to making beer. He started a new operation, which he dubbed the Western Brewery, on South Second Street, between Walnut and Elm, where the Gateway Arch now stands. The new brewery was initially designed to produce both vinegar and beer, a common manufacturing practice in those days. For the first few years, Lemp sold his beer at a pub called Lemp's Hall that was attached to the brewery. The company's total output started out at only one hundred barrels per year but between 1842 and 1845, the popularity of Lemp's beer was so great that he discontinued vinegar production and focused solely on making lager beer.

Adam Lemp

Beer historians agree that Adam Lemp was the first to brew lager beer in St. Louis. However, there are many who believe that he may have been the first to do so in the entire United States, an honor that has previously been bestowed on Philadelphia brewer John Wagner. Lemp had last been employed in Germany in 1836, working

A map / illustration of the St. Louis Riverfront, created in the 1850s

A close-up from the map showing the original site of the Lemp Brewery and saloon -- in the lower left hand corner, marked with a number 4.

in a brewery. If he brought yeast with him to America, which was commonly done, especially by a master brewer, and he began making lager beer in 1838 in his mercantile store, his lager beer would have pre-dated Wagner's by two years. But whatever the date that Adam Lemp produced his lager beer, few can argue that it was one of the first produced in America and, without question, the first brewed in St. Louis.

Beer, in the form of traditional ales and porters, was a popular American drink for many years before Adam Lemp arrived. However, lager beer was something else altogether. Lager is named for its brewing and aging process and the name itself comes from the German verb *lagern*, meaning to rest or to store. Early German brewers, like their later American counterparts, stored their beer in cooling caves during the summer months, when brewing had to be suspended because of the heat. The lagering, or aging process, did several things to the beer that only time could do, including giving the remaining yeast in the product a chance to settle, improving the flavor and allowing it to store better. The end result was a light, crisp beer that not only tasted better but because of its use of bottom-fermenting yeast, it was more stable than ale, which used yeast that fermented at the top. Lager beer became commercially important to brewers in the years before artificial refrigeration because it gave them a product that could be stored longer before it had to be consumed.

Lager beer was quick to catch on in St. Louis, eventually almost to the exclusion of other types. Its popularity in the city was owed to two things. One was the wave of German immigrants that flooded into the area in the 1840s and 1850s. Their demand for lager forced the beer market to change. One by one the makers of English-type brews switched to German lager. In 1850, most St. Louis brewers were producing a combination of lager and ale but by 1860, only two companies were making any ale at all.

The other reason for the popularity of lager in the city was the ease by which it could be made. Thanks to the fact that St. Louis was built atop a network of natural caves, it was easy to find cool places for the beer to be stored during the warm weather months.

The now sealed-off entrance to the Lemp lagering caves. The author's exploration of the caves and brewing cellars took him to underground places once used by the Lemp family and workers.

As Adam Lemp's business increased, he found that his brewery was too small to meet the demand. His main issue was a lack of space in which to lager the beer. The solution, Lemp believed, could be found in a newly discovered limestone cave just south of what were the city limits at the time, now the northwest corner of Cherokee Street and DeMenil Place. By cutting ice from the Mississippi River in the winter and storing it in the cave along with the beer, temperatures could be controlled during the lagering process.

Lemp purchased a lot over the entrance of the cave and then began excavating it for use as a storage area for his lager beer. Work began in the fall of 1844 and continued into the early months of 1845. Workmen cleared a large space for the lagering cellars and the excavations created quite a stir in the city. In the April 10, 1845 edition of the *Daily Missouri Republican*, the newspaper's editor told of his visit to the Lemp cavern and described it as extending to a depth of over fifty feet, about one hundred yards long, and averaging about twenty feet in width. Inside, he wrote, were several oak casks, each holding twenty or thirty barrels of Lemp beer, which had been brewed at the Second Street brewery and then hauled by wagon to the cave for lagering. By the end of 1845, Lemp had moved over three thousand barrels of beer into the cave.

Lemp's Western Brewery continued to grow throughout the remainder of the 1840s and by 1850, it was one of the largest breweries in the city, with an annual production of about four thousand barrels. Lemp

(Left) Rare photograph of Justine Lemp, Adam's first wife, who died from yellow fever.
(Right) Adam's daughter, Mary Lemp.

John Lemp

had established himself as a dominant force in the St. Louis brewing industry and his lager beer led to great financial success. In 1858, his beer captured first prize at the annual St. Louis fair and he was listed in the R.G. Dun Credit Reports as "the most substantial brewer in the city – has made sufficient money to make him independent – owns valuable real estate."

Lemp's Hall, the tavern attached to the brewery, was a major factor in the company's growth. It was improved many times throughout the 1850s until it eventually became the largest saloon in the city. It served only Lemp beer, no hard liquor. This policy served to foster beer sales and it gave Lemp's Hall a good reputation, making it clear that drinking took place in moderation there and that families were welcome.

In 1848, Adam brought his wife and son to America. He and Justine had two more children, a daughter named Mary and a son, John. In 1854, Justine died from yellow fever. Adam later married Louise Bauer, who helped raise the children and remained with him until the end of his life.

By 1860, brewing had become one of St. Louis' largest

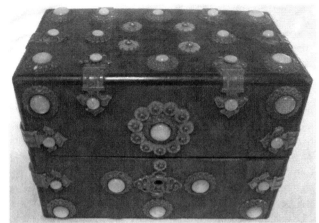

A wooden box with mother of pearl inlay that once belonged to Louise Bauer Lemp.

A formal portrait of Louise Bauer Lemp, Adam's second wife, who he married in 1854.

industries, with the Western Brewery regarded as the best in the city. Lemp planned to continue the brewery's dominance into the next decade. As part of that plan he brought in his eldest son, William, to learn the business.

William Jacob Lemp was twelve when he came to America. Adam had made his fortune by that time and William obtained an education in St. Louis schools. He attended St. Louis University and then went to work in his father's brewery. He quickly learned the art of making beer and was promoted to plant superintendent.

Then, for reasons that remain unclear, William left the Western Brewery and went into a partnership with William Stumpf, whose brewery was located at the present-day intersection of Shenandoah and Lemp avenues. Stumpf had started his brewery in the early 1850s (sources disagree on the exact date, ranging between 1850 and 1853) in the Soulard section of the city. Typical of other brewers on the south side of St. Louis, the brewery operated a storage cave and subterranean beer garden called Stumpf's Cave. It was a major attraction in its day. William Lemp remained Stumpf's partner for a number of years, even after Adam died in 1862, leaving William in charge of the Western Brewery.

William Lemp's career in the brewing industry was temporarily interrupted in April 1861 by the start of the Civil War. Like many German-Americans of that time, Lemp was fiercely patriotic. He immediately joined up with the Third Regiment of the United States Reserve Corps, which was largely made up other south side Germans. Their role as members of the home guard made them responsible for the protection of the St. Louis Arsenal, under the command of Captain Nathaniel Lyon. William even became involved in a brief, violent bit of action during his short term of service.

St. Louis was a city torn apart by the Civil War. Largely pro-Union, St. Louis had to deal with the rest of Missouri, which was sympathetic to the Confederacy. Among those was Missouri's governor, Claiborne Jackson, who came from a family of wealthy Kentucky slave owners. He nevertheless respected the March 1861 decision of the State Convention for Missouri to remain in the Union.

At the start of the war, President Lincoln called for four regiments of volunteers from Missouri, a demand that Governor Jackson called "illegal, unconstitutional and revolutionary." He refused to respond to

William Lemp as a young man

the call for volunteers and four days later, Union leaders ordered Captain Lyon to muster four regiments into public service. Among the newly enlisted home guard troops was William Lemp. Before nightfall, Lyon had his troops at the St. Louis Arsenal, supplied with both arms and ammunition.

On May 2, secessionists at the capital in Jefferson City held a special legislative session to organize a state militia to defend Missouri against Union invasion. The men were marched to an encampment in an area called Lindell Grove at the western edge of St. Louis, on what is now the Frost Campus of St. Louis University. The militia had a yearly muster and drill at Lindell's Grove and that year it was dubbed "Camp Jackson" in honor of the governor.

City leaders feared that the troops, under command of Colonel John S. Bowen, planned an attack on the arsenal. It was discovered that Governor Jackson had asked Confederate President Jefferson Davis to send cannons with which to fortify the militia. Davis returned a message stating that the South was looking "anxiously and hopefully for the day when the Star of Missouri shall be added to the constellation of the Confederate States of America." To help further that plan, Davis sent along two 12-pound howitzers, two 32-pound guns and ammunition that the Confederate government had seized from the Federal Arsenal in Baton Rouge, Louisiana.

On May 8 crates labeled "Tamaroa marble" reached the St. Louis levee in a boat called the *J.C. Swon*, flying a Confederate flag. Inside the crates were the guns and ammunition. Major James A. Shaler escorted the crates to Camp Jackson. Shaler was unaware that he was under surveillance at the time.

The day before, Captain Lyon had driven through Camp Jackson disguised in women's clothing. He wanted to look thongs over without being spotted. Unnerved the sight of about 800 members of the volunteer militia and by a few Confederate flags flying from tentpoles, he feared the troops were preparing for an attack. It probably didn't add to Lyon's peace of mind when he observed that some of the camp streets were named "Davis" and "Beauregard" avenues. Lyon (presumably returned to male attire) held a meeting with Union leaders and informed them that he believed the arsenal was in danger. He decided that even though he had no official orders, he would make the first move and would capture the camp and disarm the militia.

Early the next morning, Lyon and his home guard marched on Camp Jackson. They surrounded the camp and brought about a half-dozen artillery pieces to a ridge along Grand Avenue and to a hill near the intersection of Olive Street and Garrison Avenue. Lyon then demanded the camp's surrender on the grounds that the troops of mostly secessionists and men loyal to the Confederacy were engaging in acts hostile to the United States government.

General Daniel Frost, a secessionist and (ironically) a West Point classmate of Lyon's, protested but he admitted that he was in no position to defend the camp against Lyon's superior force. He had no choice but to surrender. Lyon offered immediate parole to all those who would take an oath of allegiance to the United States, but fewer than a dozen agreed to his terms. The home guard gathered up all of the weapons in the camp and the militiamen were formed into lines to be marched downtown, surrounded on both sides by Lyon's soldiers.

The activity had drawn a large crowd and many of the spectators began shouting taunts and threats at the soldiers who had captured the camp. The crowd began milling into the camp and wandering between the lines of soldiers, causing confusion. Finally, the column began to move, marching north on Grand and then east on Olive. Then, a pistol shot rang out from somewhere and stones and bricks began to be hurled toward the soldiers. More gunfire followed. Fearing for their lives, the home guard opened fire on the mob. Shots were returned from the surrounding area and several soldiers fell in the street. The troops re-loaded and fired again. Unarmed citizens, many of whom had been throwing rocks and stones, were now running for their lives. Many of them went down in the street, blood pooling around their bodies.

Captain Nathaniel Lyon

In the aftermath of the incident, it was reported that ninety people had been wounded, soldiers and civilians alike, and that twenty-eight of them perished from their wounds. It was widely agreed that the soldiers who fired into the mob were justified in their actions. Colonel James Peckham, who was at the scene, stated that the soldiers did not fire until several of them had been wounded.

Several tense hours followed the riot. Anger spread among the Southern sympathizers in the city and in hotels and saloons, speeches were made supporting the Confederate cause. The streets became increasingly unsafe and the police force had trouble keeping the crowds in line. At one point, officers had to line up shoulder to shoulder to prevent a mob from attacking two newspaper offices, one supporting the Union and the other in favor of the South. More rioting followed the next day. A regiment of men from the home guard marched from the arsenal up Third Street, turning west on Walnut. As the first recruits reached

Contemporary illustrations of the violence that occurred in St. Louis at the start of the war. The St. Louis Home Guard, which included William Lemp among its members, took part in what some called the "Camp Jackson Massacre"

Seventh Street, shots rang out from the steps of a church on the corner and a soldier fell dead. Panicked, the untrained troops fired down the street, killing their attackers and four of their own men.

On June 17, more shots were exchanged between soldiers and civilians. A detachment of home guard that had been patrolling the railroad tracks beyond the city marched downtown from the railroad station and turned onto Seventh Street. This time, the crowds cheered the men but between Olive and Pine streets, shots rang out and bullets tore into the center of the column. The soldiers halted and began returning fire at the balcony of the recorder's court on the second floor of the Missouri Engine House. Four people were killed and two were seriously wounded. Captain J. W. Bissell was criticized for giving the order to shoot, but experienced officers were of the opinion that he had to defend his men. The killers had mingled with the crowd with the idea that they could fire at the soldiers and the surrounding mass of people would protect them against the soldiers firing back. As soon as it was made clear that the soldiers would return fire, there were no more attacks on columns of troops.

Captain Lyon was promoted to Brigadier General for his role in the capture of Camp Jackson, but the conflict was far from over between the state of Missouri and the city of St. Louis. In June, Governor Jackson and General Sterling Price called on Lyon at the Planter's House and ordered that he disband the home guard and maintain strict neutrality throughout the state. Lyon was enraged by the command. "Rather than concede to the state of Missouri for one moment the right to dictate to my government in any matter, however unimportant," he shouted, pointing a forefinger at the governor's face, "I would see you and every man, woman and child dead and buried."

He leaned forward until his eyes met directly with those of Governor Jackson. "This means war," he said to the highest official in the state of Missouri. "In an hour, one of my officers will call for you and conduct you out of my lines."

Julia Feickert, who married William in 1861.

Jackson was insulted and angry. He countered Lyon's words with a call for fifty thousand troops from Missouri to "repel this invasion." But he fled the state capital when he heard that Union troops were on their way to Jefferson City. When he left, his office was declared vacant. A provisional governor was appointed in his place and Jackson's senators were expelled from the U.S. Congress with loyal Unionists were put in their places. On June 17, Jackson's forces were defeated at Boonville but they managed to rally at Carthage and escape the state. Jackson attempted to bring Missouri into the Confederacy, establishing a makeshift capital at Neosho, in the southwestern corner of the state. This region became a hotbed of battles and skirmishes.

Nathaniel Lyon was also sent to the southwestern part of the state. When he learned that a Southern army was moving up from Arkansas to take Springfield, he met them with an inadequate force in the battle at Wilson's Creek. This time, Lyon's bravery got the better of him. Already twice wounded, he rallied an Iowa regiment and led them back to attack again. A bullet struck him in the heart and he was killed. He left $30,000, almost his entire estate, to the government for use in continuing the war effort. Lyon had given his life to save St. Louis and Missouri for the Union.

The home guard played an important role in protecting St. Louis at the start of the war. William Lemp was mustered out of the regiment with the rank of orderly sergeant in November 1861. A few weeks later, on December 3, he married Julia Feickert, the daughter of Jacob Feickert, a St. Louis saloon owner and businessman.

The following year was the first in a long line of tragedies for the Lemp family. In 1862, William and Julia's first child died at birth and later that year, on August 23, Adam Lemp passed away, leaving an estate valued at $20,000, a considerable sum for those times. The elder Lemp had been well liked and respected and his funeral procession consisted of more than thirty carriages.

In his will, Adam left the Western Brewery jointly to his son, William, and his daughter Mary's son, Charles Brauneck, along with "all of the equipment and stock." Although no records exist to explain its source, there were bad feelings between the two heirs to the Lemp fortune. According to Lemp family members, the two did not get along and could not stand to be in the same room with one another. But in death, Adam forced them to get along. In his will was a condition that if either of them contested the division of the property, the other would receive everything. Charles Brauneck and William J. Lemp formed a partnership in October 1862 and agreed to run

Charles Brauneck, Adam's grandson, who initially inherited half of the Western Brewery with William Lemp. Bad feelings between the two of them eventually led to the dissolution of the partnership.

the business under the name of William J. Lemp & Company. The partnership turned out to be short-lived. It was dissolved in February 1864 when William bought out Brauneck's share for $3,000.

Soon after, the brewery began to thrive. Unlike many businesses that are weakened by the death of their founder, the Lemp Brewery grew under William's control. He managed to take what his father had created and transform it into an empire that was larger than Adam ever dreamed possible.

3. "The Pride of St. Louis"
The Building of the Lemp Fortune

William Lemp during the heyday of the brewery.

(Below) A match holder that belonged to William Lemp

In the first years after Adam Lemp's death, little changed in the St. Louis brewing market. The Civil War was still in full swing and the city was filled with soldiers and the various types of industries that followed in their wake. As Eberhard Anheuser had discovered, even bad beer was popular with those who didn't know any different. Nearly everyone with a brewery was made rich by the war, but William Lemp was not content to own the largest brewery in St. Louis – he wanted it to be the best.

Lemp, like many other German-Americans of the time, was a hard-working, dedicated man. He loved his wife and grieved with her when their first child died. Three years would pass before Julia became pregnant again. Their oldest daughter, Anna, was born in 1865.

William was a small, compact man, standing just five feet, one inch tall, but he and his brewery were destined to become giants in the beer industry. He realized soon after taking over the reins of the Western Brewery that the modest factory that had served his father was inadequate for the demand that he planned to create for Lemp beer. In 1864, he started plans for a new, much larger brewery.

For many years, Adam Lemp had hauled his beer by wagon from the brewery near the riverfront to the lagering cave on the south side of St. Louis. William knew that it would make more sense to have the brewing and storage facilities in the same place, so he started looking into buying land directly over the Lemp cave. In 1864, he purchased a five-block parcel around the storage house and

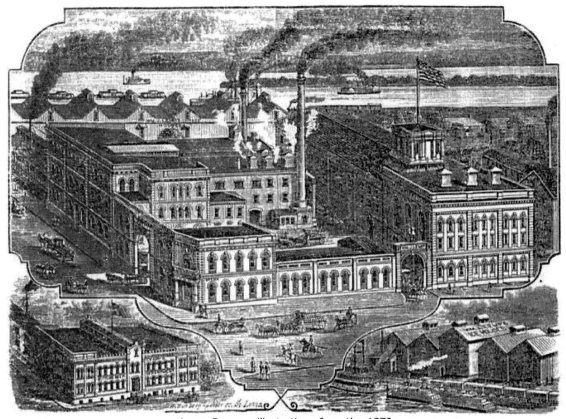
Lemp Brewery illustrations from the 1870s

lagering cave at Cherokee Street and Second Carondelet Avenue (later re-named Thirteenth Street, then DeMenil Place). He planned to build the new brewery at the site, eliminating the need to move the kegs by wagon from the facility on Second Street.

Architects and builders quickly went to work at the site. William had grand ideas and wanted nothing more than to construct one of America's premier breweries. The first building to be completed was the actual brewery, followed by the malt house, the offices and then the east front of the brewery and the ice house. Also around this time, two homes were built near the brewery. One, which is no longer standing, was for William's step-mother and Adam's widow, Louise Bauer The second, a little farther down what is now DeMenil Place, was constructed by Jacob Feickert, William's father-in-law. This imposing brick home was purchased from Feickert in 1876 and turned into a residence for William and Julia, who by then had six children.

The new Lemp brewery was unlike any other brewing operation in St. Louis at the time. The main buildings covered an entire city block, but it was the brewing plant itself that made the Lemp operation the envy of every other brewer in the city. The brewery consisted of three stories at ground level with three more stories below of cellars and caves. On the brewery's first floor was a wash house, where the empty containers were cleaned before being re-filled with Lemp beer. There was also an enormous beer kettle,

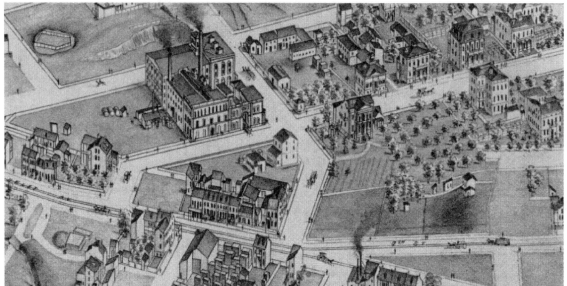

An 1875 map that shows the Lemp Brewery (just left of center) and the surrounding neighborhood. Across the street are the Lemp stables, followed by (left to right) Louise Lemp Bauer's house, homes of Edward Hoppe, J. Beauvais, Jacob Kern and Michael Keber. Below that line of homes is the DeMenil Mansion and to the right, the Jacob Feickert house, which became the Lemp Mansion.

Jacob and Elizabeth Feickert, the parents of Julia Lemp, for whom William Lemp constructed a mansion near the Lemp Brewery. It later became the home of the Lemp family.

which a capacity of one hundred and fifty barrels per day. An air pump was used to send beer to the cellars. On the second floor of the brewery were a wash tub and a second beer kettle, this one designed to hold two hundred and fifty barrels. A coil of copper tubing would be inserted into the kettle and then the beer would be boiled by steam heat. Also on the second floor was the "hop room," which routinely contained hundreds of bushels of hops.

Hops are flower clusters that are primarily used as a flavoring and stability agent in beer. They are what give beer its bitter, tangy flavor. Historically speaking, hops began to be cultivated around the eighth or ninth century in Germany but the first documented use of them as a bittering agent in beer appears in 1079. Before this period, brewers used a wide variety of bitter herbs and flowers, including dandelion, burdock root, marigold, horehound, ground ivy and heather. Hops were first cultivated in America in 1629. German beer makers of the nineteenth century used hops extensively in their brewing for their many benefits, including balancing the sweetness of the malt with bitterness, and contributing a variety of desirable flavors and aromas. Many of the traditional herb combinations stopped being used when it was noticed that brews made with hops were less prone to spoilage.

Also on the second floor of Lemp's brewery was the dining hall and a large room that was used as an employee dormitory for single men. It was a spartan arrangement, with each man assigned a cot and a wardrobe where he could keep his work clothes and personal items. The rising heat from the brew kettles made it brutally hot in the summer, but it was a place to stay for those who could not afford better housing.

The brewery's cooling room was on the third floor. It contained two vast sheet-iron pans over which currents of air would pass freely from the open sides of the room. In this way, the beer was cooled before being sent on to the fermenting tubs. Two elevators were used to move the casks and kegs between floors for cleaning, filling, receiving and shipping.

Lemp's malt house was a massive building, measuring one hundred and six feet across and one hundred and forty-two feet deep. It had three floors aboveground, plus three underground cellars, including the lagering chambers. Every season, workers prepared about 125,000 bushels of malt from the best Canadian barley.

Malting was a process that was applied to cereal grains like barley, in which the grains are made to germinate while soaking in water. They are then quickly halted from germinating further by drying them with hot air. Malting grains develop enzymes that are required to modify the grain's starches into sugars and developing other enzymes that can be utilized by yeast. Barley was the grain most commonly used for malting because of its high enzyme content. An extensive amount of work had to be done to prepare the grain for brewing and Lemp owned one of the most advanced malt houses in the city.

Three grain elevators – one each for barley, malt and sprouted barley – were used to move the grain to different parts of the building during the brewing process. The brewery's cleaning and separating machines were the largest in St. Louis, capable of processing up to one thousand bushels per hour.

Across the street from the brewery was the barrel-making shop and to the north were the Lemp stables. The entire complex was designed in an Italian Renaissance style with arched windows and brick cornices. It eventually grew to cover five city blocks. Soon after its construction, it was ranked as one of the largest breweries in the country and building and renovation continued on a daily basis.

The Lemp brewery was a marvel of modern technology for its time and a showplace of industrial design. William's fascination with mechanics and new innovations was apparent in the construction of the facility. Power was provided by a single seventy-five horsepower engine, which, while small today, was far beyond the capabilities of engines owned by his competitors. The brewery

A photograph of the interior of the brewery, taken by the author in 2003.

The cellars at the Lemp Brewery, visited by the author in 2003. The upper cellars (left) were used to store beer that was undergoing fermentation. The lower cellars (right) were used for lagering.

had been designed to be fireproof, with underground boilers that were located away from the main building. Since boilers were the main cause of fires in those days, having a separate boiler room was essential to safe operations. Steam pumps heated the offices and supplied hot water for the brewing process and for the plant and the nearby homes of William's stepmother, Louise Bauer, and his father-in-law, Jacob Feickert.

The Western Brewery, with its towering buildings and looming smokestack, was the most commanding presence on the south side of St. Louis. But as impressive as the brewery was above ground, it was no less amazing below, where Lemp's lagering cellars consisted of three levels of underground chambers, including both artificial cellars and natural caves.

The upper cellars, accessible through the brewery's basement, were used to store beer that was undergoing fermentation. In the lower cellars, which were divided into about twenty chambers, beer was stored for lagering. Depending on the time of year, there could be as many as fifty thousand barrels of beer stored in huge casks that held between thirty and sixty barrels. The man-made cellars were connected to a vast natural cave that was also used for lagering beer. The entire underground area was kept at a constant year-round temperature of between thirty-five and forty degrees by means of vents from Lemp's ice houses, which held as much as ten thousand tons of ice. There were four additional ice houses on the Mississippi River levee in south St. Louis. Workmen cut blocks of ice from the river each winter, which was then shipped to the brewery where it was used to keep beer cool through the humid summer months. Once artificial refrigeration came into use, the ice houses on the river were used for receiving cargo from Lemp river barges, which transported beer up and down the Mississippi and Ohio rivers.

Around 1877, beer began to be sold in bottles. This was an important development in the brewing industry and it was quickly adopted by William Lemp. The new technology made it possible for him to ship his beer all over the world.

At first, only European brewers bottled their own beer. In America, bottling was a separate, independent industry that was handled by companies under contract by the brewers. But after Anheuser-Busch introduced a pasteurization process for beer, making it more stable and easier to transport, it became preferable for breweries to do their own bottling. This development soon changed the entire brewing industry. The main reason for this was that the retailing of draught beer was a costly and cumbersome operation since, in a large market, scores of horses, stables and wagons had to be maintained for regular

deliveries. On the other hand, bottled beer could be delivered anywhere at a fraction of the cost. This opened new markets for beer in homes, restaurants, hotels and in distant places that brewers never dreamed of in the past.

Brewers who began their own bottling shops began to call themselves brewers and bottlers. William Lemp advertised that his beer was "Bottled in the Brewery." Initially, the bottling process was a somewhat crude process that was done by hand by workers using a hose from the barrel to fill each bottle. After filling, a pressing device was used to insert a cork into the bottle, which was then wired shut. After the beer was pasteurized, labels were glued onto the bottles and the neck was wrapped in decorative foil. When it opened the Lemp bottling plant had a capacity of twelve thousand bottles per day.

Needless to say, William Lemp's expansions allowed the Western Brewery to enjoy greater success than ever before. William had been able to turn a neighborhood brewery, albeit a lucrative one, into one of the largest and most modern operations in America. By 1877, it was the largest in St. Louis and was ranked nineteenth in size in the entire country. That same year, Anheuser-Busch, which was starting to become a serious challenger to the Lemp brewery, was ranked thirty-second.

In the late 1870s, the next great innovation in the brewing industry, artificial refrigeration, came along to change things all over again. From its earliest days, brewers like Lemp supported the advent of mechanical refrigeration, knowing that it would offer them great advantages. Brewers gave the inventors of these devices the opportunities to try out their new-fangled machines, often paying heavily for the failure of the initial prototypes. Eventually, though, the refrigeration units developed to the point that the needs of the breweries could be served and allowed them to meet the always-increasing demands of their customers.

William Lemp was eager to add artificial refrigeration to his brewery and in 1878 he installed the first refrigerating machine in an American brewery. The ammonia compression unit designed by Theodore Krausch managed to streamline Lemp's operations in such a dramatic way that he no longer had to rely on the limited capacity of the lagering cave.

4. "Wonders Below the Earth"
The Brewery Caves of St. Louis

The caves of St. Louis – in particular the cave that was once used by the Western Brewery – represent one of the most unusual elements of the city and the story of the Lemp family. The city of St. Louis is built upon a huge and complex system of natural caves. In fact, no other city on earth has as many caves beneath its streets. While most of them have been abandoned and closed off, they have not been forgotten. Many tales of their unusual history are still told today.

Caves were used as man's earliest storage cellars. Thanks to their natural coolness, food and other items could be stored in them and kept from spoiling. Their low temperatures made them perfect for lagering beer. Adam Lemp, who first brought lager beer to thirsty St. Louisians, was the first of the German brewers to put the caves to work, but he was far from the only one. Brewers altered the caves beneath the city to suit their purposes. They constructed stone arches and brick ceilings to prevent water from seeping in and paved the uneven floors. They constructed staircases and walkways and installed massive wooden kegs where beer could be stored. While the brewers initially saved money by having the caves, it was usually quite expensive to expand and renovate them. For this reason, many of the caves did double duty as not only the place where beer was lagered, but also as the place where it could be sold. A number of beer gardens and taverns were located in St. Louis caves and they became popular drinking establishments and eateries.

Many of the caves also had a rich history. In some cases, breweries might not have been built at all but for the existence of the caves beneath the earth. The Anheuser-Busch brewery cave was first discovered in 1852 by a German brewer named George Schneider. He built a small brewery on the land above it and operated it for three years before going out of business. The company was taken over by a competitor, who renamed the property the Bavarian Brewery. Later, after defaulting on loans, the brewery was taken over by Eberhard Anheuser.

In addition to beer lagering, the cave was also used by the military. During the Civil War, it was located close to the arsenal and the tunnels of the cave were used to hide arms and ammunition. The guns were concealed in beer wagons and were taken to the cave for safekeeping when a raid on the arsenal was feared. Later, when Anheuser-Busch began using artificial refrigeration in its plant, the cave beneath the brewery was abandoned and forgotten. It was rediscovered in the 1930s when excavations were being done for underground storehouses.

The story of St. Louis' caves is an important part of the city's history and an essential element to the strange story of the Lemp family.

Uhrig's Cave

In 1852, Dr. William Beaumont, a famous St. Louis surgeon and the longtime post doctor at the Jefferson Barracks, decided to sell off a portion of his land, which was notable for the fact that it had a large natural cave beneath it. The wooded tract was bounded to the north by Locust Street and to the south by Washington Avenue.

The land was purchased by two German brothers, Franz and Andrew Uhrig, who owned a brewery on Market Street, just southeast of Beaumont's property. Franz had come to America in 1836 and he arrived in St. Louis two years later. His first enterprise was ferrying cordwood to the city, down the Illinois River, from a farm that was owned by his brother, Andrew. In 1839, the brothers went into the beer business and started the Camp Springs Brewery near the present-day site of Union Station. It would later be re-named the Uhrig Brewery and it operated until 1884.

Before the early 1850s, the Uhrigs had been lagering their beer inside a warehouse at the brewery. Using ice that was cut from the river and packed in sawdust, they barely managed to keep their beer cold enough during the warm weather months. This inefficient and time-consuming method cost them so much money that they were unable to expand. When they heard about the land being offered for sale by Dr. Beaumont, they quickly bought it. The cave, which had a small spring inside, was perfect for their business.

The Uhrigs first expanded the cave's length to one hundred and seventy feet. They built brick walls and high arched ceilings to prevent water seepage and spent an estimated $100,000 to connect their cave with a series of other caverns and to install a narrow gauge railroad that could transport their beer from the brewery to the cave. It was definitely one of the most unique cave operations in St. Louis brewery history.

As further enhancement, the Uhrigs opened a beer garden in a shady grove of trees near the cave entrance. Since it was only a short buggy ride from the city's downtown, it became a popular place to enjoy a glass of beer and listen to music. Tables were placed both outside and inside the cave's largest chamber. Band concerts were held there along with dining and dancing. Other breweries with caves followed suit but Uhrig's became known

The entrance to Uhrig's Cave, one of the first beer gardens in the city.

as the original St. Louis beer garden.

During the Civil War, entertainment at the cave was suspended while it was used as the headquarters for one of the local militia units. They camped at the cave and used some of the larger areas to hold their drills. After the war ended, brewery operations resumed and customers quickly returned to the popular spot. In the late 1860s, the Uhrig brothers sold the cave to Chris Nuntz, who added a theater and turned the cave into an opera house. He continued this endeavor until 1881, when he began leasing out the cave for the next three years.

The cave was purchased by saloon keeper Thomas McNeary in 1884. He further expanded on the theater and turned the cave into a full-blown vaudeville house. McNeary and his brothers ushered in the golden age of Uhrig's Cave, attracting popular entertainers like John Drew, Julia Marlow and other stars to their stage. They also installed the first electric lights used in any St. Louis entertainment spot. During its peak, the subterranean theater drew audiences of up to three thousand people per night, all coming to enjoy music, plays, comic operas and of course, to drink beer.

The glory days only lasted for the next four years. In 1888, the McNeary brothers lost their liquor license and the cave was abandoned until 1900, when an ill-fated attempt was made to revive the place as a legitimate theater. From 1903 to 1908, the cave was used at different times as a roller rink, a bowling alley and a mushroom farm. After the failure of the mushroom farm, the McNearys gave up and offered a ninety-year lease to a syndicate called the Business Men's League, who built a large auditorium that covered the cave, the beer garden and much of the surrounding area. They planned to create a facility to host sporting events, theatrical performances and other forms of entertainment. They broke ground in 1908 and planned to call the location the St. Louis Coliseum.

The Coliseum had a grand opening in 1909 when famed British evangelist Rodney "Gipsy" Smith began a series of revival meetings at the venue. Smith attracted more than ten thousand people each night and paved the way for horse shows, circuses and for many of St. Louis' unique Veiled Prophet Balls. Many popular performers played at the Coliseum including Enrico Caruso and John McCormack. Bill Tilden played tennis there and Johnny "Tarzan" Weissmuller swam in what was called "the world's largest indoor swimming pool." It was installed in 1925 and could be covered by a removable floor when arena space was needed. One of the most popular events to be held there was a 1927 championship wrestling match between Joe Stecker and Ed "Strangler" Lewis. The Coliseum was completely sold out and the brutal match lasted until the wee hours of the morning, with the Strangler finally emerging as the winner.

The St. Louis Coliseum, built on the site of Uhrig's Cave

Despite all of this, the Coliseum was never a financial success. As early as 1914, it was cited for back taxes and for being behind in rent payments. Ownership reverted to the McNeary estate (Tom McNeary died in 1893), which held it until 1925, when it was purchased by a New York syndicate that had plans to renovate it. They tried to stimulate new interest in the place by installing the immense swimming pool and by varying the use of the building, but by then it was almost too late. The construction of the St. Louis Arena in 1929 and the Kiel Auditorium in 1934 drew most of the large events away from the Coliseum. To make matters worse, the building had no real parking available, which was not a problem in the early days but it grew to be one as automobiles became more popular. The last event held at the Coliseum was a wrestling match in 1939. During World War II, it was used as a storage depot for new automobiles, the sale of which had been frozen by government regulations at the start of the war. After the war, the Coliseum was abandoned and in 1953, it was condemned by the city as being unsafe. It was torn down later that year.

Cave explorers and historians got one last look at the old cave in 1954 when the Jefferson Bank & Trust Company building was being constructed on the site. Many of the passageways still remained, along with the man-made brickwork and the natural features like the small spring. It turned out that some of the smaller tunnels had been used by bootleggers during Prohibition. A secret entrance was discovered, as well as a distillery for making whiskey. The walls of one of the rooms, believed to have been a speakeasy, had been decorated with Egyptian-style paintings.

One has to wonder if the Uhrig's brothers had any idea, when they purchased the site in the middle 1800s, of the activity their small brewery cave would see in the years to come.

English Cave

One of the most mysterious of St. Louis' brewery caves is one that few people living today have seen. Now filled with water and inaccessible, English Cave was a place of legend in the early years of the city. Not only was it rumored to be haunted, it was also said to bring bad luck to anyone who owned it.

The original entrance to what came to be known as English Cave was located just east of Benton Park, between Arsenal and Wyoming streets in South St. Louis. The opening was a natural shaft that extended about sixty feet underground, at the end of which was a chamber that was close to four hundred feet long.

Before the French settled St. Louis, the cave was used by Native Americans. It is from this period when the legend of the curse was first attached to it. According to the story, there was a young Indian woman who fell in love with one of the men from her village. The young man reciprocated her feelings but was unable to marry the girl as she had already been promised to the tribe's war chief, a violent and disagreeable man. Rather than see her in the arms of another, the man convinced his lover to run away with him. They found refuge in the cave and planned to stay hidden there until the chief and his warriors stopped looking for them. Unfortunately, the chief tracked them to the cave and he and his men took up positions outside, intent on taking back the young woman when she left the cave. Rather than surrender, the story goes that the couple stayed in the cave and eventually starved to death.

Many years later, white settlers discovered two skeletons in the cave and were told the story of the ill-fated lovers by the Native Americans who lived nearby. As the years passed, the settlers told their own tales about the cave, claiming that ghostly sounds of weeping and moaning could be heard coming from its darkest chambers. It was believed the spirits of the doomed couple still lingered there. The ghost story took on a life of its own and over the decades, the hard luck experienced by the cave's owners gave birth to tales of the curse.

The man whose name became attached to the cave, Ezra O. English, was the first to experience the effects of the curse. In 1826, English built a small ale brewery next to the cave and east of the commons. He later set up the brewery inside the cave, becoming the first person in St. Louis to use a cave as a commercial property. Unlike those who followed his example, English did little to improve the cave's interior beside walling up the mouth, removing some of the stone and earth from the floors and carving out fifty stone steps into the first chamber, which he primarily used for his business. Beyond this was a second chamber, ten feet lower than the first. A small spring emerged from the ceiling of the cave, creating a waterfall. English used the cave as a place to store his ale and as a novelty saloon for customers who wanted to sample cool drinks.

In 1839, English took on a partner, a local businessman named Isaac McHose. They began calling the place the St. Louis Brewery. The business grew and by 1842, they had developed the first subterranean beer garden and resort in the city. While the men were expanding the business, they gained a new neighbor when the city converted the commons next door to the brewery into a public burial ground. Cholera epidemics had been striking the city and the graveyard began to grow.

By 1849, renovations to the cave had been completed and English and McHose re-named their project Mammoth Cave and Park, likely borrowing the name from the famous cave in Kentucky, which was then starting to attract visitors from all over the country. English and McHose built gardens and arbors around the property and hired a family of vocalists to entertain on Sundays. Later, they constructed a sail swing, a carnival-type ride in the form of a gondola car that swooped back and forth. They also arranged hot air balloon rides and hired a military band to play full-time.

Just when the partners seemed to be on the verge of success, disaster struck. The year 1849 was remembered in the city as the "year of misfortune," thanks to a terrible cholera epidemic and the great fire that devastated the riverfront. After those calamities, no one seemed to have much interest in the attractions that the cave offered and by 1851, English was once again the sole proprietor. Within a few years, he faded from public records.

Several years later, the city passed an ordinance calling for the removal of all bodies from the cemetery that adjoined the site. The remains were to be taken to the Quarantine Burying Grounds, located some distance south of the Jefferson Barracks military post. When all of the bodies were removed from the St. Louis Cemetery, another ordinance established it as a public park in 1866. The park was named in honor of Missouri artist Thomas Hart Benton and the cave was largely forgotten.

In 1887, two businessmen named F.K. Binz and George Schaper attempted to resurrect English Cave as a commercial mushroom farm. They hoped to fare better than their predecessors, even though they were constantly reminded of the cave's misfortunes. A newspaper article that was published at the time wished the men well "in spite of the history of failure that has hung around the place." The operation was soon in full swing and the partners tended their fungoid crop by the light of kerosene lanterns. For a time, the business was moderately successful. Regular customers paid seventy-five cents for a pound of mushrooms. Then somehow, something went wrong and the business lasted only two years before the cave was abandoned once again.

The next unfortunate occupant was the Paul-Wack Wine Company, widely acclaimed for the fine wines they bottled – at least before coming to English Cave. Soon after opening in their new location, the company began to fail. They used the cave for storage until 1897, and soon after, went out of business. The winery was the last company to use the cave for commercial purposes.

In the early 1900s a St. Louis parks commissioner attempted to put the cave back into use. He suggested opening a portion of it to visitors to Benton Park. He recommended constructing ornamental entrance to the cave from the park, believing that people would be interested in touring this unique attraction. Unfortunately, and perhaps predictably, the plans were never realized and the cave was forgotten – or nearly so. Over the course of the next few years, it caused a myriad of problems for Benton Park. On several occasions, the park's lake lost all of its water, flooding the cave beneath it. The parks department constructed a concrete lake bottom and sealed off the leak but water kept leaking into the cave.

Today, the cave is completely flooded and inaccessible. Oddly enough, though, in the middle 199os, a dry spell in the city made it possible for a few cave explorers to get into a portion of the cave. They found that entire sections of English Cave that had been renovated during the years of English and McHose remained untouched. The dry days only lasted a short time and the cave was filled with water once more. Since then, no one has entered the cave.

Does this mean that the curse of English Cave is finally over? With curious visitors and unlucky brewery owners no longer disturbing their rest, perhaps the Indian girl and her lover can live out their eternity in peace within the damp and murky darkness of English Cave, no longer bothered by trespassers from the world above.

Other St. Louis Brewery Caves

There were a number of other breweries that also used the natural cave systems of the city during the golden age of brewing in St. Louis. Ironically, many of them used different portions of the same cave, never realizing that they were actually connected. One such was part of Uhrig's Cave, generally known as the "Winkelmeyer and Excelsior Cave." It was used by four separate breweries during the middle to late 1800s.

In 1847, Julius Winkelmeyer and his brother-in-law, Frederick Stiffel started the Winkelmeyer Brewery along the western bank of Chouteau's Pond. They chose the site because of the underlying natural cave and because of the fact that the lake was a popular recreation spot at that time. Sadly, Stiffel and his wife both died during one of the periodic epidemics that were blamed on the polluted conditions of Chouteau's Pond. When Winkelmeyer died in 1867 his wife carried on the business, changing the name to the Union Brewery in 1873. It ceased operations in 1892.

In 1880, another brewer set up operations in a portion of the same cave and became known as the Excelsior Brewery. It shared the cave with Franklin Brewery, which had been started in 1855 and was located just south of Market Street. The area was cleared to make way for Union Station in 1894, but by then, all of the companies had long gone out of business and the cave they had used for lagering had been forgotten.

But it would not stay forgotten for long. In 1933, the city made plans to widen Market Street and as city engineers started their excavations, they broke into the abandoned cave. Surveyors entered the cave and found the remains of the old Winkelmeyer plant, as well as a second level of the cave that contained wooden fermenting tanks. They discovered masonry walls and brick columns and at one end of a tunnel, they found an abandoned mushroom bed that had belonged to Binz and Shaper. Beneath this level, they entered a deep cellar that was now only accessible by a shaky ladder. This large sub-cellar had vaulted arches and huge wooden chambers and vats for beer that were still intact. The cave was sealed up and remained that way for a few years until the new post office was built and the cave was surveyed again.

In 1955, re-development work was started on the Plaza, which led to a collapse of part of the cave in 1959. Engineers had tried to fill it in a few years before, but a depression developed that was almost twenty-five feet deep. They poured four thousand cubic yards of fill into the cavern, but in 1960, a sidewalk collapsed in front of the post office. Government engineers had to drive steel beams into the cave beneath the sidewalk in order to support the pavement. It had become another St. Louis cave that simply refused to be forgotten.

In 1833, a German immigrant named Christian Staehlin came to St. Louis, followed four years later by his father. Together, they opened the Staehlin Brewery at the corner of Eighteenth and Lafayette streets, choosing the site because of the

Phoenix Brewery

access to the natural cave and spring beneath the area. The company later became known as the Phoenix Brewery and the Staehlins began a plan to expand the caves by adding brick and masonry and moving lagering equipment into what visitors called a "labyrinth of tunnels."

Christian Staehlin remained in charge of the Phoenix Brewery until 1877, when he sold out to Anton Griesedieck, who changed the name to the A. Griesedieck Brewing Company. He in turn sold the plant in 1889 to the St. Louis Brewing Association. The brewery closed for good in 1920.

In 1964, the old brewery buildings were destroyed to make way for the expansion of Interstate 55. Today, a tangle of highways crosses the area above the cave and it is no longer accessible.

In 1839, another German immigrant, Carl Klausmann, came to American and settled in Louisville, Kentucky. During his brief stay there, he met a young woman named Maria Anna Uhrig, sister to the Uhrig brewing brothers of St. Louis. A short time later, she moved to St. Louis with the rest of her family and Klausmann followed. The two married in 1841 and opened a restaurant at the corner of Walnut and Third streets called Our House. The establishment flourished and so they decided to follow the family tradition and open their own brewery along South Broadway. They used a large cave that was nearby to lager their beer.

Unfortunately, just two years after the brewery was opened, Klausmann died, leaving Maria Anna to raise six children and run the business. Through her hard work, the company prospered and she amassed a considerable fortune. The beer garden that she had added onto the property, known as Klausmann's Cave, became drew large crowds. In 1877, she expanded it and added regular music concerts. The brewery also thrived. A malting operation was added in 1881 and two years later, they began bottling the beer and selling it outside of the city. After Maria Anna Klausmann died in 1898, the brewery and the cave continued as a branch of the St. Louis Brewing Association.

In 1902, the Carondelet Business Men's Association sponsored a week-long carnival at the cave and beer gardens. The crowds that attended were so large that special arrangements had to be made to have all of the streetcars on Broadway running to Klausmann's Cave. The association also convinced the ferry companies on the Mississippi to bring over visitors from Illinois.

Like it did to so many other breweries, Prohibition killed the Klausmann operation. It was too small to survive the years of forced inactivity and so the company was shut down. Eventually, the buildings were demolished. The entrance to the cave was later filled in for the safety of the children who lived in the neighborhood but it still remains there under the St. Louis streets – silent, empty and almost forgotten.

During the late 1850s, a large natural cave that was located near Sidney Street, running from the Mississippi River to Eleventh Street, was used by a total of fourteen different breweries. In most cases, the companies had no idea that they were using parts of the same large cave and each believed that clay falls and rockslides marked the ends of their own cave. They didn't realize that these were simply natural occurrences that blocked off passageways leading from one portion of the cave to another. Some of the breweries that used the Sidney Street Cave had come along after other breweries had either gone out of business or had been sold out to other breweries.

One of the companies to use the cave was the Whitteman and Rost Weis Beer Brewery, with a small factory just east of the river. There was another early brewery called Suesert and Berger, which was located on the south side of Sidney Street. It was in this area that the Green Tree Brewery was located.

The Theo. Schwer and Co. Brewery was on Lynch Street, one block south of Sidney Street and near Carondelet, now South Broadway. This brewery operated for only one year, in 1891, and bottled a short-lived label called Our Favorite.

The Excelsior Brewery was located at Seventh and Lynch streets and closed down in 1880, when all of its operations were moved to the Uhrig Brewery.

On the north side of Sidney and east of today's Broadway was the Pittsburg Brewery. It was started in 1857 and within a year was producing more than three thousand barrels of beer annually. By 1859, when that number had increased to eight thousand barrels, the Pittsburg Brewery opened a new branch called The Cave, at the intersection of Rosatti and Lynch streets.

The Jackson Brewery, which also started in 1857, stood on the same block as the Pittsburg Brewery. The company, owned by Jacob Stagner, got off to a good start, producing about one thousand barrels of lager beer the first year, but production soon dropped off and the brewery went out of business.

The Arsenal Brewery also opened in 1857. It was built by F.F. Heinscher just south of Sidney Street and west of Broadway. The company began producing about eight thousand barrels of beer with about half that number being lagered in the cave. They opened a second branch around 1875 at the corner of Rosatti and Lynch streets.

On the north side of Sidney Street, where it intersects with Buel, the Schlop Brewery was opened by Louis Koch in 1860. This company only produced about five hundred barrels of beer during its first year and a few years later, Koch built another brewery called Koch & Feldkamp's, which it operated under that name until 1875. It was later known as Schilling and Schneider.

One block west at the intersection of Sidney and Tenth streets was the Gambrinus Brewery, which was started in 1856 by Anton Jaeger. Named for St. Gambrinus, the patron saint of brewers, it produced four thousand barrels of beer during its initial year of operation. But by 1860, production had fallen by half. Apparently being named for a saint wasn't enough to bring about good fortune and the brewery went out of business. During the war, it was used as the armory.

Jaeger was an Acting Lieutenant in Company A of Major Henry Almstedt's 1st Regiment. On July 18, 1881, Jaeger was among Union troops from St. Louis who were taking the Pacific railroad west just south of the Missouri River to Hermann and then on to Jefferson City, which had been seized by Union troops the month before. Jaeger, who wasn't feeling well, got off the train at Wellsville and unloaded his horse from a boxcar. He borrowed a buggy from a local store owner and headed to Montgomery City, where he planned to attend a funeral. With him was a lawyer named Benjamin T. Sharp. A Southern sympathizer and a slave-owner, Sharp nevertheless supported the federal government. He agreed to help in convincing the Southern states to rejoin the Union. In return for raising a company of Union men, Sharp had been promised a commission to Colonel.

Sharp was supposed to go to Mexico, Missouri, and give a speech urging Union sympathizers from Audrain, Montgomery, and Callaway counties to join his company. He got into the buggy with Jaeger, who left word in town for the forty-two horsemen from Company A who were en route to Hermann to follow the buggy tracks and catch up with him and Sharp when their train got in.

No one knows why Jaeger set off with only one companion in an area that was rife with Southern sympathizers. He must have known that there had been attacks on Union troops in the vicinity but he chose to disregard the danger. Unfortunately, fate caught up with him in the form of Capt. "One-Armed" Alvin Cobb, who, along with his son and a few other men, ambushed Jaeger and Sharp outside of Martinsburg. Both men were wounded, with Jaeger's right arm nearly blown off at the elbow by a buckshot blast. Despite their wounds, the pair tried to get away but Jaeger fell out of the buggy, which then crashed into a fence. The pair were captured and Alvin accused Jaeger of killing women and children in St. Louis, a charge he denied, explaining that he was a brewer in that city. His denial did him no good. Cobb and his bushwackers killed him and Sharp.

It was just another bloody incident in a vicious and violent war that turned neighbors and kin into sworn enemies.

In 1870, Henry Anthony and Francis Kuhn purchased Jager's old brewery. Beneath it, they had access to the Sidney Street Cave. Their portion of it was described as extending in all directions from an elevator shaft. It was dry, cool and well ventilated with stone floors and walls and ceilings made of brick. Above ground were the brewery buildings and what was described as a "mammoth" beer garden and a grand pavilion where military bands often played.

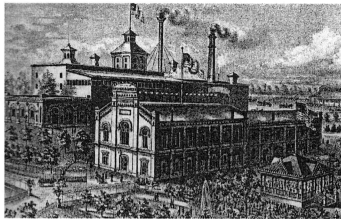

An 1879 illustration of the Anthony & Kuhn Brewing Company

The Anthony & Kuhn Brewery Company grew quickly and their section of the cavern was expanded to increase production. In 1875, they required thirty men and six beer wagons to deliver their product throughout the city. It continued to operate until the owners sold out to the St. Louis Brewing Association conglomerate in 1899. The syndicate promptly closed it down. In 1922, the building was sold to a laundry company and was later torn down.

Most of the cave was destroyed but rumors persist that a portion still remains under the south side of Menard Street. It is really quite sad to think that the Sidney Street Cave, like so many others in St. Louis, is no longer accessible. Based on the sheer number of breweries that used it in days gone by, this surely was once one of the most productive caves in the city.

The Lemp / Cherokee Cave

There is no question that the most famous of St. Louis' brewery caves was the one that would become known as Cherokee Cave. Originally, this was part of the cave that was used by Adam Lemp for lagering his beer. The cave was incorporated into the operations of the brewery that William Lemp built after his

father's death. It became an unusual entertainment venue for the Lemp family and their friends. Year later, the cave went on to become one of the most popular "show caves" in the region.

Adam Lemp began using the cave in 1845, when workmen expanded the natural confines of the cavern and fitted it for use in the brewing industry. Around 1850, at the same time the Lemp Brewery was beginning to grow, a fur trader named Henry Chatillon built a home on a piece of property that adjoined Adam's parcel on the crest of Arsenal Hill on Thirteenth Street. In 1856, Dr. Nicholas DeMenil purchased the land and began expanding what had been a simple farmhouse. DeMenil added several rooms and a magnificent portico that faced eastward overlooking a large garden and below that, the Mississippi River. The Greek Revival mansion became a favorite landmark for steamship pilots rounding a curve in the river called Chatillon's Bend.

In 1865, DeMenil leased the southwest corner of the

The DeMenil Mansion

property to the Minnehaha Brewery, which built a small, two-story wood frame brewing house on the site. For several years, DeMenil had been using a cave beneath his house to store perishable goods. He decided to lease a portion of the cave to Charles Fritschle and Louis Zepp, the owners of the brewery. Like Adam Lemp, they planned to use the cavern to lager beer. They made a number of improvements to the cave but the company went out of business two years later, unable to survive the economic downturn that followed the Civil War.

During the two years that it had been in business, the Minnehaha Brewery was using another part of the same cave as the Lemps. A wall had been constructed between the two operations, dividing the space where DeMenil's property ended and Lemp's began. The Lemp family was on good terms with Dr. DeMenil. When William began renovating the home that had belonged to Jacob Feickert for his own family, an arrangement was made to run pipelines from the brewery complex through DeMenil's cave. This furnished the Lemp mansion, along with DeMenil's home, with hot and cold running water. Another series of pipes carried beer from the brewery to taps in the mansion.

The cave was used for brewery operations until the late 1870s, when artificial refrigeration units were installed. After that, with the cave no longer played a major role in the production of beer. Instead, it was turned into an entertainment complex for the Lemp family. There was an entrance to the cave in the basement of the mansion. To reach it, the Lemps traveled by way of a quarried shaft that linked with the cave and eventually led to the lagering cellars of the brewery. William Lemp used this route to go back and forth from the mansion to his brewery office during inclement weather.

One of the cave's chambers of was used as a ballroom, where the Lemps held a few parties. Another larger chamber was converted into a combination auditorium and theater. Across one end of the space, imitation cave walls were constructed using plaster and wire screen. The walls were intended to create backstage storage space. Ironically, workmen had to tear out natural features of the cave to create the fake cave walls. Crude floodlights were used to illuminate the stage. The Lemps were believed to have hired

Vintage postcard and advertising for Cherokee Cave

actors to put on private performances there. The section of the cave where the theater was located was accessible by way of a spiral staircase that once ascended to Cherokee Street. This entrance is sealed today and the spiral stairs were cut away to prevent trespassers from entering the cave.

East of the theater was another Lemp family innovation. Just below the intersection of Cherokee Street and DeMenil Place was a large, concrete-lined pool that had been a reservoir back in the days of underground lagering. Legend maintained that in the years that followed, the Lemps converted it into a swimming pool by using hot water piped in from the brewery's boiler house a short distance away.

After Prohibition, the caves were abandoned and the entrances sealed shut. However, this was not the end for the Minnehaha portion of the cave. In November 1946, a pharmaceutical manufacturer named Lee Hess bought the Minnehaha part of the cave, as well as the old DeMenil house and grounds. He set to work developing the cave as a tourist attraction. He erected a museum building and parking lot to serve what he dubbed "Cherokee Cave." The cave became a popular tourist attraction but not without considerable work and money. Hess developed almost an obsession with the cave and nearly lost his entire fortune trying to develop it. He moved into the sprawling DeMenil house but only lived in two of the rooms. Hess and his wife shared one room and Albert Hoffman, who managed the cave for Hess, lived in the other.

In April 1950, Cherokee Cave was opened to the public. Visitors were able to stroll along on a tour that took them to "Cherokee Lake," the "Petrified Falls" and the famed "Spaghetti Room," where slender cave formations hung down from the ceiling like strands of pasta.

The cave remained open until 1960. A year later, it was purchased from Hess by the Missouri Highway Department, which had plans to demolish the museum and close the cave to make way for Interstate 55. The cave was lost but Hess battled until the end of his life to keep the state from destroying the DeMenil mansion. Eventually, he succeeded. The cave museum and the entrance that Hess had created were demolished in 1964. Today, the only reminder of this unique place is a short street near Broadway and Cherokee called Cave Street. The DeMenil Mansion became a historic site and museum.

For many years after the highway tore through the historic portion of the city, it was believed that Cherokee Cave had been filled in and completely destroyed. This was later discovered to be incorrect. Portions of the cave still exist today. While not accessible to the public, the mystery of the place remains alive.

Cave researchers and spelunkers have toured its passages in recent years but the last documented visits to Cherokee cave took place in the middle 1960s. Those who ventured into the long-abandoned cave told of seeing the labyrinth of rooms that had been constructed by the Lemps. Broken and rotted wooden casks remained where beer was once aged. The visitors described how they passed through oversized doorways and into rooms lined with brick and stone. The old pool remained, filthy and covered with mud. The theater still existed, although it was hard to imagine what kind of audience would have been willing to assemble in the clammy darkness to watch a performance there.

Ghost stories have long been told about the nearby Lemp Mansion, which once had access to the cave from its basement, but there are those who insist the cave is haunted too. Strange sounds have been reported coming from the cave and shadowy, flitting shapes have been seen that cannot be explained away as weird but natural cave phenomena. In recent times, the brewery above the cave has occasionally been the site of a Halloween haunted house attraction. There have been a few nights when the customers got a little more than they bargained for. On at least one occasion, the attraction was reportedly closed down after a staff member spotted someone in an off-limits area that led down to the cave entrance. The customers were stopped at the door while employees searched for the wandering visitor in an attempt to escort him out. After a thorough search, no one was ever found. Whoever the trespasser had been, he had vanished.

At other times, apparitions were heard rather than seen. One staff member who entered the cave claimed to have heard the sound of someone wearing hard-soled shoes walking behind him in some of the abandoned passageways. Unnerved, he began walking faster, only to have the mysterious footsteps keep pace with him. Thinking that it was only his imagination or a cave echo playing tricks on him, he stopped abruptly, fully expecting the tapping of the shoes to stop as well. Instead, they continued on for several more steps before also coming to a halt. By this time he was feeling quite frightened. Summoning his courage, he turned and shined his flashlight down the passage behind him. No one was there. Needless to say, he hurriedly left the cave.

Aside from a few unauthorized visits to the cave during the Halloween attraction, the remnants of Cherokee Cave remained dark and empty. A few forays into its depths for research purposes added to the haunted lore of the place but much as I longed to visit it myself, it seemed unlikely that I would ever have the opportunity. After discovering that the cave was no longer accessible from the house, I gave up on the idea of ever seeing it. The Lemp Caverns, and the legendary Cherokee Cave, were closed and forgotten, perhaps for all time. I resigned myself to the fact that it was a place that I would never get to see – or so I thought until March 2003.

That spring, I happily accepted an invitation from Paul Pointer, one of the owners of the Lemp Mansion, to come along on an excursion into the Lemp Caverns and Cherokee Cave.

On a chilly night in early March, a small group of us assembled at the Lemp Mansion and then followed Paul as he took us to one of the rear entrances to the brewery buildings, the only remaining access into the caves. We first had the rare treat of touring the brewery itself, even riding one of the original elevators to the top floor and going out on the roof for an incredible view of south St. Louis. The warehouse buildings at the brewery are utterly massive with huge open floors that once held machinery and beer storage casks. In later times, after artificial refrigeration, the beer had been stored in various locations in the building. As we descended to the lower areas of the brewery, it was almost like returning to the earliest days of the company, when beer had to be stored in low, cool areas to lager.

Staircases and elevators took us lower into the brewery until we finally entered areas that were underground. Here, we found massive rooms with curved archways, detailed stone- and brickwork and ceilings that had been built with individual, arched sections to add extra support for the gigantic stone buildings overhead. When the brewery had been constructed, the foundations would have had to support incredible weight in machinery, men and the huge casks of beer.

In each section that we explored, as we went deeper underground, we found remnants of the brewery and the heyday of the Lemp empire. In the upper sections, we found only occasional, worn-away emblems in the shape of the famous Lemp shield (which later became the Falstaff logo), original light fixtures, insignias on doors and glass fixtures but little else. As we descended deeper underground, however, the remains of the brewery became more noticeable and some locations appeared almost untouched, as though the last people to walk there before us had been men on the Lemp payroll.

Leaving the gigantic, arched rooms behind, we descended once again, this time through a smaller doorway. We traveled along more passages and then went down a long, curved staircase to what would be considered the brewery's sub-basement. This put us at the same level as the first portion of the cave. It was through this level that the Lemps would ascend to the brewery as they walked to work in the mornings, using the cave to travel from the mansion to their offices. It was here that William Lemp had walked as he began his descent into the depression and madness that would eventually claim his life. He became so withdrawn that he refused to appear in public and instead chose these subterranean passages to travel to the brewery each day.

Our flashlights illuminated this area of the complex, which seemed well on its way to being reclaimed by the cave from which it had been carved. The floors were covered with mud and were slippery in spots

The old Lemp "swimming pool" in the cave, which was actually a drainage pool for melt-off from the ice used in beer lagering.

The entrance to the cave from the lagering cellars in the Lemp Brewery's lower basements.

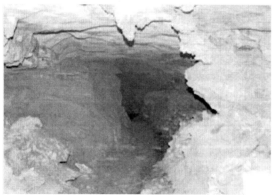

A passageway in the cave, leading back toward the Lemp Theater.

with moss and algae. Water dripped constantly and monotonously from the walls and ceilings. The old bricks were slowly crumbling from decades of dampness and moisture. It was in this cave that Adam Lemp had stored the first lager beer made in St. Louis. The original casks were housed in chambers with high, curved ceilings. Ice was cut from the river during the winter months and then placed in the chambers to keep the beer cool. As the ice melted, the water would drain off to join the water that flowed along the cave floor. The water on the sides of these long rooms was crystal clear, but it left behind mineral deposits on the stone floor, making it plain that it was unfit to drink.

We left the finished areas of the cave, with their stone floors and brick-lined walls, and entered a passageway that would take us into the natural cave beyond. To reach this section, we passed through a long, rugged corridor where the air was so damp that many of the photographs we took that night were fogged to the point that it was impossible to make out any details. Several of my own photographs were ruined but by continuing to clean my camera lens throughout the tour, I was able to take some of the first photos of the caverns to be captured in years.

This long passageway that led deeper into the cave was littered with fallen stone, mud and refuse from the old days of the brewery. Above our heads were metal brackets and chains that had once been part of a conveyor belt that transported blocks of ice into the lager vaults. A motor that at one time had powered the conveyor belt was still resting on the side of the path that led through the passage. At the end, a metal ladder dangled from the ceiling, leading upwards into a narrow, shadowy hole. During the early days of the brewery, this shaft was used to dump ice down into the cave. The ice was loaded onto cars on the conveyor belt, which moved it to the lagering areas. This hole was sealed off many years ago and the metal ladder has fallen into disrepair.

Our first area of exploration took us to the left of the passage. We traveled down a wide tunnel toward what was once the Lemps' subterranean theater. In a number of areas, cave formations, mostly stalactites, were visible. Unfortunately, many of the natural formations had been broken off and damaged. This was presumably done in less enlightened times, when people didn't realize that it takes centuries for such structures to "grow." Even touching cave formations should be avoided due to the damaging nature of the oils left behind by human hands.

One of the staircases in Cherokee Cave, marking just one of the many ruins of the commercial cave.

The old Lemp theater is in ruins today. It is an eerie and disturbing place. An archway at the rear, which led to another chamber, was one of the only remaining architectural pieces from the Lemp era. Elsewhere, the plaster scenery that had been painted to look like rocks lay in heaping piles of rubble on the floor. Here and there, patches of garish colors remained on the crumbling *faux* rocks. Overhead, an old electric light fixture that once illuminated the stage, dangled precariously, its bulbs long since been shattered and gone dark. I couldn't help but wonder as I stood there, looking around the bleak room that was shrouded in a heavy mist, just how much privacy the Lemps must have craved. I couldn't imagine descending beneath the damp earth, far underground to this dark chamber, just so I could attend private performances of popular shows with a few select friends. And how much money could the Lemps have offered to get actors to put on these bizarre subterranean entertainments? The theater was downright spooky. I would not have been surprised to learn that the ghosts of long-forgotten actors still lingered here, walking a stage that vanished long ago.

The theater marked the end of the passage, so we turned back in the direction from which we had come and once more ended up beneath the ice chute that led to the surface. Just beyond this is the Lemps' famed swimming pool. The "pool" was actually just a cement wading pool that only became used for recreational purposes after electric refrigeration was installed in the brewery. Prior to that, it was a reservoir for run-off from the melting ice. I could still see the smooth walls of the reservoir but over the years, it had been heavily clogged with rocks that had fallen from the cave's ceiling and by copious amounts of mud and clay. It now bore little resemblance to any sort of wading pool and was certainly not inviting enough for me to consider rolling up my pants legs and walking in. The pool is still filled with approximately two feet of water, and is a habitat for the blind, white fish that dwell in caves. The animals are fairly rare but they can be found in the old Lemp Caverns.

Once we traveled past the reservoir, we entered what I considered to be the actual passages of Cherokee Cave. Here, the natural contours of the cave had been opened up and the floor had been artificially smoothed and fitted with curbs on each side of the path to keep the most of the water away. These improvements, along with the remains of electrical wiring and light boxes, had been left behind when Lee Hess had been forced to abandon the cave back in 1960. They were just a few of the signs of the commercial cave that we would find in the passages ahead.

As the trip progressed, the commercial aspects of the cave became more and more obvious. At one point, we reached a ravine that cut across the path and we had to use a metal ladder to climb down and cross to stone steps on the other side. An alternate route opened to the right and we descended another flight of steps that ran between metal handrails had been installed more than fifty years before the time of our visit. As we went up these stairs, we discovered more signs of the days when Cherokee Cave was a tourist attraction in stripped-out electrical lines and carefully constructed walkways. It was this passage that had originally connected the cave and brewery to the Lemp mansion. The entrance from the house has long since been sealed off and was no longer accessible but I looked forward to seeing it from inside the cave, rather than from the bricked-up passage in the mansion's basement. However, as we began to get nearer to the house, the water that covered the floor began to grow progressively deeper. To make matters worse, Paul Pointer began to get concerned about the air quality in the passageway. This has been a problem with some of the cave exploration that has been done in recent years. On one occasion, one member of a group of spelunkers had to be bodily carried out of the cave after passing out from lack of oxygen. We tried checking the air with a flame from a lighter and we watched the flame grow weaker the farther we walked along the passage. Eventually, it flickered and went out and we had to turn back. I was the last to turn back, feeling a great sense of loss. I wondered if the others had the same sense of the history that we were privileged enough to be experiencing, walking where very few had walked in nearly half a century. This was, I realized, a haunted place, but whether by ghosts or by the passage of time, I was unable to say.

One final passage awaited us and led us deeper into the cave. If we had visited Cherokee Cave when it was in business, it would have led us outside. This was the original shaft that had been opened by Lee Hess, the one that ended at the cave's visitor center that was demolished in the early 1960s.

The passage made a sharp right turn. Ahead of us was a man-made basin that had been built to catch run-off from a small spring that flowed from the cave wall. A trickle of water was still running into the basin after all of these years. We turned into this last passageway but only traveled for a short distance before coming to what Hess had dubbed "Cherokee Lake." A stone bridge had been built across the lake decades ago but the path on the opposite side ended abruptly at a stone wall. The wall had been built by the Missouri Department of Transportation during the construction of Interstate 55. When the visitor center had been razed, the cave was been sealed off, bringing an end to an element of St. Louis' most mysterious and colorful history.

Our journey back through the labyrinth of cave passages, doorways, staircases, lagering chambers and brewery corridors took us much less time to complete than it had when we were descending. I was surprised to discover that we had been underground for almost an entire night.

I remember walking back down the corridor where the conveyor belt system had been, the one which led from the cave to the lagering caverns, and looking back into the darkness and mist behind us. I am not sure what I expected to see or hear ---- the sound of other, more ethereal explorers following behind or perhaps the specters of the Lemps still trudging to the brewery after all of these years? I don't know for sure, but I know that I expected something.

I wish that I could tell you that I had had some ghostly experience while exploring these haunted caverns but unfortunately, I cannot. The ghosts were certainly there, at least in a figurative sense, because no one can enter the cave and not feel the very tangible spirit of the past. It was a night that I will never be able to experience again, and one that I will certainly never forget.

5. "First Beer from Coast to Coast"

One of America's Great Breweries Comes of Age

From the late 1880s to the early 1910s, America saw a surge in the demand for beer. These were prosperous days for the brewing industry and the amount of beer being brewed increased with each passing year. In spite of this, the actual number of brewers was decreasing. Many of the smaller companies were falling behind, unable to keep up with larger breweries, which were using improved methods of production and distribution. This meant that fewer breweries were producing more beer. Though most breweries of that era were small, local enterprises, making all of their own deliveries using horse-drawn wagons, it was the few, large and highly mechanized breweries that were able extend beyond their own neighborhoods and towns and control the market. Their profits enabled them to spend considerable sums on marketing and advertising, reaching customers who would never hear of the small breweries that were struggling to make ends meet.

As the demand for beer increased on a national level after the Civil War, many small brewers found it impossible to keep up with their larger competitors. In the past, every brewer had known the limits of his market and had been able to maintain it with very little trouble. But the development of the railroads and improvements in communication had brought America closer together, figuratively making the country much smaller. Thanks to this, as well as to the technological advances in the brewing industry, it was now feasible for brewers to look for new customers outside of their immediate area.

This period began the rise of the "national brewer," a new concept in the industry that had only been made possible by the advent of the industrial era. As with most of the other developments in the brewing industry, William Lemp was at the forefront of this exciting time. In fact, Lemp was the first brewery to establish coast-to-coast distribution, essentially becoming the first American brewer to compete on a national level.

Before William was able to attempt this, he had a number of problems that had to be overcome. The basic requirement for such an undertaking was a reliable and well-maintained distribution system, which usually consisted of agencies in leading cities. Lemp maintained branch offices in hundreds of towns and cities around the country. While many of them were nothing more than small ice houses located near railroad depots, others were substantial operations with large warehouses that were designed to take orders and make local deliveries.

The standard practice of loading (overloading, according to the rail lines) railroad cars with huge quantities of ice to make sure that shipments wouldn't spoil eventually created problems between the brewers and the railroads. Other difficulties arose, from labor issues to accusations of unfair pricing, and to avoid these, many large brewers began buying up railroads. By running their own trunk lines, the major shipping breweries were able to control the conditions under which their beer was transported to market.

William was among the first to do this and began operating his own railroad, the Western Cable Railway Company. It connected all of the plant's main buildings with its shipping yards near the Mississippi River

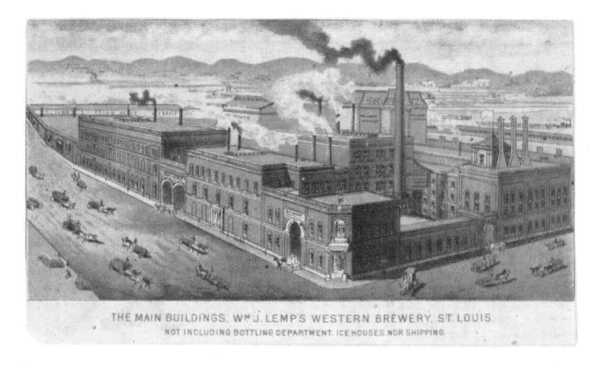

THE MAIN BUILDINGS, WM. J. LEMP'S WESTERN BREWERY, ST. LOUIS.
NOT INCLUDING BOTTLING DEPARTMENT, ICE HOUSES NOR SHIPPING

and from there, linking to other major area railroads. Eventually, new advances made it possible to refrigerate the railroad cars and William was by then transporting his product in more than five hundred refrigerated cars, averaging ten thousand shipments each year.

With ownership of a railroad, advances in bottling and pasteurization techniques and the vastly increased potential to reach hundreds of thousands of new customers, Lemp's beer was being shipped to every corner of America.

It was during this era that advertising became highly significant for national brewers. For most beer makers, local customers were already aware of the brewery and the product it offered. The most common methods for increasing sales were ads in local newspapers and display cards in stores and taverns. As the big companies began expanding out of their local areas, they began the extensive use of labels, trade names and symbols to advertise their beers. They also began using national expositions and competitions, which awarded medals and prizes to the best

A Lemp railroad train takes on its product at the St. Louis brewery

A collection of Lemp advertising trays. The trays on the right (upper and lower) feature Sir John Falstaff, an iconic symbol of the good life, who had a Lemp brand of beer named for him.

Lemp advertising signs

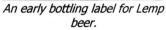

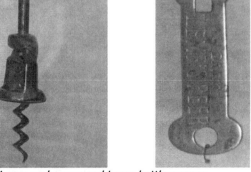

An early bottling label for Lemp beer.

A Lemp corkscrew and Lemp bottle opener

 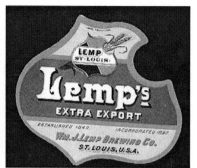 

Three of the Lemp Brewery's beer labels, all created during the heyday of the company.

beers, to advertise the high quality of their wares.

As one of the country's first national brewers, William Lemp was well aware of the importance of advertising in a quest for a larger share of the beer market. Unlike many smaller companies, he was able to afford to offer labels, trademarks and a wide variety of promotional devices. One of the first areas that he explored was a redesign and standardization of labels for the company's various brands of beer. He moved away from the flowing, ornate designs of the past in favor of a simpler Lemp shield trademark. The new labels were basically the same design with additional text describing the beer. Two varieties of Lemp beer were "Standard" -- the basic Lemp lager -- and "Extra Pale."

In 1899, William introduced what became the company's most famous brew, Falstaff. The beer was named for Sir John Falstaff, a comic character in Shakespeare's *Henry IV*, and *The Merry Wives of Windsor*. As the irresponsible, fun-loving companion of Prince Hal in *Henry IV*, Falstaff is portrayed as cowardly, gluttonous, and amoral, blessed with a wonderful sense of self-deprecating humor. William saw the jolly Falstaff as the embodiment of a rollicking good time and he wanted drinkers to associate the feelings conjured up by the classic loveable buffoon with what was to become Lemp's most popular beer. Pictures of Sir John soon began appearing in many of Lemp's advertising posters and cards. The image was said to have been based on a portrayal of Falstaff by St. Louis actor Ben de Bar.

Sir John Falstaff

In addition to labels, William also used scores of promotional postcards. Over one hundred and thirty different designs were produced during the brewery's heyday, many of them humorous and many of them using photographs of the sprawling Lemp brewery. One of the postcards featured the tall smokestack – with the name LEMP proudly emblazoned on the brick -- and an early airplane soaring off into the sky to the right. The postcard is printed with the caption, "Falstaff is the first bottled beer to be delivered by aeroplane." Another postcard showed a flimsy-looking plane with a wooden crate of Falstaff beer being loaded on board. It was printed with the same caption.

Apparently, there was a story behind these two advertising cards, one that indicated the caption was not entirely accurate. The Lemps were supporters of early aviation (Louis Lemp even became a pilot) and these two postcards were often handed out at flying events that were sponsored by the brewery. They had been issued to celebrate the first delivery of beer by airplane in the world, which allegedly took place in 1912. According to J.D. Smith, an early airplane pilot and mechanic, he was hired to follow an aviator named Tony Jannus as he flew one of the first Benoist "airliners" from St. Louis to New Orleans. The flight was sponsored by the Lemp Brewery and as a publicity stunt, Jannus was supposed to deliver a case of Falstaff beer to the mayor of New Orleans, a gift from the mayor of St. Louis.

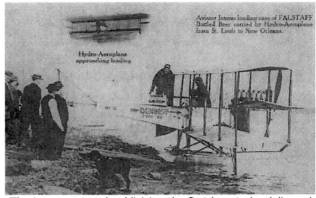

The Lemp postcard publicizing the first beer to be delivered by aeroplane.

Smith followed Jannus by land, ready to lend a hand if anything went wrong with the aircraft's engines. The flight started in St. Louis with the mayor and several officers from the Lemp Brewery strapping a case of Falstaff to the wing, just behind the pilot's seat. The flight was made in short, daily hops. On the first day out, Smith, who met up with Jannus at a pre-designated landing strip near the Mississippi River, noticed the pilot seemed to be in an exceptionally good mood. When he looked closer, he realized that the pilot had opened the case of beer during the flight and was happily enjoying his twelfth bottle. Jannus explained that the plane would fly much better if the case were empty!

So, the mayor of New Orleans never received his case of St. Louis beer and while Falstaff still might have been the first beer to be delivered by air, it didn't happen on the flight that was piloted by Tony Jannus in 1912.

Many other promotional items were given out to saloons and to individual consumers. Items included glasses that were etched with Lemp logos, corkscrews (not only a necessity in the early days before beer bottles had caps but ideal advertising devices, being small and inexpensive to produce), beer steins, mugs, letter openers, serving trays, and many others.

The brewery's clever advertising introduced Lemp beer to scores of new customers every week. So much money was rolling into the company coffers that construction of new buildings, and updating of old ones, was virtually continuous at the brewery complex. The entire place had been built (and remodeled) in the Italian Renaissance style, featuring arched windows, pilaster strips, and brick cornices decorated with the Lemp shield. Eventually, the brewery would occupy five city blocks.

By the middle to late 1890s, the brewery proper was employing more than seven hundred men. Over one hundred horses were being used to pull forty delivery wagons in St. Louis alone. Even more beer was being shipped across the country – and beyond. After expanding the distribution network throughout America, William continued to expand overseas. By the turn of the century, Lemp beers were being shipped to Canada, Mexico, Central and South America, the Caribbean, the Hawaiian Islands, Australia, Japan and Hong Kong. Lemp beer was even available in London and Berlin, both well known for their local brews.

By the early 1900s, the Lemp empire was in its glory. The company was the largest brewer in St. Louis and the eighth largest in the U.S. With Americans still having a powerful thirst for good beer, business could only get stronger – and the brewery owners become even wealthier – in the years to come. But dark clouds were already starting to gather on the horizon. In the midst of great happiness and success, the Lemp family's troubles were about to begin.

6. "The Rich Are Different"
Truth, Legends and Lies of the Lemp Family

On November 1, 1892, the Western Brewery was incorporated under the name of the William J. Lemp Brewing Company and officers were named for the first year of business. They included William J. Lemp, president; William J. Lemp, Jr., vice-president; Louis F. Lemp, superintendent, and Henry Vahlkamp, secretary. It was a closed corporation with all of the stock owned by members of the Lemp family.

William Jr. (or Billy, as he was known to his family and friends) and Louis were sons of William Lemp and both were qualified for the positions in which they had been placed. They had received some of the finest training available in the brewing industry. Billy had learned the trade at the acclaimed United States Brewers Academy in New York City and returned to St. Louis to take up the position of vice-president of his father's company at the age of only twenty-five. Louis, who was three years younger than Billy, was trained by some of the most skilled brewers in Germany and for many years, he ranked among the greatest brewmasters in America.

While they were William's oldest sons, they were not their father's first choice to take over the business. That honor was supposed to go to William's favorite son, Frederick, who was nineteen at the time of the incorporation. Billy and Louis both had to wonder if they were merely warming the chair, so to speak, until Frederick was of the proper age to manage the company himself. Tragically, they would never find out. It would be the death of Frederick Lemp that would begin the two-decade-long destruction of the Lemp brewing empire.

While most of what we know about the Lemps focuses on a few family members and their unfortunate deaths, they were a complex, fascinating and often troubled family. They have been the subject of strange rumors and perplexing myths over the years and in the chapter that follows, I'll try and clear up some of the misconceptions about who the Lemp family really was.

Anna

The first child born to William and Julia Lemp was an infant who died soon after birth in 1862. Three years later, their daughter, Anna, was born. Anna would be eighteen years older than her youngest sibling,

Elsa, but the two women would be very close throughout Elsa's life. After the death of Julia Lemp in 1906, Anna would take over the role of mother figure to her young sister. She later moved to New York, where she spent most of the later years of her life.

Anna (or Annie as she was commonly known) was married to Alexander Konta, a St. Louis businessman, banker, stockbroker, playwright and influential dabbler in world affairs. Konta was responsible for creating a replica of the city of Jerusalem for the 1904 World's Fair in St. Louis. The exhibition, which covered more than ten acres, had three hundred buildings, twenty-two streets, and over one thousand workers who were brought over from the Holy Land for the attraction. Konta had close ties to the Turkish rulers of Palestine and Jerusalem at the time and sent a personal invitation to his friend, Kazim Bey, the governor of Jerusalem. A number of years later, just before the United States entered World War I, Konta testified before a U.S. Senate committee that was looking into German ownership of a Washington newspaper, worried about the spread of pro-German propaganda. Konta had only a fleeting acquaintance with the owner of the paper and was called to testify because of a letter than connected him with a bank loan and his

Annie Lemp

wife's German connections. Konta was cleared of any involvement in the situation.

Annie and Alexander had one son, Geoffrey, who later became personal attorney to newspaper publisher William Randolph Hearst.

During her life, Annie wrote two books, *The History of French Literature* and *A Plea for Moderation: Based Upon Observations of an American Woman in a Belligerent Country.* The latter was an anti-war booklet that was written at the outbreak of World War I. America had not yet committed to the war with Germany and the vast majority of the American public wanted to stay out of it. Such writings and thoughts would later be turned against German-Americans when America finally entered the war, in spite of the fact that the majority of citizens had shared the same sentiments a few years before.

Annie was the queen of New York society during her era and was the member of many exclusive clubs. She was an elegant spectacle when she walked her two giant Russian wolfhounds along Fifth Avenue. Among her close friends were Evalyn Walsh McLean (owner of the infamous Hope Diamond), art collector Isabella Stewart Gardner and James Buchanan "Buck" Duke, father of heiress Doris Duke and founder of

Annie's husband, Alexander Konta

Duke University. Annie traveled all over the world, spending extensive amounts of time in Asia, Australia and Europe. She reportedly met with the Dalai Lama during her travels. When she returned, Annie would often bring back exotic foods for her staff to learn to prepare. Like other members of her family, she loved the sporting life and was an avid tennis player.

Annie Lemp Konta died in 1939, having lived a full, exciting and lavish life.

William, Jr.

William Jacob Lemp, Jr. was the eldest son of William and Julia, born in St. Louis in 1867. He attended St. Louis public schools, followed by Washington University, where he pursued an education in science, which would prepare him to take part in the family business. He also attended the prestigious United States Brewers Academy in New York, from which he graduated in 1885. After returning to St. Louis, William, Jr. became the superintendent of the Western Brewery and a few years later, when it was incorporated as the William Lemp Brewing Company, he was named as vice-president.

William (or Billy, as he was known to his friends and family) had a number of diverse business interests throughout his career, not all of which were connected to the brewery. He served as the president of such businesses as the Joplin Ice and Cold Storage Company in Missouri, the Columbia Manufacturing Company of Dallas, Texas, and the Ardmore Light and Power Company in Oklahoma. His brewing interests extended out of state to Arkansas, where he was president of the Little Rock Brewing and Ice Company. He also became director of the German Savings Institution and the Kinloch Long Distance Telephone Company. He was a prominent member of the Merchants Exchange and the Business Men's League.

To those who knew Billy only through his business interests, he came across as a serious and intent young man. Alvin Griesedieck, a fellow brewer and contemporary of Billy, stated that while not unfriendly, he was "by nature rather cold and crisp. He was strictly business. He was honorable to the last degree and expected everyone with whom he came in contact to be likewise. He prided himself in the fact that his word was as good as his bond. He was known to be unrelenting toward anyone who, in his opinion, had double-crossed him or lied to him. Likewise, he seldom forgave an insult, imagined or otherwise, even among members of his immediate family."

This was a side of Billy that was known to the brewers, businessmen and bankers of St. Louis. A tidy, compact man, like his father, who worked hard and yet took every advantage of the wealth that had been afforded him by his

Billy Lemp as a young child

family's lucrative business.

However, there was another side to Billy that was known to his friends and his family – an eccentric, often reckless man with an obsession with guns and according to some, violence. Billy was well known for being a fun-loving playboy who would "go to the limit" for those he liked. He was a hard drinker and brawler and was quick to use his fists on nights when he and his companions "let down the bars." In his younger days, he earned a fearsome reputation as a fighter, despite his short stature, and he wrecked saloons on more than one occasion. His family connections and wealth managed to keep him out of trouble and even those who ran up against his bad side found him quick to let bygones be bygones.

Billy had many passions, aside from women and drink, and was especially fond of horses. One of the organizations that he joined was the St. Louis Jockey Club. He was an avid sportsman (he was also a member of the Western Rowing Club) and thoroughly enjoyed hunting. Going out into the woods to shoot served as a healthy outlet for his intense preoccupation with guns. He collected a large assortment of rifles and pistols and even formed the Lemp Hunting and Fishing Club in 1898 at the confluence of the Illinois and Mississippi rivers.

William J. "Billy" Lemp, Jr.

Like many prominent young businessmen, Billy had memberships in a number of exclusive clubs of the era, including the St. Louis, Mercantile, Noonday and Glen Echo clubs. He was a member of the Masonic Order for many years and the Liederkranz Club, the roster of which was filled with the names of St. Louis' wealthiest and most respected German-Americans. He had his family's passion for new and exciting innovations and he also joined the Aero Club, as well as the St. Louis Automobile Club.

After moving out of his family's home, Billy maintained a residence directly across the street, one block away from the Lemp Brewery. He was a colorful and flamboyant man whose taste for the finer things in life was reflected in his home. Billy was fascinated by Asian furnishings and art and his house was filled with Oriental curios, draperies, furs, ivories, bronzes and figures, all of which he picked up during trips to the Far East.

Perhaps more than any of his brothers and sisters, Billy took the greatest advantage of the money that was made from the family business. It was often said of him that, even though he had many interests and was plagued by many obsessions, "his greatest passion was living life to the hilt – and spending his great fortune on himself and his friends along the way."

In 1899, the carefree bachelor made the fateful decision to get married. In what was perhaps the most extravagant ceremony in St. Louis society history, Billy was wed to one of the most beautiful socialites

Lillian Handlan

in the city, Lillian Handlan. The ceremony took place under two interlocking hearts of white roses, with the name "Lemp" spelled out in purple violets. Not only did the marriage connect the families of two prominent local businessmen (Alexander Handlan manufactured fixtures for railroad passenger cars), it also brought together two of the city's most eligible young people. But from the beginning, it was far from a perfect marriage.

To start with, there was the religious issue. The Handlans were devout Catholics and the Lemps were Lutherans. In those days, a mixed marriage of this sort was almost unheard of and it seems odd that the families would have allowed it to take place. Perhaps the couple felt that they could get past whatever difficulties their religious differences might pose – or, more likely, the marriage was arranged by parents who thought it was more important that their children marry someone of suitable social status than one of identical faith.

But this would not turn out to be Billy and Lillian's biggest problem. They soon began to clash in a variety of ways, mostly caused by the fact that they were both very eccentric, outgoing individuals with fiery tempers who were used to selfishly getting whatever they wanted out of life. The marriage would be a disaster, almost from the start.

The lavish wedding took place on October 24, 1899 at the Handlan residence on Lindell Boulevard. No one was present except for the two families and there were no bridesmaids or groomsmen. After a wedding breakfast, the couple departed for New York, where they stayed in a suite at the Waldorf-Astoria before embarking on a three-week honeymoon. After returning to St. Louis, they moved into Billy's home on Thirteenth Street, presumably to spend the rest of their lives enjoying the wealth and position that was given to them by one of the greatest breweries in America.

But none of that was meant to be. The turbulent marriage lasted only until 1906 when it ended in one of the most scandalous courtroom trials in St. Louis history. Soon afterward, the Lemp brewing empire, destroyed by Prohibition, crumbled into dust.

Louis

Born in January 1870, Louis Lemp found his greatest achievements in life away from the family business. Although Lemp beer had made him a wealthy man, he earned his real reputation in the sporting and political arenas. Louis was certainly qualified to be a brewer. He learned the trade in Germany and was ranked as one of the greatest brewmasters in America for many years. When the Lemp Brewery was

Louis Lemp as a young boy and then as a successful businessman (right). He made a fortune for himself outside of the family business of beer brewing.

incorporated in 1892, he was named as the superintendent and then went on to serve as its second vice-president until 1906. After that, he sold his interest in the company to his brothers and moved to New York, where he lived for the remainder of his life. He also kept residences in Paris and Boulogne-sur-Mer, France.

Louis (or "Louie" as his friends and family knew him) was very active in St. Louis politics and cultivated a great interest in the sporting life. Even more than his brother Billy, he loved horses and successfully bred and raced some of the best in the city. Although popular in political and social circles, he was best known for his stable of magnificent show horses. He organized the stable with noted veterinarian C.W. Crowley and the horses, headed by the famous mare May Queen, became almost unbeatable in the show ring. Louis financially backed the very first St. Louis Horse Show, which was held in the old Coliseum. Soon, his horses were known from coast to coast.

Louis later went into the racing business with Dr. Crowley, on whose St. Louis County farm many of their horses were bred. One of their colts, Wounded Knee, was behind one of the greatest

Louis on one of his famous racing horses

wins in American horse racing history. Louis and Dr. Crowley kept the horse a closely guarded secret for several years, training him to race without drawing any publicity. When he was finally taken to the track one day, the unknown horse was given 50-1 odds. Wounded Knee shot out of the gates and galloped over the rest of the field. It was estimated that the owners won more than $100,000 on that single race, drawing bets from all over the country.

Louis and Crowley also raced Elastic, a famous sprinter that broke records at tracks throughout the West. Those who saw him race called him a "giant of a horse" and he unbeatable for years.

Louis and his wife, Agnes, had one child, Louise, born in 1909. She later married her cousin, Edwin Pabst, the son of Hilda Lemp Pabst and Gustave Pabst. Louise was raised in Paris and she became an exceptional illustrator and artist who was widely known for her portraits. She was awarded a silver medal at the 1935 exhibition of the *Societe de Artistes Francais*. Louise and Edwin Pabst died within a few months of one another in 1977.

Charles

Charles A. Lemp was born in 1871 and had only a small role in the family business. Although he held the office of treasurer at the turn of the century and was promoted to role of second vice-president in 1911, most of his fortune was made from banking and real estate interests. Charles was a lifelong bachelor and

 lived at the Lemp family home until 1911, when it was renovated into offices for the brewery. He moved into the St. Louis Racquet Club after that and ended his association with the Lemp Brewery to take what would be the first of his many banking and financial positions. In 1917, he became vice-president of the German Savings Institution in downtown St. Louis. He went to the Liberty Central Trust in 1921, where he

Two rare photographs of Charles Lemp... as a young man (left) and a baby photo, taken in the early 1870s.

stayed for a number of years. Eventually, Charles went into the automobile casualty business as president of the Indemnity Company of America. He was joined there for a time by Billy's son, William J. Lemp III, who served as the treasurer and vice-president of his uncle's firm.

Charles was largely unaffected by Prohibition and the closing of the Lemp brewery. He was wealthy in his own right and continued to look after his real estate holdings and his investments. Among his varied businesses, he was the owner of the St. Louis, Columbia and Waterloo electric railroad line before it went out of business in 1932. His many investments remained strong during the Depression.

Like his brother Louis, Charles was active in St. Louis politics. He was a powerful member of the Democratic Party and was said to control many of the south side wards. His influence was particularly felt in the Tenth Ward. He was one of the biggest financial

A European Art Deco incense burned that Charles brought home from one of his trips to France.

supporters of the Tenth Ward Democratic Club and for a time, served as the treasurer for the state Democratic Committee.

Charles, like so many other members of his family, loved to travel. He visited Spain, Italy and England and once went on safari in West Africa. He was an avid collector of European Art Deco and also bought paintings by Picasso, Salvador Dali and Georgia O'Keefe.

In 1929, after the death of his brother Billy, Charles moved back into the Lemp's family mansion, reverting it to a residential dwelling. Charles had always been eccentric but his return to the Lemp mansion seemed to aggravate his condition. He developed a number of unusual habits and quirks. For instance, he only allowed his staff to use round ice cubes because he hated the sound of ice clinking against his glass. He became obsessed with germs and often took showers five or six times a day. Any money that he handled had to be washed. When he had his shoes polished, the entire shoe had to be cleaned, soles and all. Guests were not allowed to wear shoes inside the house. They had to be left at the front door and the staff always polished them before they left. Charles hated the smell of coffee and forbid it to be served at the house. He woke up every morning at 5:00 a.m. and any overnight guests were expected to get up at the same time. Charles would go and knock on the doors of their rooms until he roused them out of bed. Actor Vincent Price was a close friend of Charles and stayed at the mansion several times. One has to wonder what he thought of the early-morning morning wake-up knock.

Charles became increasingly reclusive as he got older until eventually, no visitors were allowed to call. He wandered around the old house alone, aided by his two remaining staff members, Albert Bittner and his wife, Lena. His only company was a pet parrot and his German shepherd dog, Cerva, named after the short-lived "near beer" the Lemps had manufactured just before Prohibition. In his later years, he developed arthritis and walked hunched over and in constant pain.

In 1949, his eccentricities and chronic pain finally caught up with him.

Frederick

Although Billy was named vice-president of the William J. Lemp Brewing Company when it was incorporated in 1892, he was not his father's first choice when it came to taking over the business someday.

Frederick Lemp, William's favorite son, and the child whose death would set in motion a series of tragic events that eventually destroyed the family.

It's likely that Billy not only knew this, but approved of the fact that he would not be tied to the brewery for his entire life. Billy was well aware of the fact that William's choice for a successor was his younger brother, Frederick, a young man who was passionate about the business and about beer, a passion that his brothers never really shared.

Frederick was born in 1873 and was named for William's close friend and fellow brewer, Frederick Pabst. Pabst had been born in Germany in 1836 and came to America at the age of twelve. He found his first job in a Chicago hotel and later worked for the Goodrich steamship line, traveling between Chicago and Milwaukee. He eventually became the captain of the steamer *Huron*. In 1862, he married Marie Best, the daughter of Phillip Best, the first lager brewer in Milwaukee. The following year, he became a partner in his father-in-law's firm, the Phillip Best Brewing Company. Pabst soon turned the company (which was later given his own name) into the leading brewer in Milwaukee. He expanded the company's sales and production and turned it into a national operation. The Lemp and Pabst families became very close over the years and they intermarried two times. Frederick Pabst died soon before William Lemp committed suicide and many believe that his friend's death was the final straw that drove Lemp to end his life.

It would be Frederick Lemp's death, however, that would set events into motion.

Perhaps because of his great interest in the brewing business, Frederick was always considered William's favorite son and heir apparent. He received a degree in mechanical engineering from Washington University, where he was also a popular member of several social and fraternal groups. Like his older brother Billy, he was a graduate of the United States Brewers Academy.

In 1898, Frederick married Irene Verdin of St. Louis in a small, private ceremony at the Lemp home. The wedding, held just before Irene's twentieth birthday, was a quiet affair since the bride's family was still mourning the recent deaths of Irene's father and her ten-year-old sister. No public announcement of the wedding was made.

Frederick was twenty-five at the time of his marriage. He was a handsome young man with a stylish mustache and was described as hard working and ambitious. Although he was utterly devoted to his work and his new wife, he still managed to find time for his friends and was prominent in St. Louis' social circles. Irene was a beautiful young woman, tall and slender with wavy, ash-blond hair and blue eyes. The couple was deeply in love and by 1900, Irene had given birth to a daughter, Marion.

Frederick continued to throw himself into his work. He was dedicated to the expansion of the brewery and worked long hours, concentrating on distribution networks and merchandising. In the summer of 1901, he began to have problems with his health. His condition became so severe that in October, he and his family relocated temporarily to Pasadena, California, in hopes that a change in climate might do him some good. For a time, it seemed as though Frederick was improving. William and Julia traveled to California to visit in early December and Frederick seemed much better. He was active again and seemed to be more like his old self. William returned home to St. Louis confident that his favorite son was on his way to a full recovery and would soon be back to work at the brewery. Unfortunately, Frederick never came back to St. Louis alive.

Soon after his parents departed, Frederick suffered a relapse and on December 12, 1901, he died of heart failure at the age of twenty-eight. His young wife was left a widow with a one-year-old daughter to raise. Irene never remarried. She received a generous sum from her father-in-law when William purchased Frederick's share of Lemp stock from her a short time later.

The family learned of Frederick's death by telegram. Having assumed that he was getting better, news of his passing was a great shock to everyone. It was especially devastating to William who was stunned when he heard what had happened. Brewery secretary Henry Vahlkamp later wrote, "...suddenly the grief of the father was most pathetic. He broke down utterly and cried like a child. It was the first death in the family. He took it so seriously that we feared it would completely shatter his health and looked for the worst to happen."

William Lemp was never the same after the loss of his favorite son. As a tribute to Frederick, he constructed a large mausoleum for the family in Bellefontaine Cemetery. Frederick's body was returned from California to be entombed there and many other members of the family joined him as the years went by.

Hilda

Little is known about Hilda, the Lemps' second daughter, who was born in 1875. Even remaining family members don't recall much being said about the plump, golden-haired young woman, who left home to marry into the Pabst family in 1897 and had little contact with the Lemps in the years that followed. Described as "flighty" and somewhat shallow, she made little impression on history, although her husband held a place of some notoriety in the brewing world as the son of Frederick Pabst.

Hilda Pabst

Gustav G. Pabst undoubtedly met Hilda through the connection that existed between the Pabst and Lemp families. No record remains as to whether this was an arranged marriage or one of romance, although it is suspected that it may have been the latter. The wedding was originally scheduled to take place during the fall of 1897 in St. Louis. However, Gustav grew impatient and pursued his fiancée to Europe, where the Lemps were vacationing that summer. He convinced her to advance the wedding date and they were married during a simple ceremony on the Isle of Wight in the English Channel.

This was the second time that Gustav Pabst allowed impulse to lead him down the aisle. Historical accounts show that Hilda was not his first wife. He had been married briefly in 1892 to a Canadian actress named Margaret Mather. This was during an era when being on the stage was not seen as a socially acceptable profession for a woman and Milwaukee society was said to be "shocked" by this development. Gustav and Margaret had been married in secret in San Francisco and the Pabst family did not learn of it until two weeks after the

The Gustav Pabst mansion in Milwaukee

wedding. Frederick Pabst refused to comment on the nuptials but the newspaper noted that "it had been known for some time that [Gustav] was infatuated with Miss Mather." The news writer went on to surmise that the Pabst family would undoubtedly try to induce the young man's bride to leave the stage.

But Margaret was no mere chorus girl. She played lead roles in a number of productions, always to mixed reviews. She was striking in her physicality and bearing but critics found her to be overbearing – as did her young husband. The marriage turned out to be short-lived. They divorced after Margaret threatened Gustav with a whip. She toured the country as Juliet in Shakespeare's classic romance during the last years of her life. She suffered from a chronic illness and actually died on stage. She was buried in her Juliet costume in Detroit's Elmwood Cemetery.

After they were married, Hilda moved to Milwaukee, where she lived in splendor with her new, wealthy husband. After the death of his father in 1904, Frederic took over the leadership of the Pabst Brewery until 1921. After that, he turned his attentions to real estate development and was a member of the board of directors of many Milwaukee business and banking establishments. In his later years, he was a respected conservationist and devoted his time to the propagation of upland game birds and the breeding of Holstein dairy cattle.

Hilda and Gustav had three sons, William; Gustav, Jr. and Edwin L. Pabst, who was born in 1907. Edwin later married Louise Lemp, the daughter of Hilda's older brother, Louis. Hilda passed away in 1951.

Edwin

Born in 1880, Edwin was the youngest son in the Lemp family and while he served the family business dutifully for a number of years, he eventually disassociated himself from the brewery and retreated into a reclusive life of books, nature and outdoor living. A handsome, friendly, yet timid boy, he grew into a quiet, withdrawn young man who became disillusioned with the world. In 1913, his unhappiness led him to abandon his hectic life and leave the business world for good. He was lucky enough to be wealthy in his own right and he planned to live off his investments for the remainder of his days. In 1929, he reflected on his decision to retire at age thirty-three:

It was simply that I saw no need to make more money. It seems to me that this is the curse of America. Everyone is always making more money. I was confident that I could organize my life in the way I wanted to. Of course, I was very fortunate in having an income.

Free from the requirement of making a living, he was able to devote his life to the things that he loved the most, including his love of nature and animals. During a camping trip along the Meramec River, he

*Two rare childhood photographs of Edwin. (Left) Edwin's christening photo from 1880.
(Right) Formal portrait around the age of three.*

discovered a wonderful wooded site near Kirkwood, Missouri, and later built his magnificent home, *Cragwold*, on that spot. The sprawling mansion seemed almost too large for one man, but Edwin filled it with works of art, books, a gourmet kitchen in which he loved to cook and closets overflowing with expensive clothes. A large atrium grew to contain one of the largest and most valuable collections of tropical and semi-tropical birds in the country. Over one hundred birds could be found there, along with

numerous trees, shrubs and plants. Edwin kept twenty-four varieties of parrots and the same number of finches. The parrots were mostly kept in cages but the finches and other small birds were allowed to fly free. He also kept a large menagerie of exotic animals on the estate, one of the most varied private collections in existence at the time. He was a well-known benefactor of the St. Louis Zoo, and it was from Edwin that the zoo received its first lions.

Toy horse that once belonged to Edwin

Edwin collected books and artwork from all over the world and his appreciation for fine things was also reflected in his love of good food. He became an expert chef and earned a reputation for giving thoughtful and perfectly planned dinner parties.

Unlike most members of his family, Edwin was

Edwin as a young man.

adverse to the idea of joining the business and social clubs in the city. For a time, however, he was on the roster of an exclusive German-American social organization, the Liederkranz Club, but his tenure in the society ended with an angry resignation. On New Year's Eve 1911, Edwin, who was then vice-president of the Lemp Brewery, appeared at a party at the club without being dressed in the required evening clothes for the night's festivities. He arrived at 4:00 a.m. wearing a business suit and danced with the female relative of a club member. Edwin was aware of the dress code but didn't think that it would be enforced so late into the party. He was dancing when Moritz Elyssel, the president of the club, interrupted and ordered Edwin to leave the dance floor. Edwin laughed and with a shrug, walked out. The next day, friends told him that Elyssel was spreading the rumor that Edwin had brought a prostitute into the club on New Year's morning and that he'd been thrown out because of it. Angered by the lie, Edwin resigned from the club and never joined another social organization again.

As he grew older, the dapper, compact Edwin (like other members of his family, he was a small man, standing only five feet, two inches tall) grew increasingly reclusive. Unlike his brother Charles, who preferred his own company, Edwin was frightened of being alone. Perhaps his family's legacy of death and despair – of which he never spoke – haunted him during the lonely hours of the night. Because of this macabre terror, he almost always kept a companion with him at *Cragwold*, one of whom was Thomas Dooley, father of Dr. Thomas A. Dooley III, the U.S. Naval physician who became famous for his humanitarian activities in Sotheast Asia in the 1950s. Another of Edwin's companions was George Vierheller, former director of the St. Louis Zoo. But his most loyal friend was John Bopp, who lived at *Cragwold* for the last thirty years of Edwin's life. During that time it is believed that Bopp was never away from the estate for more than five days in all.

Edwin's peaceful life was a sharp contrast to the lifestyle of the rest of the Lemp family and more will be written about him and his magnificent home later in the book. He was a colorful, complex man who distanced himself from the problems that plagued the rest of his family. He died quietly in 1970 at the age of ninety.

Elsa

Born in 1883, Elsa was the last of the Lemp children. While only three years younger than Edwin, she was eighteen years younger than her oldest sister, Annie. She was always the baby of the family and lived a different life than her older sisters and brothers. She was beloved by all of them, but instead of becoming spoiled as many last-born children do, she became an independent, resilient young woman who made the most of her short and often turbulent life.

Elsa was only twenty-three when her mother died in 1906. Julia had inherited William's entire estate,

Rare photographs of a lovely, rich young woman in St. Louis' Gilded Age, Elsa Lemp. (Left) Elsa's confirmation photo for the Lutheran Church. (Right) A formal photograph of a headstrong young woman.

which was divided among the children when she passed away from cancer. This made Elsa the wealthiest unmarried woman in St. Louis when she claimed one seventh of the $10 million estate. Under the terms of Julia's will, Elsa received an additional $100,000 when she married.

Always a headstrong free thinker, she joined the suffrage movement in 1910s, working hard for women's right to vote. She became the founder of the first suffragette society in St. Louis. She also became fascinated with Spiritualism, which was in its heyday at the time. She held many séances at the Lemp Mansion during the time that it was a private residence and became acquainted with a middle class homemaker named Pearl Curran, who was making quite a sensation in St. Louis at the time with her alleged spirit communications with a ghost named Patience Worth. Curran had first made contact with the spirit through a Ouija board but she later began to receive direct messages from her and put those messages on paper. The relationship between Pearl and Patience Worth produced numerous writings, poems and even several novels --- works that the largely uneducated Curran would never have been able to produce on her own.

The most eligible heiress in the city became even wealthier in 1910 when she married Thomas Wright, the president of the More-Jones Brass and Metal Company. The ceremony was a small but opulent affair. Elsa's dress, which she paid for herself (along with her wedding ring) was a Worth original. After the wedding, they took a year-long honeymoon, traveling to Cairo, Bangladesh, Calcutta, Bombay and Nairobi. When Elsa traveled, she took along twenty-eight pieces of Louis Vuitton luggage. When they returned to St. Louis, the couple moved into a beautiful home in Hortense Place, one of the private neighborhoods in St.

A novelty photograph of Anna and Elsa

Two of Elsa's crystal perfume bottles and a facial powder box.

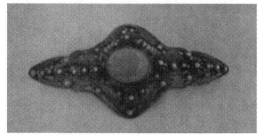

Broach that belonged to Elsa

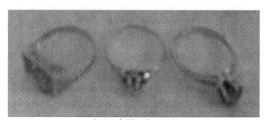

Set of Elsa's rings

Elsa's childhood dolls. The doll in the middle is wearing Elsa's baptismal gown.

Some of Elsa's jewelry and a necklace

The Lemps loved to travel and this photograph was taken aboard an ocean liner in the early 1900s. Elsa can be found on the bottom row of the photo, third from right. Thomas Wright is also on the bottom row, fifth from right. Edwin Lemp smiles widely on the bottom row, far left.

Louis' Central West End. Elsa's independent nature and her husband's dismissive attitude did not mix well and their marriage was a stormy one from the start.

They had frequent screaming matches that often turned violent. During one such episode, Elsa hit Wright with a vase, opening a large gash on his forehead. Wright was unfaithful to Elsa almost from the start of their marriage. Once, she caught him in bed with one of the servants and chased him down the street wielding a fireplace poker. After finding him in bed with yet another woman, she got into her Pierce-Arrow automobile and rammed it into his prized Duesenberg three times. It was not uncommon for the staff to find broken pieces of china and shattered furniture when they came on duty in the morning.

Elsa had one child, a little girl named Patricia Lemp Wright, and tragically, she was stillborn. Elsa blamed her husband for the baby's death. Eventually, they separated in 1918.

On February 1, 1919, Elsa filed for divorce. In her petition to the court, she stated that her husband had destroyed her peace and happiness by his conduct and had long since ceased to love her. She also stated that Wright treated her with coldness and indifference and absented himself from their home in order to avoid her. All of these things, according to the papers that were filed, caused her great mental anguish and impaired her physical health. Unlike Billy Lemp's sensational divorce trial, Elsa did not go into specifics about the events of her married life. Whatever it was that occurred, the case was expedited so that within an hour after it was filed, a divorce was granted on the grounds of general indignities. The question of alimony was never mentioned in the courtroom, but it was understood that a settlement had already been reached.

Elsa spent the next year alone, traveling and visiting with friends and family. At some point, she reconnected with her former husband. They traveled together for a time and eventually reconciled. On March 8, 1920, they were remarried in New York City and then returned St. Louis and a home filled with flowers from friends and well-wishers.

A few days later, Elsa was dead.

Her death was officially ruled a suicide and generally accepted as one considering the fact that her father killed himself in 1904 and two of her brothers would take their own lives in the years to come. But did Elsa really commit suicide? Not everyone believes that she did...

The "Other" Lemp:
Debunking the "Monkey Boy"

What about the other Lemp child – the one that, as it turns out, never existed at all?

Perhaps the greatest myth connected to the Lemp family is that of "Zeke," the so-called "Monkey Boy," whose ghost is said to haunt the attic of the Lemp mansion. Plainly stated, he never existed, despite the rumors, legends and outright lies that have been told on internet websites, in questionably researched books and articles and on tours of the mansion.

But, without question, there was no "Monkey Boy" and the Lemps never had a child named Zeke.

There are several versions of the story. One claims that the boy, who was born mentally handicapped, was the illegitimate son of Billy Lemp. The child of an affair with a servant girl, he was kept locked in the attic of the house, away from the prying eyes of the public. Occasionally, a passerby saw his deformed face peering out of the attic window and the legend of the "monkey" or "monkey-faced" boy was born. Others claim the child was a sibling of Billy, born to William and Julia Lemp during less enlightened times. Due to his handicap, he was locked in the attic, where he eventually died. Still other sources claim that "Zeke" was the child of a servant with no connection to the Lemps other than that Julia Lemp provided a place for him to live in the attic rather than have him be turned over to an institution.

The truth is, he never existed.

The "Monkey Boy" story comes from a few wild imaginations and questionable sources that claim the story is true. Apparently, the "Monkey Boy's" ghost has communicated with a few people in the attic of the house – a neat trick considering that he never lived. The same people who perpetuate the legend of the "Monkey Boy" have also erroneously claimed on occasion that the Lemp home was once a school or an orphanage. Other erroneous "facts" hbeen passed along by these same sources, each allegedly gleaned from behind-the-scenes knowledge of the Lemp Mansion, but these are too numerous and silly to recount.

But what of the Monkey Boy?

It's unfortunate that such a tale has managed to take root in the history of the house and even more unfortunate that so many people are gullible enough to believe it. It is a tale with no substance or truth and yet it has been allowed to damage the character of the entire Lemp family for a number of years. It's sad that the story has been accepted as fact when absolutely no evidence exists to prove it is anything other than a terrible piece of bad fiction. It's true that you cannot slander the dead, so people are allowed to say whatever they like about the departed Lemps without consequence, but it's sad when people are willing to believe things that have no evidence to support them.

7. "And it All Began to Crumble..."
The Beginning of the End

By the late 1890s, the Lemp brewing empire had reached the summit of its greatness. The size, growth and phenomenal wealth of the business had the family looking with great anticipation toward the new century. They believed, for good reason, that only greater success was coming their way in the 1900s.

New construction and renovation were constantly being carried out at the brewery. By the turn of the century, William Lemp had installed a pipeline between the stockhouse and the bottling plant that was unlike anything else in the industry. Fellow brewers, and general tourists, came from around the country to see the pipeline, which had been encased and insulated so that beer could be transported to the bottling machines without any loss of quality or flavor. The new conveyance system was just one of many of William's modern marvels.

By this time, the brewery covered eleven city blocks if the count included the extensive shipping yards that were located along the Mississippi River. It was producing over five hundred thousand barrels of beer every year with annual sales of more than $3.5 million. The Lemps employed five hundred and fifty men, with another six hundred and fifty working in other departments. The brewery was producing six brands of beer, many of them award-winning, including Tip Top, Standard, Extra Pale, Tally, Culmbacher and, of course, Falstaff. They used more than six hundred refrigerated railcars to get the beer to the marketplace

The death of his beloved son Frederick nearly broke William Lemp. He recovered, only to be dealt another crushing blow in 1904.

and shipped it throughout America and to ports around the world.

The future certainly looked bright for the company and for the Lemps themselves as the new century dawned – but in truth, their future was anything but bright. Just one year later, the first in a series of tragedies occurred with the death of Frederick Lemp.

The events that followed his death became the first indication that the once-mighty empire was beginning to fall apart.

William Lemp had always been a volatile and passionate man, even though, as a good German, he kept most of those feelings bottled up inside. Those hidden feelings were what made him a good businessmen and his drive for success was what changed the Lemp Brewery from a small, moderately successful local company into a giant national business that had become a force to be reckoned with in the brewing industry. He was a man of great passion, capable of excitable highs, and as his family and friends soon discovered, horrific lows, as well.

When his beloved son Frederick died in December 1901, William plunged into an abyss of despair. His family and close associate Henry Vahlkamp feared that he might never come out of it. William's friends and even his employees at the brewery said that he was never the same after Frederick died. It was obvious to all of them that he was not coping well and he began to slowly withdraw from the world. He was rarely seen in public and chose to walk to the brewery each day by using the cave system beneath the house. Before his son's death, William had taken pleasure in personally paying the men each week. He also would join the workers in any department and work alongside them in their daily activities or go among them and discuss any problems or questions they had. He took great pleasure in teasing the chiefs of the various departments at the brewery, asking them questions that seemingly had no connection to the business of the day. In order to answer, his men had to not only keep the immediate record on their minds, but they also had to know something about the entire history of their department. After Frederick died, these playful practices ceased almost completely. When he did visit the different departments, it was apparent that he was just there to pass the time. William was distracted and disinterested and his joking manner and quick smile were absent.

This went on for nearly two years. William had ordered the construction of a grand mausoleum for his family on Propsect Avenue in Bellefontaine Cemetery, where the city's captains of industry were buried. It was the largest in the cemetery and cost $60,000, an amount worth over $1.6 million today. Frederick had been laid to rest there and William frequently visited the tomb. Eventually, he seemed to find a little peace and hints of a return to his former self began to appear in his manner. He finally seemed to be coping with the death of his favorite son, but it was not meant to last.

On January 1, 1904, William Lemp suffered another crushing blow with the death of his close friend, Frederick Pabst. This loss made William even more withdrawn and soon he became indifferent to the details of running the brewery. Although he still came to the office each day, he paid little attention to the work and those who knew him said that he seemed nervous and unsettled. It began to seem as though his physical and mental health were beginning to decline.

By February 13, 1904, his suffering had become unbearable.

That morning seemed to be an ordinary one for William Lemp. He arose at his customary hour of 7:00 a.m. and took his time in his personal bathroom, which included a barber's chair, a marble tub and a massive glass-enclosed marble shower stall that was the first of its kind in St. Louis, which William had imported from an Italian hotel for his own use. After dressing, he ate breakfast but remarked to one of his staff that he was not feeling well. Rather than go to the brewery, he excused himself and went back upstairs to his bedroom.

At 9:30 a.m., William shot himself in the head with a .38 caliber Smith & Wesson revolver. There was no one else in the house at the time except for the servants. Julia had gone downtown to do some shopping and Billy and Edwin, the only children in St. Louis at the time, were already at work at the brewery.

William Lemp's closest friend, Frederick Pabst

A servant girl, upon hearing the sound of the gunshot, rushed to the door but she found it locked. She immediately ran to the brewery office and summoned Billy and Edwin. They hurried back to the house and broke down the bedroom door. Inside, they found their father lying on the bed in a pool of blood, a bloody wound in his right temple and the revolver still gripped in his right hand. At that point, William was still breathing but unconscious.

One of the boys telephoned the family physician, Dr. Henry J. Harnisch, who came at once. He was soon followed by Dr. Henry Schulz, Dr. Andrew Harscher and Dr. Herman L. Nietert, the former head of the city hospital. They quickly examined William but they knew there was nothing that could be done for him. Dr. Nietert pronounced the wound fatal and waited next to William's bed until death came to claim him.

Meanwhile, one of the staff had managed to reach Julia Lemp at a downtown department store and her driver rushed her home. She arrived only moments before her husband's succumbed to his wound. He was pronounced dead at 10:15 a.m.

William had been dressed for work when he ended his life and there was nothing to suggest that he had made any preparations for suicide, or that he had even contemplated it. There were rumors that he had written a letter detailing his plans and bidding farewell to his family, but this was not the case. There was no suicide note. While it is likely that William took his own life in a fit of depression, there is no way that we will ever know for sure. The motives that he hid deep in his heart will always remain a mystery.

A short time after the shooting, the Lemp home was closed to everyone but relatives and those who had been summoned by the family. Brewery employees were posted at the front of the house to intercept callers and newspaper reporters, who flocked to the scene when word spread of the tragedy. All of the curtains were drawn and the mirrors were draped in black. A dark silence settled on the house, which might have appeared vacant if not for the grim-faced brewery workers who were stationed outside.

Billy and Edwin refused to speak to the newspapermen who had gathered. Edwin returned to the brewery office for a short time in the afternoon but he turned away everyone who came to offer condolences. He did confirm through his assistant that his father had committed suicide and the only explanation that he could give was that he was despondent over the deaths of his son and his friend, Frederick Pabst. Henry Vahlkamp agreed with Edwin and added:

Mr. Lemp had been looking extremely bad for some time. When he came back from the funeral of Captain Pabst, he was a changed man. They were lifelong friends and the relations between them were very close – so much so that Mr. Lemp felt the death of Captain Pabst as keenly as that of his own son three years ago.

I remember when he received word of Fred's death how he went into street and paced up and down. I walked with him and tried to console him, but it was useless. The death of Captain Pabst brought the former trouble back on his mind. He brooded over these matters constantly. I exchanged greetings with him yesterday and noticed that his condition was the same as it had been ever since his return.

A broach worn by Julia Lemp to William's funeral.

The Lemp family mausoleum in St. Louis' Bellefontaine Cemetery. It was built to hold the family's remains after Frederick's death.

Funeral arrangements began to be made the following day and family members had to tracked down from all corners of the world. Charles was in Chicago and bought a ticket on the first train returning home. Annie was on a tour of the Orient and her husband, Alexander, was in Europe. Hilda and Gustav rushed to St. Louis from Milwaukee when the news reached them. They were accompanied by Elsa, who was in Milwaukee for a visit. Louis was on his way back from a trip to Japan and his steamship was due to arrive in San Francisco on February 16. He finally arrived home, along with Annie, after the funeral had already taken place.

Services were held in the Lemp mansion on February 14. The body was placed on display in the south parlor, next to the conservatory, which was filled with plants and flowers. Before the funeral took place, more than one thousand Lemp employees filed through the house to view the body and pay their last respects. The brewery had been closed for the day. Once the long stream of men, some openly weeping, had departed, family members and friends gathered for a simple memorial service conducted by Dr. Max Hemple of the German Ethical Society.

After the service, a cortege of forty carriages traveled to Bellefontaine Cemetery. Julia, Elsa and Hilda were too grief-stricken to go to the burial ground. Eight men who had worked for William for more than thirty years served as pallbearers and honorary pallbearers included many notable St. Louis residents, including Adolphus Busch, the owner of the Anheuser-Busch brewery, who had liked and respected his principal competitor. William was placed inside the family mausoleum next to his beloved son, Frederick.

There is no question that William J. Lemp left an indelible mark on the city of St. Louis and the history of American brewing. He was well liked, admired and praised by not only his friends and the people of St. Louis but by his competitors, as well. He was a modest and unpretentious man who did business fairly and honestly. He could dine with the cream of St. Louis society and drink a beer with the lowliest worker on his payroll and get along famously with both. His employees saw him as not only a good boss but as a man that they knew they could go to for aid and advice. Even though most people didn't know it – because it was not his way to speak of his own virtues – William gave away immense sums to charity each year and never thought of his generosity as anything special. He was a fine man but one who allowed his grief and pain to get the better of him, ending a good life before its time.

According to his will, dated February 1, 1904, William left his entire fortune to Julia. The will read:

I, William J. Lemp, hereby make, publish and declare this to be my last will and testament, hereby revoking all previous wills. I direct the payment of my debts and the closing of administration on my estate as rapidly as the law will permit.

I give, bequeath and devise to my wife, Julia, all my property, real and personal or mixed, wheresoever situate or whatsoever title held, absolutely.

I make no gift her to my children, Annie L. Konta, William J. Lemp, Louis F. Lemp, Charles A. Lemp, Hilda L. Pabst, Edwin A. Lemp, and Elsa J. Lemp, and I make no gift here to my grandchild, Marion Lemp, having perfect confidence that my wife will without any request on my part, and none such is here made, will do best for them.

I hereby appoint William J. Lemp, Jr., Louis F, Lemp, Charles A. Lemp, Edwin A. Lemp or either or any of them that may accept and qualify my executor or executors without bond.

In witness whereof, I have hereunto set my hand this 1st day of February, 1904.
[signed] William J. Lemp

At the time of his death, the brewery was estimated to have been worth about $6 million and William's personal estate was valued at $10 million.

8. "The World Came to St. Louis!"
The Louisiana Purchase Exposition of 1904

William Lemp's death came at a terrible time as far the Lemp Brewery was concerned. In the days that followed, there was little time for mourning. St. Louis was preparing for the opening of the Louisiana Purchase Exposition and this "World's Fair" was going to be the greatest event to ever occur in the city. Not only had William been elected to the fair's board of directors, but the brewery was also involved in beer sales and displays for the exposition. He had accepted the role on the board in 1901, helping to plan and administer the event. Billy had no choice but to step into his father's shoes. He took William's place on the agriculture committee and supervised the William J. Lemp Brewing Company's display in Agriculture Hall, where brewers and distillers from around the world assembled to show off their products.

It was a moment of shining glory for the Lemp Brewery. No one knew at the time that it would be one of the last.

The Louisiana Exposition was proclaimed as the "greatest World's Fair to ever be held." St. Louis had campaigned hard for an earlier fair in 1893 but the Columbian Exposition had gone to Chicago. The loss of this event instilled a great desire on the part of the eminent citizens of St. Louis, especially David R. Francis, who would soon be elected governor of Missouri, to snag the next gala event to come along. A few years later, people began to talk of a fair to celebrate the centennial anniversary of the Louisiana Purchase in 1904. What better place to have it than in St. Louis, the Gateway to the West? Civil leaders pledged to raise $15 million to the event, the same amount Jefferson paid for the Louisiana Purchase, and the 1904 World's Fair came to St. Louis.

After lengthy debate, the western side of Forest Park was chosen as the site of the fair. Businessmen of the south side (like William Lemp) were very unhappy with the decision, stating their part of the city was a more attractive and viable location, mostly thanks to the proximity of the Mississippi River, but their lobby was unsuccessful. It would not be until the construction of the Jefferson Hotel and the improvement of streetcars and other city services that much enthusiasm could be raised about the fair being held on the west side. By 1903, though, ninety-four hotels had been built to meet the needs of fair attendees and fifteen more were completed by April 1904.

The section of the park that was chosen for the fair covered a little more than six hundred and fifty acres but it was soon obvious that more land would be needed. Additional tracts were leased from the new, but unoccupied, Washington University campus and this nearly doubled the size of the fairgrounds. Preparations ran at a feverish pitch for several years and as the actual centennial date of April 1903 approached, it was obvious that the fair was not going to open on time. A dedication was held anyway on April 30, 1903 with thousands of troops parading through the grounds and President Theodore Roosevelt on hand to deliver the opening address. Right after that, everything was shut down again and Congress

granted the request for a postponement of one year to 1904. This gave the organizers more time to obtain foreign exhibits and to get more companies to plan displays.

By the cold spring of 1904, the Exposition was ready to open. Organizers began to panic, though, on April 20 when a late snowstorm slowed all of the operations. Luckily, the snow was cleared away and on April 30, the fair opened. The (second) Opening Day ceremony was held in the Plaza of St. Louis and included prayer, music and an assortment of speeches. John Phillip Sousa led his band and a choir of four hundred performed a song called "Hymn of the West," which had been written for the occasion. William Howard Taft, the United States Secretary of War, made the principal address and Mayor David Francis touched a gold telegraph key that alerted President Roosevelt to officially start the fair. At that same moment, ten thousand flags unfurled, fountains began to spray geysers into the air and the fairgrounds opened to almost twenty million visitors from around the world over the course of the next seven months.

The architecture and design that went into the fair was breathtaking. A few years before, Peninsular Lake in the park had been re-shaped and re-designed. The lake acquired a new name, the Grand Basin, and it was connected throughout the park with lagoons to provide waterways for boating during the festivities. Above the lake, on the natural semi-circular hill now known as Art Hill, was the Festival Hall, the centerpiece of the fair and one of its foremost

The Grand Basin at the Fair.

More scenes from the Fair, along the Great Basin.

attractions. It had a gold-leaf dome that was larger than the one atop St. Peter's Basilica in Rome. On each side were smaller pavilions from which three cascades of water descended 400 feet from the top of the hill to the lake. Along the cascades were large staircases that were adorned with statues, benches and landscaped gardens.

The Colonnade of States, linking Festival Hall and the many fair pavilions, was flanked by giant seated figures, seven on each side, each representing a state that had been carved from the Louisiana Purchase. Eight ornate exhibition palaces surrounded the Great Basin. These included Mines and Metallurgy, Liberal Arts, Education and Social Economy, Manufacturing, Electricity, Varied Industries, Transportation and Machinery. The building that housed the Palace of Machinery had parking space for the 140 automobiles that had been driven to the fair from as far away as Boston. That fact alone was almost as much a marvel as the other wonders of the fair. Long-distance driving was still in its infancy and it was only the year before, in 1903, that an automobile had been driven from coast to coast for the first time. Each of the exhibition palaces was different in design and all were massive in size, each covering several acres.

Although the buildings were detailed, highly decorated and looked as though they had been built to stand forever, they were actually made from temporary, insubstantial materials. They had been constructed from what was called "staff," a mixture of fibers such as burlap and manila fibers soaked in gypsum plaster, commonly known as plaster of Paris. The hardened material was very adaptable and could be used just like wood. By pouring staff into molds, many ornamental pieces that appeared to be carved by hand in marble could be achieved in a short time. The structure under the staff was always steel or wood so that the buildings didn't simply collapse.

The great Ferris Wheel from the 1893 Fair in Chicago made its last appearance in St. Louis.

A few of the fair structures were meant to be permanent. One of these was the Palace of Art, constructed of limestone. The building that would be used by more than twenty nations to house priceless works of art during the exposition. Two temporary buildings flanked the center one and a smaller sculpture building was located on the south, creating a beautiful courtyard between them. The temporary buildings

The Agricultural Palace, where the Lemp Brewery and other brewers and distillers from around the country showcased their various products.

were removed after the fair and the Art Palace was donated to the city and today houses the St. Louis Art Museum.

The area of the park now occupied by the St. Louis Zoo was called the Plateau of States, where many states erected houses to greet visitors and to show off their individual attractions. Some of the buildings were replicas of important historic sites like the Cabildo of New Orleans where the Louisiana Purchase had been signed, Tennessee's Hermitage and Virginia's Monticello. Missouri, the host state, constructed a lavishly decorated building made entirely of native materials. It was designed to be permanent, with a large dome and a heating and cooling system, something that no other building on the fairgrounds could boast at the time. Unfortunately, on November 19, just two weeks before the end of the fair, the building and all of its contents were destroyed by fire. The fire was caused by faulty electric wiring. Electric lighting, still in its infancy in 1904, was a requirement in all the buildings for its decorative effect. Some of the furnishings were saved from the blaze and are on display today in the Governor's Mansion in Jefferson City. No attempt was made to replace the structure.

The U.S. Fisheries building was one of the fair's most popular attractions. It had forty glass-fronted fish tanks that surrounded a center pool for seals. Nearby was the Bird Cage, the largest of its kind ever built. It was created by the Smithsonian Institution to allow sightseers to walk through the cage and interact with the numerous species of birds inside. After the fair, the cage was donated to the city and it became a part of the St. Louis Zoo. Visitors can still experience it today.

The Grand Basin was the focal point of the fair's activities. Boat parades were held daily along the lagoons and waterways that led away from the Basin and flowed between the exhibition buildings. North of the Basin was the Plaza of St. Louis, where the official proceedings were held. The Plaza was graced with a tall monument for the Louisiana Purchase and the statue of St. Louis. Stretching away from the Plaza was Louisiana Way, the main thoroughfare of the grounds. On one side of it was the United States building and on the other was the French Palace, honoring the two countries involved in the Louisiana Purchase.

The hill to the west of Forest Park provided a space large enough for the agricultural exhibits and the largest building on the fairgrounds, the Agriculture Palace. It was here that the Lemp Brewery and other

Natives of the Philippines were brought to the Fair and put on display so that visitors could see how "exotic people" lived.

brewers and distillers from around the country showcased their wares. The Agriculture Palace had an eastern facade that was one-third of a mile long. The area was covered with displays showing various types of grasses, pools containing water plants, and windmills. Livestock shows took place there every day. Near the north entrance to the Agriculture Palace was a giant floral clock that was one hundred and twelve feet in diameter. It was made from flowers and foliage and had giant hands that were operated by compressed air. The hands were controlled by a master clock in a small pavilion at the top of the clock at the number twelve. The gardens were illuminated at night with thousands of lights hidden in the foliage, a breathtaking sight when artificial lighting was still a novelty. Thomas Edison himself was brought to the fair to oversee the proper installation of the electrical exhibits.

Washington University's new campus not only provided much of the space needed for the fair, but it also served as the model for the ideal university. The Administrations Building (Brookings Hall) was the site of all the official meetings and the receptions for important guests. Other buildings furnished space for exhibits and offices and meeting rooms. At the western end of the campus, the athletic fields and gymnasium were used for an elaborate physical culture program and also for the Olympic games of 1904.

At the eastern end of the campus were halls representing foreign countries, including China, Sweden, Brazil and others. The British Building was a copy of Queen Anne's Orangery at Kensington Gardens. After the fair it was purchased by the university and for years it housed the School of Fine Arts. The college abandoned the building in 1926 when the school was moved into the new Bixby Hall.

Perhaps the most fascinating of the exhibits at the fair to turn-of-the-century visitors was the Philippines Reservation. This was the largest and most expensive of the foreign displays and it brought eleven hundred Filipinos to live in St. Louis for almost seven months. One of the goals of the fair's Anthropological Division was to show

Americans how people of "exotic" cultures lived. The U.S. had taken control over the Philippines from Spain in 1898 and people were curious to see the various communities of "primitive" people set up on forty-seven acres around Arrowhead Lake. Each tribe constructed its own village of thatched huts and houses on stilts along the water. The tribe's customs and homes fascinated visitors and in turn, the Filipinos were enthralled by the trappings of modern society. One tribal chief created a problem when he refused to let his tribe be viewed until a telephone was installed in his hut. Another tribe caused a scandal with their demand for dogs, the main staple of their diet.

What most people remembered when they later recalled the 1904 World's Fair was the Pike, an inviting one-mile section along the northern edge of the fairgrounds. This area was like a giant amusement park with concessions and attractions that had not yet become standard at fairs everywhere. It was here that hotdogs and ice cream cones were first sampled. Fairgoers were introduced to "fairy floss," a new treat that was to become known as cotton candy. The fair popularized peanut butter and Dr. Pepper, billed as a "health drink." The forerunner of the ice pop also made its first appearance at the Pike. Known as the "fruit icicle," it was made of fruit juice frozen in a narrow tin tube. Another welcome "first" from the Pike was iced tea. It was first served almost as a fluke. A tea house was having a hard time selling hot tea on summer days and one of the employees suggested that they try serving it over crushed ice.

The attractions of the Pike undoubtedly influenced the design of future fairs and amusement parks, just as the White City at the Columbian Exposition in 1893 had influenced the St. Louis event. At the eastern end of the Pike was the spectacular Tyrolean Alps concession, which had been created by the brewers of St. Louis. A castle had been built, along with other structures, to create the illusion of life in the Alps. There were yodelers, musical shows, and a

Views of the amusements on the Pike, the Fair's most popular attraction.

The Tyrolean Alps concession on the Pike, where the Lemps and other brewers sold their wares.

storybook Alpine village. The massive manmade mountain range was crowned with real snow. Visitors could take a train ride into the mountains and dine in the Great Hall, where many official gatherings were held. President Roosevelt was honored there at a banquet given by the brewers. An elevator took guests to the peaks of the Ortler, where a waterfall tumbled into the lake. The whole exhibit was a stunning display created from humble paint, canvas, rock and plaster. It left quite an impression on fairgoers, most of whom would never have the opportunity to visit the real Alps. It also sold enormous quantities of cold beer, which was what it had been designed to do.

Next to the Alps was an Irish village with reproductions of medieval buildings. It featured a restaurant, a facsimile of Blarney Castle, and a theater where visitors could enjoy a show. Also on the Pike was Hagenbeck's Animal Paradise, which attracted large crowds in those days before modern zoos. There, visitors could see bears and an assortment of exotic animals.

All types of foreign cultures were represented, as were displays about topics as diverse as the deadly Galveston flood, the North Pole and the Siberian wastelands. When visitors had enough of education, they could enjoy entertainment. Fairgoers could catch a performance by a little-known comedian named Will Rogers or hear the new ragtime music, which originated in St. Louis. Scott Joplin, one of the most famous ragtime composers, wrote "Cascade Rag" in honor of the fair. Other rags at the time were "On the Pike" and "Strolling Down the Pike." In addition to hearing the strains of "Meet Me in St. Louie," visitors might experience the Magic Whirlpool, the Water Chutes or the Scenic Railway.

There was no greater ride at the fair than the immense Observation Wheel. The two hundred and fifty foot-high wheel was created by George Ferris, an engineer who debuted his creation at the 1893 Columbian Exposition in Chicago. The "Ferris Wheel" was so successful that it was brought to St. Louis. Sadly, the wheel never left the city at the end of the fair. It was scheduled to be taken to Coney Island but the demolition contractor for the fair found it to be too much trouble to disassemble. So, he dynamited it and sold the scrap for $1,800. The original wheel became the model for all such attractions to follow, but there has never been another of such gigantic proportions.

The visitors came throughout the summer and into the fall of 1904. But as December approached, a sense of sadness filled the air. The Exposition closed down at midnight on December 1. From early morning right up until the time the clock struck midnight, thousands gathered to stroll the Pike one last time and to pay homage to David Francis, the man responsible for bringing the fair to the city. Schools and businesses closed for the day. It was like a carnival that was tinged with grief. The fair's closing night became one of the wildest nights ever witnessed in St. Louis with the authorities on high alert, should the celebration turn overly buoyant.

As the midnight hour approached, Mayor Francis made a final speech from the Plaza of St. Louis and then he threw a switch that plunged the entire fairgrounds into darkness. A band played "Auld Lang Syne" and then suddenly the air was filled with blinding fireworks as "Farewell" was spelled out, followed by "Good Night."

The Louisiana Purchase Exposition of 1904 had come to an end.

The destruction of the fairgrounds began on December 2. Demolition was started by the Chicago Housewrecking Company, which had been awarded the $450,000 contract to remove the fair buildings. Even though the fair was officially closed, visitors were able to view the demolition for a twenty-five cent admission. The demolition process produced mountains of staff, the fiber and plaster of Paris material from which nearly all of the pavilions had been constructed. Useful only for landfill, it was hauled away over miles of railroad tracks that had been laid down before the fair for the construction and removal of the buildings on the grounds. The tracks were covered with asphalt during the fair and then opened again to remove the debris when the fair ended.

The exhibition buildings were removed quickly, as the contract specified that the demolition be completed within six months, but many of the concessions on the Pike remained in place for months. Some of the buildings were so unusual that it was believed that buyers could be found for them. One of them, a cabin that once belonged to General Ulysses S. Grant had been moved to the fairgrounds to be used by the Blanke Coffee Company. No one knew what to do with it at the end of the fair but it was finally purchased by Adolphus Busch and moved to Gravois Road. It is now a part of the Anheuser-Busch company attraction, Grant's Farm.

The buildings representing the various states and countries were the easiest to get rid of. Many of the ones made from permanent materials were purchased and hauled to nearby sites for use as homes. The New Jersey building was moved to Kirkwood, where it served as an apartment building for a time. The New Hampshire house, after undergoing alterations, became a home on Litzinger Road. The Oklahoma structure was taken to El Reno, Oklahoma, where it became an Elks Lodge. The Michigan and Minnesota structures became permanent fair buildings in their home states. The New Mexico building became a public library in Santa Fe. The Iowa building become an asylum for alcoholics. Belgium's building was purchased by Anheuser-Busch and was used for many years as the company's glass works. The Swedish building was taken to Lindsborg, Kansas, where became the Art Department for Bethany College. The fifty-foot statue of Vulcan, a donation from the city of Birmingham, Alabama, was removed to its home city on seven freights cars and while it rusted in storage for years, it was later restored on Red Mountain overlooking the city. Many other statues from the fair were given to the city of St. Louis and were assigned to parks and public places.

An attempt was made to preserve the Pike as a permanent attraction in St. Louis, with the reproduction of the Alps being the major benefit of the plan. However, officials at Washington University viewed an amusement center of this sort as being too big a distraction for the students and lobbied against the idea. Adolphus Busch finally purchased the Alps, planning to install them as an attraction in Forest Park, along with a summer theater. This plan never came about and eventually the mountain range was destroyed.

Although little remains from the fair in the city today, the Louisiana Exposition has never been forgotten. Never again would a World's Fair be held that had the magnitude of the St. Louis Fair and while others would follow, the magnificence of that brief season in 1904 would leave a lasting mark on the country, and perhaps the world.

9. "Desertion, Cruel Treatment & Indignities"
The Lemp Divorce Trial of 1908

As for Mrs. Lemp, it is very difficult not to be rude and stare, because she is so handsome a lady."
St. Louis Mirror, 1906

Bill just up and tells the public that he couldn't stand it with Lil and had to get out. But of course, Bill was never noted for tact.
St. Louis Mirror, 1906

On November 7, 1904, during the waning days of the Louisiana Purchase Exposition, Billy Lemp officially succeeded his father as the president of the William J. Lemp Brewing Company. The fair had served as Billy's initiation as the brewery's new leader and he had managed to navigate his way through the myriad of problems and challenges it presented. The company came out of the event in great financial shape and Billy looked forward to its having a bright future.

But the troubles of the Lemp Brewery – and of the Lemp family itself – had only just begun with the deaths of Frederick and William Lemp. There was much worse to come.

The brewery began facing a much-altered St. Louis beer market in 1906 when nine of the large area breweries combined to form the Independent Breweries Company. The formation of the company left only Lemp, Anheuser-Busch, the Louis Obert Brewing Company and a handful of small neighborhood breweries as the only independent beer makers in St. Louis. Of even more concern was the expanding temperance movement in America. The growing clamor of those speaking out against alcohol was beginning to be heard in all corners of the country.

On a personal level, it was discovered in 1905 that Julia Lemp was suffering from cancer. By March 1906, her condition had deteriorated to the point that she was in constant, agonizing pain. She died at home on April 18 with her children at her side. The funeral for Julia, who at the time of her death was the

Billy Lemp

richest woman in St. Louis, was held in the Lemp home. She was laid to rest next to her husband in the family tomb at Bellefontaine Cemetery.

After Julia's death, her children received most of the massive fortune left behind by their father. Amounting to more than $10 million, it was divided equally between them. The girls were allowed to divide their mother's jewelry and both sons and daughters had a share in distributing the household items, horses, vehicles and other personal effects. Julia specified that each child should receive one of the paintings from her collection. Billy, Charles, Annie, Hilda and Louis received their inheritance immediately but the shares given to Edwin and Elsa were held in trust for them by their brothers until they reached the age of thirty. When Elsa was given her share, she became the wealthiest unmarried woman in the city.

Their mother's death was a shattering blow to the Lemp children, especially after losing their father to suicide just two years before. Perhaps the hardest hit by her death was Billy, who had been the closest to his mother. He was very affected by her passing, weighed down by the responsibilities of running a company that he had never intended to run.

But Billy's problems were only just beginning – or perhaps, more accurately, they had really started in 1899 when he had married St. Louis heiress Lillian Handlan.

Lilly May Handlan (she changed her name to Lillian before her marriage and from that point on refused to acknowledge anyone who called her by her old name) was born on April 29, 1877 to Millie and Alexander

Lillian's baby bonnet

Lavender dress that Lillian wore as a child

Lillian as a young girl

Lillian Handlan Lemp, the so-called "Lavender Lady"

Handlan. Her father was one of the wealthiest businessmen in St. Louis who made his fortune making lamps and other fixtures for railroad cars. Although Lillian had two sisters and three brothers, she was a favorite of the family, adored by everyone for her pert manner and happy exuberance. There was no denying that she was a pampered, spoiled child but there was no reason not for her to be. She was a girl of immense wealth, born in America's Gilded Age. It seemed unlikely that from the time she was an infant, she would ever want for anything.

Lillian managed to win over everyone with her charm, from European royalty to the cream of New York and St. Louis society. She moved easily among the wealthiest and most famous people of the time, largely due to her family's money, Alexander Handlan's many political connections, her numerous friends, her outgoing personality and her great beauty. She enjoyed her place as one of the city's most beautiful and most popular socialites. Those who threw parties could only pray that she would accept the invitation and when Lillian hosted an event of her own, everyone in St. Louis' social scene lobbied for an invite. She was so adept at entertaining that after she married Billy, he called on her to plan all of the major functions for the Lemp family.

Lillian loved attention. She openly craved it, but not in a way that would be distasteful. Her station in life simply would not allow it. She always managed to stand out in a crowd, even in church. She was expected to behave in a conservative manner and yet she always chose taffeta as the material for her Sunday dresses, so that the stiff fabric would allow her to make as much noise as possible as she swished down the aisle. That way, she would be noticed by everyone in the congregation and yet it would not seem as if she was purposely drawing attention to herself

Another way that Lillian used her clothing to attract stares was by wearing the color lavender. She included it in every ensemble that she wore, often down to her undergarments. She even had a lavender rosary made to match her dresses. Even her carriages – she had a different one for each day of the week – were upholstered in lavender, including the leather on the horses' harnesses. This earned her the nickname

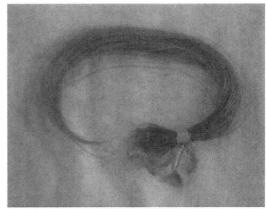

A lock of Lillian's blond hair, carefully preserved by family members over the years.

Some of Lillian's combs and hair decorations.

Bracelets and earrings belonging to Lillian

Pair of Lillian's handmade lace gloves

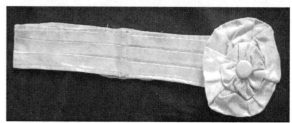

Lillian's lavender rosary

Belt that Lillian wore on her wedding day

of the "Lavender Lady." Lillian stood only four feet, eleven inches tall and was reputed to have an eighteen-inch waist. Her wardrobe included hundreds of gowns that were made by a full-time staff of seamstresses.

Lillian created a sensation everywhere that she went. Many recalled her visits to downtown department stories, like Famous-Barr, where employees and customers alike were delighted by her boisterous laughter and entertaining behavior. She talked and joked with everyone, leaving harried employees in her wake, as she went from department to department, always followed by several servants, who carried the day's purchases.

When she traveled by train, it was not uncommon for Lillian to be greeted at the station by a crowd of admirers. When this happened, she would smile graciously and wave one small, gloved hand before she entered a waiting carriage. Along the same lines, an evening at the theater became a major event when Lillian was in attendance. She always waited until a large enough crowd had assembled in the auditorium before making her dramatic appearance.

Despite her love for attention and her sometimes odd behavior, Lillian could be charming and demure. She was loved by almost everyone who knew her and liked even by those who didn't. Although she was wealthy her entire life, she never looked down on anyone and the eccentric and vivacious woman had friends ranging from royalty to common maids. Lillian loved life and all it had to offer but if there was a single thing that nearly destroyed her, it was her short, turbulent marriage to Billy Lemp.

No one could ever really say what happened but it soon became obvious that the two strong-willed, independent and eccentric young people should never have wed. Both of them were used to getting whatever they wanted, whenever they wanted and neither was open to compromise. The marriage was rocky from the start but it soon became a disaster – as everyone in St. Louis was about to find out.

On March 19, 1908, Lillian filed for divorce from Billy. In a long petition, she charged him with desertion, cruel treatment and indignities, all of which were painstakingly detailed. Lillian further stated that Billy entertained women in their home when she was absent and that these women were allowed to use her boudoir and private rooms. Billy answered the divorce petition with his own charges against Lillian. He claimed that she was guilty of improper conduct, foul language and other offenses, including the excessive wearing of the color lavender to attract public attention and violating the terms of the prenuptial agreement that had been signed before their marriage.

Both wanted custody of their only child, William J. Lemp III, who had been born on September 24, 1900. [Note from author: I could find no reason why Billy and Lillian's son was not mentioned in William's will, which had been filed only a few weeks before his suicide, other than to assume that he found it unnecessary. No money was being left to children or grandchildren and perhaps Marion was only mentioned because her father, Frederick, was deceased.] There was no question that both Billy and Lillian loved the little boy dearly. In fact, a few family friends believed that Billy and Lillian might actually reconcile for the sake of William III.

But that was not meant to be. The couple was simply too stubborn and too angry with one another to try and work things out. Family members hoped that they would at least sort out their differences in private, thus avoiding embarrassment for everyone, but instead, they chose to expose their sordid domestic problems to public scrutiny – and reveal the private lives of Lemp family. The public soon learned that the people they had placed on pedestals as glamorous members of society were just like they were – fallible, ordinary people whose extraordinary problems were largely brought about by their wealth and privilege.

"Let me tell you about the very rich. They are different from you and me," F. Scott Fitzgerald would write in 1926. He was not writing about the Lemps, of course, but be very easily could have been.

The divorce trial – Lemp v. Lemp – opened on Monday, February 8, 1909. Judge George Hitchcock presided over the case, which was already being speculated about as the most sensational in the city's history. When Billy, Lillian and their respective attorneys arrived at the courthouse in downtown St. Louis, they were greeted by a crowd of people, most hoping to catch a glimpse of Lillian in one of her spectacular lavender dresses. They turned out to be disappointed. Lillian walked into the courtroom wearing a simple black suit and a white hat with a veil that partially obscured her lovely face. She was accompanied by her parents. She took her place next to attorney John S. Leahy at a table across the courtroom from her husband. Billy was represented by his attorney, Frederick W. Lehmann.

Lillian, the plaintiff in the matter, was the first to testify. After seating herself in the witness chair, she raised

The old St. Louis courthouse, where the Lemp divorce trial was held.

John S. Leahy, *attorney for Lillian Handlan Lemp*

her veil and carefully folded it onto the brim of her hat. She waited patiently as John Leahy approached and asked his first question. "Mrs. Lemp," he said, "please state a circumstance that took place in your bathroom in October 1904."

According to Lillian's testimony, Billy had been out drinking with friends all evening and returned home around 10:00 p.m. "I was in my bath arranging bottles in the medicine case when I heard him enter the front door," she said. "He came into my bathroom and knocked me down."

Frederick W. Lehmann, *attorney for Billy Lemp*

As Lillian struggled to her feet, she said Billy hit her again and then once more when she tried to stand up. After the third blow, she said, he began yelling at her and calling her vile names. Lillian said she scrambled away from him and ran for the telephone with the intention of calling her father. But Billy caught up with her and slammed her against the wall. Her head snapped backward and cracked against the plaster. As Lillian dizzily swayed, he pushed her and she tumbled down the stairs. She came to a stop at the bottom of the staircase, unconscious. "When I recovered," she told the court, "I looked around and he was gone. I went to my room and looked in the mirror, and saw how badly my face was battered. I then went to the ice box and got a piece of raw meat and bound it to my blackened and swollen eye. Then I went into my room and locked the door."

When Billy heard her go into her room, he immediately came to the door and began pounding on it with his fists. Lillian claimed that he demanded that she open it, giving her a two-minute deadline before he knocked it down. When she refused to answer him, she said he yelled that he was going to get a police officer to take it down. She heard him leave the house and return a short time later. She heard him talking to someone but never saw anyone else in the house. A few moments later, she said the door crashed open as Billy broke the lock. He walked into her room, looked at her, and then went upstairs to bed.

"Did Mr. Lemp drink?" her attorney asked.

Lillian replied. "Yes, a great deal. He drank whiskey, cocktails, absinthe, and all varieties of wine."

As Lillian continued her testimony, she revealed more about the couple's tumultuous personal life. She claimed that Billy would sometimes refuse to speak to her for days at a time. On one occasion, she said his "silent treatment" lasted for an entire three months. She also testified that between 1904 and their separation in 1906, Billy frequently stayed away from home all night and would sometimes be gone from home for long periods of time, refusing to reveal his whereabouts. During this same period, Billy often refused to occupy the same bedroom with Lillian and took a separate one on the second floor of the house.

In addition, she said, he seldom came home for meals and when he did, he often refused to sit at the table with his wife.

In spite of what seemed to be his indifference toward her, Lillian said that Billy was violently jealous. "He never wanted me to go out or to have company. If he went out, he wanted me to go upstairs in a room by myself," she testified. If company came to the house, Billy would become angry when she was nice to the visitors. Lillian stated that he often cursed and swore at her after they left.

As further evidence of her husband's pathological jealousy, Lillian told about a trip to her favorite vacation spot, Palm Beach, Florida, in 1905. She stated that after Billy paid for the trip, he hired a detective to follow her and see what she was up to while she was out of town. After her arrival in Palm Beach, Lillian alleged that the detective smiled and winked at her and tried to engage her in conversation. When this failed, he tried to befriend her son, who had accompanied her on the trip. He even rented the room next to hers in the hotel and tried to listen through the door to what she did and said.

During cross-examination, Billy's attorney asked her how she knew the detective was trying to eavesdrop on her.

"Because I looked under the door and saw him standing there," Lillian snapped. Her response caused a ripple of laughter through the courtroom. Further testimony revealed that the hotel's desk clerk, who had become acquainted with Lillian during her previous trips, informed her of the detective's identity.

According to Lillian, Billy deserted her on October 13, 1906. She said that he never returned to her and ceased to provide for her in May 1907. After that, she said Billy would send her, through their son, bills that had been sent to him by her creditors. In the spring of 1908, Lillian returned home to live with her parents.

Testimony returned to Billy's violent temper – and his habit of carrying firearms. Lillian testified that he always carried a gun in his hip pocket. He was never without it, she said, and he would often take it out at the slightest provocation. Once, only a few weeks after their son had been born, they were driving on Lindell Boulevard and ran into a passing parade. The men in charge refused to open the ranks and allow them to pass through, so Billy charged on ahead. When their carriage was stopped, he started to get out and draw his revolver but Lillian stopped him. He wasn't always so easy to control, she stated, and would even sometimes draw his gun when their carriage was blocked by another at the theater. As their marriage deteriorated, Lillian said, he often threatened to shoot and kill her. She told the courtroom that she had every reason to believe he would make good on his threats.

Leahy's questioning eventually got around to what would become one of the most significant issues with the marriage – the couple's different religious faiths. Lillian explained that she was a Roman Catholic and that her husband "had no religion" (the Lemp family were Lutherans) and that Billy especially despised the Catholic Church. He would constantly criticize their son's religious training and when Lillian had the boy baptized, she did so against Billy's wishes and actually kept the baptism a secret for almost three years. Whenever Lillian spoke to their son about God, Billy would laugh and tell him there was no such thing as God and that she was silly to believe there was. He further annoyed his wife by making the boy eat meat on Fridays, which, at that time, was against the teachings of the Church.

When Lillian was cross-examined by Billy's attorney, problems emerged with parts of her story. Frederick Lehmann produced the Lemps' prenuptial agreement and pointed out where she had promised that if a child were born of the marriage she would leave all decisions regarding religious and academic educations to Billy's discretion. Lillian denied ever seeing the paper before, despite the fact that she had signed it. When Lehmann showed her the signature at the bottom, she admitted that it was hers but stated that she never would have knowingly entered into an agreement that would give Billy total control of their child's education. In turn, Lillian produced a contract of her own in which Billy agreed that any children of the marriage would be instructed in the Catholic faith. It had been signed in the presence of Archbishop John Joseph Kain. However, it was the contention of Billy's attorney that he had been obliged to sign the waiver before their marriage could be overseen by an official of Lillian's church. Billy had required the prenuptial agreement later, which revoked the initial waiver, and made him the sole authority as to the education and religious upbringing of their son. However, Lillian argued that when Billy made her sign the paper, it had been folded in half and that she had been unable to read what was written on it. She had trusted her husband to act in her best interests, she said, a mistake that she later regretted. Lillian claimed that she did not know the second contract existed until after the divorce was filed and Billy's defense became a matter of public record. Unfortunately, it was impossible to know who was telling the truth. Both contracts bore the same date -- October 21, 1899.

On Tuesday, February 9, the trial entered its second day. The courtroom was even more crowded. Word had spread through rumor and newspaper reports about the sordid aspects of the case and seemingly everyone in the vicinity of Saint Louis wanted to listen. A deputy sheriff had to be posted at the door to keep out the hundreds who tried to get inside after the courtroom was filled. Three policemen had to be stationed outside to try and keep the noise of the crowd to a minimum.

Lillian returned to the witness stand, looking worn and tired from the questioning that she had endured the previous day. Lehmann's cross-examination had gotten to her and she seemed very nervous. Trial observers had to lean forward in the gallery to hear her strained words as she continued to describe the terrible treatment that she claimed to have endured during her marriage.

As she had the day before, Lillian spoke of her husband's unreasonable jealousy. This time, she recalled a trip she had taken to Chicago in 1903. Billy led her to believe that he was not going to accompany her and then surprised her by showing up at her hotel room at 10:00 p.m. He seemed disappointed to find her sewing. "He came in and looked under the bed and went into the closet and pushed back clothing and looked behind it and went into the bathroom and searched all corners," Lillian testified. "When I asked him what he was looking for, he made no reply." After Billy finishing searching the hotel suite, she said he drank a bottle of wine and fell asleep.

The next series of witnesses called by Lillian's attorney were all presented in an attempt to further discredit Billy. All of their testimony concerned his behavior when Lillian was away from home. Mrs. Lena Corey, a former laundress for the Lemps, told of wild parties that were held in the house when Lillian was out of town. During these parties, drunken guests overturned tables, broke chairs, shattered glasses and spilled liquor all over the floor. She said the sounds of drunken singing, laughter and debauchery could be heard throughout the house.

Billy's driver, Robert L. Johnson, told of many late-night automobile rides with with his employer, all of them involving women and alcohol. On some occasions, the women ended up at Billy's house and other times, he spent the night at theirs. Leahy asked Johnson if he recalled taking Billy to a residence on Garrison Street, near Laclede Avenue. The chauffeur admitted that he did and said that Billy told him to park around the corner from the house and wait. He parked for about thirty minutes while Billy went inside. Lillian's attorney asked if he knew whose house it was and Johnson said that it belonged to a Mrs. Howard.

Billy's attorney objected but Leahy insisted that the question was relevant. He stated that he expected to prove that the society editor of the afternoon newspaper lived at the address and that Billy went there to give her derogatory stories about his wife. The day after his visit, an article appeared that referred to Lillian as the "Lavender Lady." Leahy contended that Billy had invented the name. The judge sustained the defense's objection and the testimony was ruled out.

Wednesday morning, February 10, brought frigid temperatures to St. Louis, shrinking the size of the crowd outside the courthouse. Lillian and Billy were likely relieved by this development as both were showing signs of fatigue from the past two days of the trial. One has to wonder if they were starting to regret their stubbornness and dislike for one another, which had prevented them from settling the matter in private.

The entire morning session of the third day was filled by the reading of two depositions. The first was that of Jacob Rosenstein, the owner of a women's clothing store in Chicago. He said that in his work, he dealt with both society ladies and those of the "underworld." Among the latter group was Lulu Morrison, who ran a brothel on Chestnut Street. According to Rosenstein, he had seen Billy in her "resort" several times after he was married to Lillian. He also told of seeing him in other sporting houses in the city. The second deposition, collected from a woman named Pearl Richey, who was also from Chicago, stated that she had seen Billy in a local St. Louis brothel that was owned by a Molly Edwards. The story behind Miss Richey's deposition was an interesting one. Apparently, she had been visited by an "elderly, gray-haired gentleman" when she was sick in a Chicago hospital. After hearing that Pearl had seen Billy in a St. Louis sporting house after his marriage, this mysterious man offered to pay all her expenses and bring her to doctors at Mullanphy Hospital in St. Louis. She was registered in this prominent Catholic hospital under the name "Mary Carter" and her deposition was taken. While Pearl never revealed her benefactor's identity, the description fit that of Alexander Handlan, Lillian's father.

In the afternoon session, Billy presented a deposition of his own -- an impressive document more than three hundred pages long that offered extensive details on his financial status. It was presented as evidence to guide the court in fixing the amount of alimony that would be given to Lillian. Her attorney claimed that the facts in the document showed Billy to be worth around $1.5 million but the defense maintained that he was worth much less, well under $1 million.

Billy stated in his deposition that he owned 3,760 shares of William J. Lemp Brewing Company stock, worth $100 per share. As president of the company, he was paid an annual salary of $12,000. He declared that his entire annual income, including salary, was $33,000. In addition, he was allowed $5,000 in expense money each year to be spent in taverns in cities throughout the country to promote Lemp beer. The deposition stated that although Billy was the president of several other small breweries and ice companies, he didn't draw a salary from any of them.

Only a dozen or so people returned for a special night session of court that evening, which had to be called because of the length of Billy's deposition. When court adjourned at 10:15 p.m., only a little more than half of the document had been read. Lillian did not attend the session and even Billy left at 8:00 p.m.

The trial resumed on Thursday, February 11, with the conclusion of Billy's financial statement taking up the entire morning. Shortly before noon, Alexander Handlan was called to the stand. Handlan was asked by Lillian's attorney to recall the details of a conversation that he had with his son-in-law in which Lemp told him that he wanted to separate from his wife.

He also testified about a heated verbal exchange that the two men had at the Mercantile Club in 1905 when Handlan confronted Billy about his treatment of his daughter. Handlan remarked that Lillian had "every ground for divorce in the law dictionary" except that of infidelity. He claimed that Billy smirked at him and said that, if necessary, he would give her that ground, too.

Court recessed for the day at 12:30 p.m. In honor of Abraham Lincoln's birthday, February 12, no session was held on Friday.

The trial resumed on Saturday, February 13. For the first time, Billy took the stand. After a brief overview of the Lemp Brewery and his association with it, he was given a chance to tell his side of the rocky -- and what he claimed was disastrous -- marriage.

As expected, he denied the majority of Lillian's allegations, stating that he did not strike his wife or push her down the stairs. He said he never broke down her bedroom door, cursed at her, pointed a pistol at her, and had never disparaged the Catholic Church. He said he didn't mind his son being brought up in the Catholic faith. There was nothing true about his wife's testimony, he said, and in fact, it had been Lillian who made his life miserable, not the other way around. One of the most aggravating examples of this was her constant wearing of the head-to-toe lavender, which caused people to turn and stare at them whenever they were out in public. It had become so embarrassing to him that Billy dreaded going anywhere with his wife.

Billy's version of the attack in the bathroom in October 1904 also differed dramatically from the story that Lillian had told. He claimed that he had not been out drinking but had been at his mother's house. He said he returned home between 8:00 and 9:00 p.m. and Lillian started to argue with him almost as soon as he took off his coat. Billy said that Lillian began talking about his mother, brother and sisters, saying that he was their "tool" and that they were "using" him. He told Lillian to be quiet, that he didn't want to hear that kind of talk. Billy said that when he left the room, Lillian followed him with a book or a magazine in her hand, getting ready to strike him with it.

"I pushed her into the dressing room," Billy admitted. "She ran past me to the telephone. I went out, and in passing her I told her that if anyone wanted me, I would be at the brewery. I went across the street to the office and remained there about an hour, then I returned with the night watchman."

Lillian was in her dressing room with the door locked when Billy returned. He asked her to let him in, he told the court, but she refused. He swore that he did not threaten to break down the door, nor did he try and enter it by force. "I simply said 'Please open the door,'" Billy said. "The nurse, Roxie Saxenberg, suggested that I go to the guest's room, and I went there and slept."

"Did you strike her?" Frederick Lehmann asked him.

"I did not," Billy replied.

"Did you knock her down?"

"I did not."

"Did you push her down the stairs?"

"I did not," Billy answered, half rising from his chair. Newspaper accounts say his right hand was extended and his face was flushed with anger. He nearly shouted at his own attorney. "I know of no worse crime than for a husband to strike his wife, the mother of his child," he said. Lillian glanced over at her attorney after this statement and shrugged her shoulders.

Billy's frequently criticized Lillian during his testimony. There were many allegations made and one startling disclosure, a photograph that was introduced as evidence by his attorney. The audience in the courtroom collectively gasped at the photo, which showed Lillian dressed in men's clothing and smoking a cigarette, a habit in which no respectable woman of the era indulged. Lillian explained that her brother took the photograph as a joke long before she even knew Billy. She added that Billy knew the circumstances behind the photograph and always told her that it was one of his favorites. Lillian offered a plausible explanation for the scandalous photograph but the courtroom had been shocked by it. The damage had been done.

Billy spoke with disdain about Lillian's housekeeping abilities. He said that she would often be without necessary servants and that the house would not be property cleaned. "Time and again I came home and the meals were not ready," he said. "Often she would leave the house with the boy and give the servants no instructions regarding meals for me." Lillian often remained away for most of the day and late into the night leaving only the laundress on duty. She failed to hire any new servants and often told Billy that if he didn't like the situation, he could hire new servants himself; she was tired of bothering with it. Billy failed to explain, when asked by Lillian's lawyer, why he never went ahead and hired any servants himself. It was, quite simply, a wife's duty to handle such things.

Billy also spoke of how much he disliked his wife's sister, Vella Handlan Bisbee. He said that Lillian aggravated their already troubled home life by continuing to allow Vella to visit, even though he had asked repeatedly that she be kept away. He claimed that Vella had "shown great discourtesies" to him, even daring to ignore his presence and refusing to speak to him. Billy said that he disliked his sister-in-law so much that he couldn't stand to eat at the same table with her.

During cross-examination, John Leahy returned to the subject of the disputed prenuptial agreement and asked Billy when he and Lillian had first discussed giving him control of the religious training of their children. Billy replied that it had been when they had first become engaged, in June 1899. Leahy asked him why he had waited until they were married before deciding to put this into a contract, but Frederick Lehmann objected and Billy didn't answer the question.

Leahy persisted, "At the time you signed the contract in the presence of the archbishop, providing the children were to be raised Catholics, did you intend to keep the agreement?"

Billy sniffed before he replied, "No, I can't say that I did."

Billy returned to the stand on Monday morning, February 15. Throughout his testimony on Saturday, Lillian had sat facing him at her table, taking copious notes, her pencil flying across the

Lillian's sister, Vella Handlan Bisbee, who Billy blamed for the collapse of he and Lillian's marriage.

paper. At other times, she sat watching Billy's face as he spoke. All of her notes were passed on to Leahy, who used the information that she gave him to attack Billy on the stand. The newspapers had already given Billy high marks for his demeanor on the witness stand. He had answered all of the questions posed to him in a calm, deliberate manner, which could be difficult under grilling by the experienced Leahy, who was both loud and dramatic in the courtroom. On Monday, Leahy once again began hammering Billy with questions.

Leahy first asked him about his annoyance with Lillian's attire, making him admit that he disliked high lace and linen collars and that he hated his wife's constant wearing of lavender. Leahy asked him if she had been wearing lavender before they were married and Billy said he didn't remember.

"You say you can't remember what your wife wore before her marriage?" Leahy asked, in a disbelieving tone.

"I have no recollection."

"Now, wasn't it purple, instead of lavender, that she wore?"

"Sometimes it was purple."

"Was it the color you objected to?"

"It was the almost constant wearing."

"You wanted change and variety now and then?"

Billy shook his head. "I didn't want her to be conspicuous by wearing the same thing all the time."

Leahy asked him about the origin of the newspaper article that first referred to Lillian as the "Lavender Lady." Billy said that he did not solicit the interview. He said that Mrs. Howard had come to his office and asked him for a statement. He was allowed to look over her article and after he returned it to her, it was published the next day. He said he did not agree to be interviewed for the article; he only wanted to look at it and make sure that it was correct. When questioned by Leahy, he stated firmly that he had not written any of it and had not concocted Lillian's nickname.

Leahy then turned to Billy's interest in guns. He asked him why he always carried one and Billy had a ready explanation. "When I was 22 years old, they made a brewmaster out of me," he explained. "I weighed only 120 pounds and I had to go all around through the brewery alone at all hours of the night. That is why I carried a pistol." Billy confessed that carrying a gun became something of a habit for him but, despite what Lillian claimed, he did not carry it all the time.

Billy was forced to explain his actions involving a pistol and a member of the household staff, which Lillian had earlier testified about. Either version of the story presents an alarming view of life in Billy and Lillian's household. In Lillian's version, she and Billy were eating dinner when the doorbell rang and a butler named Donaldson went to see who it was. It was a man delivering some hats, but Billy thought it was someone else. When Donaldson returned to the dining room, Lillian said Billy swore at him, drew his revolver, placed it to the man's head and threatened to kill him.

Billy gave a different version of the incident. He stated that the butler had standing instructions to always announce whoever rang the bell at the front door. On the night in question, Billy, Lillian and the baby were seated at the dining room table and when Donaldson opened the door, he simply called out "Hats!" Lillian asked him what hats he was taking about and the butler answered, "Why, your hats, of course," in a rude and surly manner. Billy, offended at the way Donaldson had spoken to his wife, followed him into the kitchen. He ordered him to come back out and apologize but he refused. Billy said the butler backed toward a table where the cook kept the carving knives.

"Then I drew my revolver in self-defense," Billy testified. "I covered him with the revolver and said, 'You have been insolent to Mrs. Lemp, and here is your chance to apologize.'" Donaldson quickly did so and Billy said that he put away his gun and finished his meal.

The trial, which had originally been predicted to last three days, finally ended on Tuesday, February 16. During a short bit of morning testimony, Lillian returned to the stand to deny most of her husband's allegations, including those that dealt with her taste in clothing. Leahy asked her if she tried to get attention with her manner of dress. Lillian stated that she absolutely did not.

"Do you wear lavender to the exclusion of other colors?" he then asked her.

"I don't remember ever wearing lavender in my life," Lillian replied, which was an obvious mistruth. She stated that she preferred black, white, violet and sometimes tan and gray and that her husband had always greatly admired her wardrobe.

Lillian then denied ever having spoken badly about Julia Lemp, Billy's mother. During his testimony, Billy claimed that Lillian said Julia was "using him." He also said that his wife neglected his mother during the time when she was bedridden with cancer. He said she only visited her twice each week and only occasionally brought flowers. Julia was on her deathbed, Billy said, and Lillian should have cared for her more. Lillian insisted that she and Julia "were devoted to each other."

Her testimony ended at noon and soon after, the attorneys began their closing statements, starting with Frederick Lehmann. "Every divorce is a tragedy," he said. "It calls for the severance of holy ties, the breaking apart of two united for life's tenure. All are accompanied by revelations of the inner heart's emotions. When affection becomes soured and embittered, then the altar fires of love, burning softly, cast pleasing shadows in a life of trust and domestic bliss, then turn to very hate, the same shadows take on grim and sordid shape in the higher and fiercer light of new emotion. The whole horizon of view is changed and the one who loved may come, when love is changed to hate, with a different attitude toward every circumstance and things which in a home of love and trust may seem fraught with kindness and consideration, when viewed in the later hours of hate become cruelties extreme."

Lehmann held his audience spellbound and spoke for more than an hour. The only sounds in the courtroom were sobs from some of the female spectators. The attorney paced back and forth, dramatically comparing his client to Shakespeare's Othello, who loved his wife and yet was inspired to frenzied jealousy. Billy couldn't control himself, his attorney cried, and who would not have been jealous after the damning letter that he found among his wife's things?

Lehmann referred to Exhibit No. 1 in the case, or the "Dear Little Pal" letter, as the newspapers called it. The startling note had been written by Lillian and discovered by her husband, which he claimed was proof that she was involved with another man. Lillian claimed, however, that the letter was a fabrication, written to make Billy jealous and intentionally left where he was sure to find it. After his discovery of the note, Billy snatched it up and took it to the brewery office, where he photographed it. He then returned it to the spot where he found it. He did not mention the letter to Lillian until it was produced during the divorce trial. The letter read:

My Dear Little Pal,
I wish you could see what I am going through to make "him" take me to the show tonight. Of course, the day is not over and I may still succeed. If I fail, then I shall go anyway, with Ham and Ella. However, "he" does not know that. Tomorrow I will again take Vella to the matinee. Although I cannot be with you, to watch you at a distance or to feel your presence is my only happiness and my greatest recreation. Do telephone me when you can, as I usually answer the phone now. In case I do not you can always put up the phone again or else say my brother wishes to speak to me. "He" us going hunting next week and I wish to heaven he would never return. I am completely worn out and God alone knows how much longer I can stand this loathsome bondage.

Was it a real letter, written to a lover or would-be lover, and accidentally discovered by Billy? Or was it, as Lillian claimed, merely an attempt to make her husband jealous. The truth will never be known but to Frederick Lehmann, it didn't matter. Whether genuine or a fabrication, he saw the letter as proof that Lillian was causing Billy to behave in a jealous and erratic manner. The letter, viewed in either light that the court cared to take, was a monstrous and awful thing. "It was written either to gladden the heart of another or to crush the heart of her husband," he said. "Either of these theories is replete with room for thought. I am not sure that it is not worse for a woman to have written the letter, intending that her husband should see it, than to have written it for another."

Lehmann went on to attack various parts of Lillian's case, including the statement that was given by Pearl Richey, which he called "a most unreasonable and impossible contravention, clever in its very lack of definition."

In the end, Billy's attorneys stated that he had been the injured one in the case because Lillian had brought criminal charges against him and then failed to prove them. Thus, Billy had suffered an indignity that entitled him to a divorce, as well as the custody of his son. It was also added that Billy did not desert his wife – he had just cause for leaving her because she had intentionally made his life miserable. Billy was entitled to have pleasant surroundings, they said, but when Lillian insisted on having her sister Vella as a regular visitor, Billy's life became wretched.

The senior attorney for Lillian was Judge Daniel Dillon and he was the first to make a statement on her behalf. Up until now, John Leahy had largely handled the case but Dillon's reputation earned him great respect in the courtroom, which he felt would work to his client's advantage. Dillon asserted that, even though his lawyers denied it, it had been proven conclusively that Billy had deserted Lillian. He stated that this, regardless of any other charges, was enough to earn his client a divorce. He further urged that she be given custody of William III. "Mr. Lemp has told you that he has no religious beliefs," Dillon said. "You should remember this in thinking of the child's future, and you should also remember the testimony about Lemp's associations with evil women after he was married."

As Dillon continued to speak, Lillian, finally showing her exhaustion, burst into tears. As her attorney spoke about her terrible marriage, she sat with her head bowed and a handkerchief dabbing at her eyes. She soon regained her composure, but it was obvious to everyone that the long days in the courtroom had taken a toll on her.

Dillon spent much of the time during his statement dealing with the matter of Billy's income and just how much of it Lillian should get. He urged the court to give her a large, lump sum payment rather than smaller, periodic ones. He attempted to paint a picture of Billy as a cruel, bitter man who might not make the payments that were required of him if the alimony stretched on for years. He had already lied about his net worth, Dillon claimed, and might also lie about whether he could be trusted to keep up with his payments. In addition, if the brewery business declined and his wealth was wiped out at some future date, what would happen to Lillian then? And what if he got married again? If his wealth was reduced to an ordinary income, how could he still provide for Lillian?

Dillon also pleaded for the welfare of William III, stating that Billy had never shown the proper regard for his child. He claimed that Billy had been just across the street for six weeks after his separation from Lillian and had never come to see the child. "The court must take into account the father's former life," Dillon said, "the fact that he has no religious beliefs and the treatment of his wife, in determining the future custody of this child. This child is entitled to religious training, which he would never get if left in the care of his father. Mr. Lemp has shown himself a man not to be relied upon. Any man who would sign the agreement he signed before the archbishop with an intention to disregard it is not worthy of belief by this court."

As Billy saw listening to Lillian's senior attorney speak, he managed to repress any emotions that he might have felt as he was berated and ridiculed. However, when Dillon stated that he had, by his action, showed that he had no love for his little boy, Billy's eyes filled with tears and he turned his face away from the courtroom audience.

Billy was moved to tears again a few minutes later, after John Leahy took over the closing statements for his client. He also launched a scathing attack on Billy, detailing how terribly he had treated his wife during their marriage. As he spoke, Lillian pulled her veil down over her face and turned toward the window, unable to look at the audience behind her. Billy himself hid his face behind his hands and wept as Leahy's words rang out in the crowded room.

Like Lehmann, Leahy was a skilled speaker and was able to captivate the audience in a way that even the more experienced Judge Dillon had been unable to do. He spoke at length about how the case he presented proved beyond a doubt that Billy had committed sufficient indignities to warrant a divorce decree from his wife. He spoke of the poor treatment and the violence that Lillian had suffered at Billy's hands. He defended his client for her writing of the "Dear Little Pal" letter, which he still maintained was merely a ploy to deceive Billy. No man had yet been able to know what a "discarded woman" might do or how she might act under circumstances like the ones that Lillian endured. He asserted that Billy was not a jealous man, merely a clever one, and spoke of the two separate prenuptial agreements and Billy's photographing of the letter.

"The facts are that the defendant was tired of the woman he took as his wife," Leahy said. "He tired of her dress; he sought to prevent her from associating with relatives; he sought to prevent her from christening her child. He was through, and he said to himself, 'Bring on the next.' Mr. Lemp was never jealous of anybody but himself. Now he comes into court and asks 'Give me a divorce. Send her forth childless and homeless, and still dependent for a living. Send her back to the unfaltering love of her parents. Let me continue to live on the profits of Gambrinus.'" [Gambrinus was a legendary king of Flanders, and an unofficial patron saint of beer or beer brewing]

The overly dramatized (often bordering on histrionics) closing statements concluded at 4:30 p.m., marking an end to the most publicized and bitter divorce trial in St. Louis history. Even many years later, after all of the proverbial dust has settled, it's hard to say who the clear winner was in the courtroom portion of the proceedings. The stories of both Billy and Lillian were filled with holes, often bordering on outright lies. By the end of the trial, it was obvious by the expressions on both of their faces that the public spectacle that they had presented had been a serious lapse in judgment. But, just as their married life had been, the divorce was a poorly thought out, hasty affair, filled with anger and recriminations. One has to wonder what might have happened if only cooler heads had prevailed. Or even if things might have been different if William and Julia Lemp had still been alive. It's likely that Billy would have been able to avoid the pressures of running the company and perhaps the lack of stress would have made him a different – much better – man.

Or perhaps not. It's another mystery of the Lemp family that will never be solved.

The presiding judge, Judge Hitchcock, handed down his decision on February 18. Neither Billy nor Lillian were in the courtroom that day to hear the decision. The judge granted Lillian an absolute decree of divorce, as well as control of the education and religious training of William III. She was also awarded alimony of $6,000 per year, payable in quarterly installments. Billy was required to execute a bond for $30,000 that would be held against him making the regular payments.

Billy was allowed custody of his son from 9:00 a.m. each Saturday until 8:00 p.m. on Sunday, starting on February 20, 1909. During the summer, Lillian could take her son to a resort, as she usually did each year, provided that he had visited with Billy for two consecutive weeks in advance of the trip. This was to compensate Billy for the loss of his weekend visits.

According to Judge Hitchcock, Billy had managed to refute every allegation made by his wife except for the charge of desertion. The divorce was granted on that charge alone, but it was enough. Billy's attorneys saw the trial as a victory in their favor. When asked for a quote, one of them said, "I wouldn't like to talk about it. I never like to exult over the misfortune of a loser in a suit."

John Leahy was disappointed by the amount of alimony that his client had been awarded. "Such an allowance practically creates license for a rich man to get as many divorces as he wished," he said. "A millionaire may have fifty wives at that price and get rid of them all by divorce, as far as the financial part of it is concerned." He added, however, that Lillian was very happy to be divorced, but was sorry that the custody of her son was not more absolute, in that she would be tied down to one place so that William would always live close enough for Billy to carry out his weekly visits.

Billy never spoke publicly about the divorce trial and he refused to give a statement to the press. It should be noted, however, that a small piece did appear in the afternoon edition of the *St. Louis Star*:

Soon after the decision in the Lemp case, "Billy" Lemp, going west on Washington Avenue in his automobile and turning south on Twelfth Street, heard the cries of the newsboys calling the extra edition of the Star. *Lemp caused his machine to be stopped and purchased a paper, the first page of which he perused for a moment. Shaking the paper before him, he laughed heartily as if in great amusement, and, slapping his chauffeur on the back repeatedly, handed the paper to him and passed several joking remarks. Then, folding the paper and putting it into his pocket, he directed his chauffeur to drive on. As he passed out of sight he still seemed to be very much amused, giving every appearance of not being affected by the court's decision.*

But Billy wouldn't be laughing for long. Just over one day after the divorce decree had been handed down, attorneys Dillon and Leahy filed a motion for a new trial. The motion was denied on March 11, 1909 but they did not give up the fight. Ultimately, the case was taken all the way to the Missouri Supreme Court. On March 28, 1913, Lillian not only won sole custody of her son, she was awarded alimony of $100,000. At the time it was the largest sum ever awarded in the state.

Lillian and her son went to live with her parents at their home on Lindell Boulevard. In 1915, she moved to New York and took a suite at the Chase Hotel, where she was living when reporters caught up with her and asked for her thoughts on Billy's new wife.

In 1922, Lillian, William III, and Lillian's sisters, Vella Bisbee and Marie Hornsby, sued her brothers over money from her late father's estate. Alexander Handlan had died in May 1921 and left behind real estate holdings and a sizable bank account. The shares in the Handlan-Buck Company that Lillian's father owned were worth a large fortune, but at the time of his death, the shares were taken over by Lillian's brothers, Eugene, Edward and Alexander H. Handlan, Jr. They claimed the shares because their father had been drawing interest from them at the time of his death and they had never been transferred into his estate. Lillian and her sisters believed that their father would have wanted them to receive a portion of the money. Eventually, the case was settled out of court and a trust was set up for the sisters. Lillian managed to use this money, along with the money she received from Billy, to live on for the rest of her life.

In New York, Lillian lived the same sort of flamboyant, eccentric lifestyle that she had maintained as a society favorite in St. Louis. She threw lavish parties where her guests rubbed shoulders with movie stars, writers and politicians. It would not be a surprise to come to her house and find Cole Porter on the piano, providing the evening's entertainment. Visitors who dropped in during the day might find her in a $2,000 evening gown.

She managed to live in extravagance for many years and only returned to St. Louis near the end of her life. Lillian never re-married. She died in 1960, having outlived both her former husband and her son.

10. "An Approaching Storm"

The Lemp Years Before Prohibition

After the strain of the divorce trial, both Billy and Lillian dropped out of the public eye. Lillian went to live with her parents and then left St. Louis altogether. Billy sought refuge outside of the city in what was then near- wilderness near Webster Groves in St. Louis County. In 1910, high above the bluffs overlooking the Meramec River, Billy built a magnificent country estate, which he called *Alswel*.

He was not the first of St. Louis' wealthy men to seek solace among the hills, forests and rivers west of the city. St. Louis County had been a retreat for city-dwellers since the eighteenth century, when colonial Governor Zenon Trudeau built a country home near Spanish Lake. Some of the houses were used as summer homes or weekend lodges, while others became primary places of residence. Among those who sought the quiet of country living were William Clark, the last territorial governor and who, along with Meriwether Lewis, was one of the most famous men in American history. Clark had a large country estate on Natural Bridge Road. St. Louis' first millionaire, John Mullanphy, had a retreat called *Taille de Noyer*, (French for walnut-size) near Florissant. The house grew from a two-room fur trading post into a stately 22-room mansion. *Talle de Noyer* is believed to be one of the oldest homes in St. Louis County. Mullanphy's daughter, Jane Chambers, later made it her permanent home, while a second daughter, Catherine Graham, settled in a nearby house called *Hazelwood*.

James Lucas and his sister Anne Lucas Hunt once owned most of the land that became downtown St. Louis. They also had a vast estate in Normandy, where Lucas and Hunt Road is named for them.

In the 1850s, the railroads made it easier for people to live farther outside of the city and still maintain their business interests there. William McPherson, president of the Pacific Railroad, built a house at Glendale Station, where his neighbor was Hudson Bridge, a director of the railroad and president of both the Mercantile Library and Bellefontaine Cemetery, both of which were important St. Louis institutions. The Pacific Railroad had plans to become a transcontinental railroad and had very little interest in suburban commuting, but some lines were specifically intended for that purpose, mostly to appease the prominent men who lived on country estates.

Toward the end of the 1800s, new development came to the banks of the Meramec River, which has its origins in the Ozarks and flows through St. Louis from west to east. Midway through the county, it makes a long southern bend and the high bluffs along the north and east banks offer breathtaking views of the plains to the south and west and the distant hills beyond. In the early nineteenth century, there had been hopes that the Meramec could support river navigation, but water levels proved to be too irregular and the river remained undeveloped for most of the century. In 1895, however, a resort called Meramec Highlands opened at a bend in the river about three miles from where Billy constructed *Alswel*. Served by the Missouri Pacific Railroad, it had a large hotel, cottages, a dance hall and many recreational pursuits for summer

Billy Lemp's escape from the city, Alswel

resort-goers who wanted to escape the heat of the city.

Over the course of the next few years, brewer Joseph Griesedieck and stove maker Louis Stockstrom acquired adjacent properties about a mile south of Meramec Highlands and built private retreats. Others began to be attracted to the area and a number of houses for year-round occupancy were built. Edwin Lemp built his home *Cragwold* on a hill overlooking the river in 1911, the same year that brewer August Busch built the magnificent estate at Grant's Farm on Gravois Road, closer to the city. The next year, Anheuser-Busch converted a nearby restaurant into the Sunset Hills Country Club. In 1913, Adolphus Busch III built *Grandview* adjacent to it. The area was attractive to many of the brewers in part because it was easy accessible to the southern part of the city, where most of the breweries were located, using Gravois Road.

The homes that were built along the Meramec differed greatly in style. *Cragwold* had a half-timber exterior, *Grant's Farm* was a French chateau and *Grandview* was a Colonial Revival. *Alswel* stood out from the others because of its unusual architectural style, combining a Swiss chalet with a Craftsman bungalow.

Alswel still stands today. It a large cypress-clad house sitting atop a two-hundred-foot bluff that overlooks the Meramec River. The house has two full stories with a third level tucked under the gable roof. From the entrance side, an embankment nearly hides the ground floor. The upper stories were surfaced in cypress planks, applied shiplap-style on the second story and vertically on the third. *Alswel* was designed by Guy Norton, the staff architect at the Lemp Brewery. It was modeled on a Tyrolean chalet, a German form of home that was developed in the Chiemgau region south of Munich and taken into the Lower Inn Valley of

Austria by Bavarian settlers. *Alswel* looks just like one of these houses with its relatively low-pitched roof, its long balconies and its belfry-like chimneys.

The interior of the house, though, was pure American, reflecting the Arts and Crafts movement of the era. It was unusually arranged, with most of the public rooms on the level below the entry, a large reception hall and four bedrooms on the entry level, and four more bedrooms on the third floor.

From the main drive, visitors entered a large parquet-floored living hall, which extended through the center of the house to the balcony in back that overlooked the river. It was designed with a high ceiling that had exposed trusses and an art-glass skylight. On one side was a massive stone fireplace and on the other was a staircase that descended to the first floor. At the corners of the entry floor were large bedrooms with *en suite* bathrooms and dressing rooms. A service staircase was set back off the left of the entry.

The staircase led down to the ground floor living room, an irregularly shaped area with a large alcove that was nestled under the overhead balcony. This room had a large fireplace and bookcases with leaded-glass doors. The dining room, paneled in mahogany with a built-in buffet, was also located on the lower floor. At the southwest corner of the house was a breakfast, room called the garden room that was separated from the dining room by glass doors. It had a tile floor, half-timbered walls, a beamed plank ceiling and a huge fireplace with an iron hood and ornamental spit. On the north side of the house was an entry area that was walled in red brick and had a bathroom on one side. This entry led to the billiard room with a tile floor, beamed ceiling and walls surfaced to wainscot level with gray-brown brick. The fireplace was trimmed with stones and flanked by cabinets with glass doors. The service rooms on the ground floor included a kitchen, a butler's pantry, a scullery and a boiler room, which extended under the entrance porch and dropped about ten feet below the level of the other ground floor rooms.

Four more bedrooms and two baths were located on the third floor, which had a large center hall. Occupying most of this area was the art-glass window that emitted light into the hall below.

Steps descended on both sides of the house from the entrance drive to the backyard, which extended in a gentle grade about one hundred and twenty feet to a stone retaining wall. At the north end of the wall was an octagonal pavilion with a cupola, while a little beyond the south end was a circular stone tower with a flat wooden roof that was designed as a viewing platform. Just on the other side of the wall, the ground dropped sharply down a wooded hillside to the Meramec River.

Billy loved *Alswel* and it became his permanent home in 1914. He lived there almost until the end of his life. He found peace and solitude away from the city and from the prying eyes of the public that had been so fascinated with his sensational divorce trial.

A stone cupola at the corner of the property looked out over the Meramec River

Billy's second wife, Ellie Limberg

He also had the land and freedom to indulge in two of his favorite pursuits, hunting and fishing. He never regretted moving away from his home near the brewery and secluding himself in the woods of St. Louis County.

The next few years after Billy's divorce were busy times at the Lemp Brewery. Business had remained strong and profits continued to pour into the company coffers. The year 1911 turned out to be a significant one for the brewery. In the spring, Charles Lemp moved out of the family home and the house was remodeled and converted into the new offices of the William J. Lemp Brewing Company. The stately mansion underwent many extensive changes, forever altering its design. The house had already been remodeled once in 1904, when the grand wooden staircase had been replaced with an elevator that helped the aging Julia Lemp to more easily reach the second floor, but the 1911 renovations were startling. One of the most visible changes was the immense bay window that was added atop the atrium on the south side of the building. Inside, the front of the house was rearranged into private offices, lobbies and work space for the clerks.

Also in 1911, giant grain elevators were added to the Lemp brewery complex, making it possible for the company to increase its daily production for the first time in several years. No one knew it at the time, but these were the last major improvements that would be made to the brewery.

A year after moving to *Alswel*, Billy married for the second time. His new wife was Ellie Koehler Limberg, the widowed daughter of Casper Koehler, who founded the Columbia Brewery. Koehler was another German immigrant who made his way to America in 1855. He settled in Fort Madison, Iowa, and worked in a brewery owned by his brother, Henry, who had, coincidentally, started his career at the Lemp Brewery. Koehler came to St. Louis in 1874 and started the Columbia Brewery in 1892. He and his wife, Josephine, had four children, including Ellie Amelia. Ellie married Rudolph Limberg, who started the Excelsior Brewery and later joined his father-in-law when he started the Columbia Brewery, before passing away in 1910.

Julius Koehler, Ellie's brother, owned land adjacent to *Alswel* and although they were business rivals, the

Koehler and Lemp families had been good friends for years. It became widely known among their friends that Billy and Ellie were more than just "passing fond" of one another after Billy took a family cruise with the Koehlers in 1914. The two of them began to be seen together at social functions and rumors of an engagement persisted for months, but the stories were always denied.

Then suddenly, without any announcement, Billy and Ellie were married at the Waterman Avenue home of the bride's son, Edward Limberg. The ceremony took place on May 18, 1915, attended only by a few close relatives. Reverend John W. Day, pastor at the Unitarian Church of the Messiah, presided over the event. Anyone who inquired at the house that day was told by the servants that the family was "out" and it would be denied for some time afterward that the wedding even took place.

The newspapers eventually broke the story. Billy's infamy had only slightly died down from the days of the divorce trial and his second marriage was just interesting enough to grab the attention of newspaper readers. Coincidentally, Lillian (who was living in New York by then) was in St. Louis when the story broke. When told of Billy's unexpected re-marriage, she said that she was surprised but refused further comment.

The *St. Louis Globe-Democrat* noted about Ellie Limberg: "Mrs. Lemp is considered very attractive and is so youthful in appearance and manner that she looks more like her son's sister than his mother." One can only assume, after seeing Ellie's photograph, that the newspaper writer was being kind. Not only was Billy's new wife an unattractive woman (and, according to family members, an unfriendly one) she was four years older than her new husband.

After their honeymoon, Billy and Ellie went to live at *Alswel* but contrary to the whimsical name that Billy had given to the estate, all was far from well in the brewing business. At the Lemp Brewery, Billy had failed to keep up with current industry innovations. Without the passion for the business that his father had, Billy had allowed much of the brewing facility to become outdated and it was starting to show signs of age.

Even worse, the entire brewing industry was in trouble. The dark clouds of Prohibition were beginning to gather on the horizon and those opposed to alcohol began to use every method at their disposal to try and bring down the brewing industry, including boycotts, protests and even accusations of treason.

America Goes Dry:
The "German Threat" and the Push for Prohibition

By the early 1910s, a strong push for national Prohibition was underway, led by organizations like the Anti-Saloon League. However, Americans of the time were, for the most part, not interested in outlawing alcohol. Prohibition was an extreme measure that smelled of coercion and invasion of privacy. Not to mention, alcohol was a powerful and well-entrenched part of American culture. One could find beer, imported rum or locally made liquor and cider in almost every frontier household. Almost everyone, young and old, drank. A pitcher of beer was often found on the family supper table simply because the local water was unfit to drink. Alcohol was a basic ingredient in most old medicinal remedies and many mothers put cranky babies to sleep by adding a few drops of whiskey to their milk. When neighbors got together to raise barns, harvest crops or just to socialize, there were always jugs of whiskey on the table next to the platters of food.

Even America's greatest heroes were proponents of alcohol. Daniel Boone operated a store that sold liquor. Davy Crockett found that taking a jug of whiskey along when he went "electioneering" helped him win votes. George Washington, Thomas Jefferson and Benjamin Franklin all brewed or distilled their own alcoholic beverages, and the young Abraham Lincoln operated a tavern. A daily ration of rum was given to American soldiers and sailors. Frontiersmen felt so strongly about their liquor that in 1794, the farmers of western Pennsylvania almost went to war with the federal government over a tax on whiskey in what came

A group of women from the Anti-Saloon League gather outside of a tavern in protest against the evils of alcohol.

(Left) Flyers and posters were used to promote the fight against alcohol and the drive to ratify an amendment that would bring about Prohibition.

to be known as the Whiskey Rebellion.

So, how did the Anti-Saloon League manage to weasel its way into the halls of the United States Congress and force a change to the Constitution that would make alcohol illegal? Part of the group's success can be attributed to the times themselves. Many believed that drastic measures were needed in a society that had been shaken by the speed in which the new industrial economy had taken hold. People were free to do as they pleased, many believed, as long as it didn't place additional burdens on their neighbors or the government. Alcohol, the "drys" believed, burdened society in terms of lost productivity, families harmed, wages wasted, health destroyed and lives damaged beyond repair.

But what the group managed to do starting in 1913 stands as a testimony to the tenacity, passion and devious skill of the nation's first single-issue lobbying group. They had been working for several years convincing Americans to ban liquor on a local level but now they took the extreme step of pushing their beliefs through Congress. Had the electorate been asked to vote directly on the measure, it would have undoubtedly failed, but the mechanism used to ratify changes to the Constitution worked to the Anti-Saloon League's advantage. The issue would never go before the voters themselves. Instead, ratification would fall to the members of the state legislatures and only they could vote on the amendment.

The process began in Congress, where two-thirds of the House and Senate had to authorize submission of the amendment to the forty-eight states. Ernest Cherrington, the Anti-Saloon League official who was the strategist for the group, planned a test vote in Congress in 1914. The group then planned to devote 1915 and 1916 to electoral warfare, getting rid of "wet" congressmen and replacing them with "drys" of their choosing. If the plan worked out, a dry Congress would approve the amendment in 1918 and send it on to the states, where the league, having by then filled the legislatures with sympathizers to the cause, expected no trouble in gathering the necessary thirty-six votes.

It was a simple plan, but not an easy one. They faced an uphill batter and in the hands of other organizers, the fight would have been lost before it began. But the members of the league, seeing this as the final battle, brought great passion to the fight. Petitions, letters and telegrams rolled in by the tens of thousands, burying Congress under a mountain of paper. League spies sent daily updates to headquarters so that league officials knew every move the wets made.

Another great asset to the Anti-Saloon League was the indifference of the opposition. The "wets" simply refused to take the "drys" seriously. They ridiculed their efforts but the jokes were no defense against the self-righteous solemnity of the Prohibition movement. The only significant argument rested on theory rather than fact. As one article stated, a ban on booze would "breed deceit, hypocrisy, disrespect of law and encourage evasion, lying, trickery, and lawlessness." It added that enforcement would "require an army of United States officials, paid spies and informers." All of this turned out to be true, but in 1913, it was an argument that had no real effect. The Anti-Saloon League made sure of that. Their newspapers, magazines and press releases only spoke of the decrease in crime wherever local Prohibition was already the law. They left

In the 1850s, the brewers had managed to fight back against those who believed beer should be lumped in with all forms of alcohol but by the 1910s, the prohibitionists did not believe that beer was a beneficial drink.

out the instances of corruption, violence, bootlegging and the rise of "blind pigs," as illegal retail outlets for alcohol were called.

And so, the campaign for constitutional Prohibition continued. By late 1914, five more states had gone dry. Fifty percent of the American people now lived under Prohibition and more than seventy breweries had closed their doors.

The Anti-Saloon League had greatly benefited from the mysteriously clueless and seemingly indifferent brewing industry. Still resting on their laurels from the middle nineteenth century, when beer was "proven" to be beneficial to one's health and had not been a target of the Prohibition movement the way that hard liquor had been, the brewers paid little attention to what was happening around them.

But the new Prohibitionists did not believe in moderation, or that beer was a beneficial drink. They believed that you either did not drink or if you did, you were doomed to damnation along with the gamblers, heathens, fornicators and godless foreigners. Female temperance fighters marched with banners emblazoned with slogans that proclaimed sentiments like, "Lips that touch liquor will never touch ours." Preachers claimed that the "wine" that Jesus and his apostles drank was only grape juice and ranted about the dangers of drinking, which they said included blindness, insanity, poverty and babies that were born sickly, already addicted to the devil's brew. They plastered walls with posters of bartenders who were demons in disguise; hopeless drunks staring in despair at empty liquor bottles; and ragged children standing outside the doors to taverns, watching in despair while their fathers were inside drinking away the grocery money. They dragged derelicts out of gutters and put them on display as examples of what alcohol could do to a man. This was all-out war for groups like the Anti-Saloon League and beer would not be able to get by this time.

The brewers hemmed and hawed and it was not until the spring of 1913 that the dwindling membership of the United States Brewers' Association finally decided to wake up and get serious about their enemy. The group's executive officers voted to found an organization that was specifically designed to fight back against the Anti-Saloon League. To lead it, they hired Percy Andreae, an Ohio brewery executive who had mounted a successful counter-offensive against the league in his own state.

Andreae became the head of the National Association of Commerce and Labor, an alliance of brewers, glass and bottle-cap manufacturers, corn and rice processors, wholesalers and retailers, saloon keepers and hotel workers – all of whom benefited from the production and sale of beer. Andreae used membership dues and funds from the Brewers' Association to hire a full-time staff of researchers and writers who studied congressional and state legislative elections and analyzed candidates and issues. He also contracted with writers who planted articles in newspapers and magazines blasting the coercive nature of the proposed amendment. The articles reminded readers of beer's virtue as a "temperance" drink of moderation, and touted its nutritional value. A group of sympathetic experts traveled on a lecture circuit that took them to trade and professional conventions, women's clubs, and any church group that was willing to listen to them. The group funded two "wet" magazines and even supported an acting troupe that presented a play about a respectable German saloon keeper who managed to outwit the "drys" who wanted to put him out of business.

Andreae knew, though, that no matter what he did or how quickly he worked, the brewers were far behind their opponents. In order to even the odds, he needed to get more men into action, raise more money and implement his ideas more quickly and efficiently. Looking for a group to help him compete with the Anti-Saloon League, he latched onto the National German-American Alliance.

The alliance had been founded in 1899 by Charles Hexamer, a civil engineer from Philadelphia whose parents were German immigrants. He started the group as a way to celebrate and preserve German heritage, history and culture in the United States. The alliance lobbied against immigration restriction and for German language instruction in public schools. It also supported German language newspapers and funded historical studies. But as the Anti-Saloon League began growing larger and becoming more of a threat to the brewing industry, the alliance's leadership began diverting its energy and funds to defending beer.

On its own, the German-American Alliance couldn't match the organization skills of the Anti-Saloon League. The biggest problem they had was the cultural arrogance of the members. The educated middle-class men who made up the membership regarded German culture as superior to the American way of life and saw themselves as the spokespersons for a unified German-America. This explained the organization's limited membership and also proved to be a fatal mistake. Most German-Americans of the time wanted nothing than to assimilate and regarded themselves as Americans first and only incidentally as Americans of German descent. Many of them supported Prohibition and thousands more disdained the alliance's need to celebrate all things German. Most people who opposed Prohibition, but who were not German-Americans, saw no reason to ally themselves with an ethic organization.

As far as Andreae was concerned, however, the alliance was an asset that could be used to his advantage. It had a membership that was devoted to the "wet" cause, a printing press, and access to thousands of German-American social, political, religious and labor groups. In the late summer of 1913, Andreae offered Hexamer a cut of the brewers' funding in exchange for access to the alliance's network of contacts.

Hexamer needed the money, but he resisted the idea of linking beer's increasingly unsavory reputation with the good name of the German-American Alliance. Andreae managed to work out a way to pay the alliance under the table and soon, laundered money was being distributed to alliance field agents who placed anti-prohibition articles in national magazines and newspapers. In this way, both groups benefited. The alliance received a steady flow of cash and the brewers enjoyed access to an organized political action group that had no obvious connection to the alcohol industry.

But no matter what Andreae did, he couldn't compete with the Anti-Saloon League. Their propaganda overshadowed everything that he tried to do. He spent over a half million dollars of the United States Brewing Association's money and yet the House of Representatives still came perilously close to approving a Prohibition amendment. Meanwhile, every town and county across the country that voted to become dry put another brewer out of business. Since 1904, nearly five hundred breweries had failed. In January 1915, the Brewers' Association, now led by Hilda Lemp's husband, Gustav Pabst, stripped Andreae of his authority.

It became clear just how badly Andreae and the brewers had failed in their efforts when, in April 1917, the United States entered World War I, which by that time had been raging for almost three years. Congress banned alcohol from a five-mile "dry zone" around military bases and imposed abstinence on all servicemen, soldiers and officers alike. As the war continued, Congress turned to the task of rationing food and supplies. The Anti-Saloon League seized the opportunity and turned the debate over bread into a new call for Prohibition.

They cried out over the absurdity of rationing bread to the "laboring man" and the "starving babe" when the brewers were permitted to use those same grains to make "a beverage that kills the body and damns the soul." If the breweries and distilleries were closed, they claimed, America could save the equivalent of eleven million loaves of bread each day. Senator William Thompson of Kansas stated, "There is no patriotism among the liquor interests of this country." He added that the brewers and distillers would gladly "sell liquor under the government of the Kaiser as under that of the President, and chances are they would prefer to do so."

Prohibition supporters flooded the House and Senate with petitions and promised that they would "pray for the prohibition of the manufacture and sale of all intoxicating beverages during the period of war." And it worked – Congress banned the sale of grain to distillers for the duration of the war, a move that effectively closed the doors of the entire industry.

The United States Brewers' Association still had enough clout to succeed in keeping beer out of the bill, but as a compromise, Congress empowered the president to ration the brewers' supplies whenever he thought it to be necessary. President Wilson did just that in early 1917, when he ordered the alcohol level in beer reduced to 2.75 percent and slashed the industry's grain allotment by thirty percent.

August Busch, who now presided over Anheuser-Busch, criticized the new rules saying, "We cannot tell just how the public will take to the change in taste. It may be readily accepted, but a falling off in consumption is a possibility." Otto Stifel, who owned St. Louis' Union Brewery, told reporters, "I do not think the expected saving of food products will be brought about, but the food value of beer will be decreased." Beer was food, in Stifel's way of thinking, one that provided as much nutritional value as milk.

But worse news was coming. The Senate had already approved the Prohibition amendment resolution. The House had argued over the wording for several months, but on December 18, four years after the amendment first appeared in Congress, the House voted 282 to 128 to send it to the state legislatures. The Anti-Saloon League was certain that it had enough support in the various states to approve the ratification, but they weren't taking any chances. It planned one last move, this one aimed at rallying the public's support for amending the Constitution. They would, the leadership decided, discredit what was left of the brewing industry once and for all.

To carry out this task, the league chose Wayne Wheeler, who began his anti-liquor career in 1893 when he helped to start the anti-saloon crusade. He managed league affairs in Ohio but spent most of his time in Washington, D.C., where he strong-armed hesitant lawmakers and helped plan the league's political strategies. In 1915, he had moved to Washington to work as the league's general counsel, chief lobbyist and manager of legislative affairs.

Wheeler was a shrewd and dangerous man whom one critic claimed would "cohabit with the devil

Prohibition crusader Wayne Wheeler

himself to win." On the surface, he was a respectable, middle-class paper pusher who dressed in a proper suit and tie, with a well-trimmed mustache and a prissy pince-nez on his long, straight nose. However, the gleam in his eyes and the occasional smirk that crossed his lips gave evidence of the zealot lurking behind the mask. Wheeler was a born crusader, one of the many that emerged in the America of the 1890s, all fighting for or against civil rights, female suffrage, child labor, white slavery and more. Unfortunately for the country's brewers, Wheeler's crusade was against alcohol.

Wheeler had been working for years to defeat America's distillers and brewers and by early 1918, he had the brewers in a corner. Two years earlier, a Pennsylvania grand jury had indicted most of that state's brewers and the officers of the United States Brewers' Association on charges of violating corporate tax law and the federal corrupt practices act. The defendants had pleaded no contest before the case could go to trial, but the biggest payoff had been the confiscation of two trunks and a suitcase filled with the brewers' records.

Through his many connections, Wheeler managed to get hold of the records and found evidence of Percy Andreae's payments to the German-American Alliance. Wheeler persuaded William King, a senator from Utah, to introduce a bill to repeal the alliance's congressional charter on the grounds that the group had violated the charter when it lobbied against Prohibition, an issue with no direct connection to German heritage, and therefore outside the bounds of the alliance's stated aims. Wheeler also convinced King to hold hearings on the matter. King agreed and Wheeler stacked the witness list with people who make the effort worthwhile. Over the course of six days, he managed to tear apart the backroom practices of both the United States Brewers' Association and the German-American Alliance and expose it to the public.

Wheeler finally had what he wanted – he had created a link between German treachery and American brewers. It was well planned and carefully carried out, especially in light of the fact that many (if not, most) of the brewers were of German descent. It turned out to be the right tactic at the right time. The war had started an outpouring of hatred and violence toward German-Americans. A mob in Collinsville, Illinois, lynched a German-American man who they believed – wrongly, as it turned out – to be a spy. In Milwaukee, a gang of "patriots" set up a machine gun in front of a theater as a way of warning people to stay away from a performance of *Wilhelm Tell*. A Lutheran minister in Texas was publicly whipped for delivering sermons in German. All over the country, mobs beat, tarred and feathered suspicious German-Americans. They were often dragged through the street and forced to kiss the American flag. Homes and churches that belonged to German immigrants were vandalized with yellow paint. German books were burned and streets, newspapers and foods with German names were changed.

John Strange, the former lieutenant governor of Wisconsin, gave a speech in which he wanted of not only the Kaiser's minions in Europe but of German enemies in America, too. He said, "The worst of all our German enemies, the most treacherous, the most menacing, are Pabst, Schlitz, Blatz and Miller. They are the worst Germans who ever afflicted themselves on a long-suffering people. No Germans in the war are conspiring against the peace and happiness of the United States more than Pabst, Schlitz, Blatz, Miller and

A sign warns children that only "Loyal Americans" are allowed in the park and that there is "danger" for Pro-Germans!

(Right) Posters urged Americans to ration and "eat less wheat" a sentiment that the Prohibitionist managed to use against the brewers and distillers and shut them down during the War.

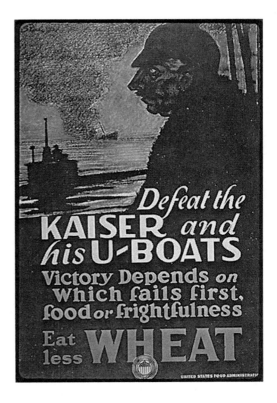

others of their kind."

Strange was joined in his rhetoric by others who linked German-American breweries with the enemy of the United States. The brewers were called "an organization so brutal, so domineering, and so corrupt" and demands were made for "firing squads" to go and dispatch this enemy. A writer for *American Issue* accused the "German breweries in America" of aiding the enemy. Every bushel of grain destroyed in a Busch, Pabst or Lemp brewhouse "serves the Kaiser just as well as a bushel sunk by a submarine at sea." Beer was being denounced as the "most brutalizing drink" available. Even the war was blamed on beer. If the Germans had not been drinking it for centuries, critics claimed, their moral sense would not have been deadened and they would not have started the war in the first place.

It was the perfect atmosphere for the Prohibitionists and one perfectly suited for the work of A. Mitchell Palmer, who had been appointed to the position of Custodian of Alien Property in 1917. The position was created when Congress passed the Trading with the Enemy Act. Among other things, it forbid Americans from doing business with enemies during times of war. Palmer was charged with seizing and administering properties in the United States that were owned by enemy nationals. These were, it turned out, worth millions of dollars. Palmer had no qualifications for the job, other than that he was loyal to the party. He had served in the House of Representatives several years earlier but lost a Senate bid in 1914. Since then, he had practiced law and had helped get Woodrow Wilson re-elected in 1916. Wilson offered Palmer the position of Secretary of War, but Palmer refused because of his Quaker upbringing. He did take the custodian's post, however, which originally only authorized him to seize and hold enemy property for the duration of the war. Palmer, who was no stranger to wheeling and dealing, eventually convinced Congress to let him sell the seized property.

A. Mitchell Palmer was named to the position of Custodian of Alien Property by President Woodrow Wilson, who immediately began going after German-American brewers.

To Palmer, there was little difference between enemy-owned property and property owned by Americans of German descent. In early December 1917, he started an investigation into the financial affairs of Clara Busch von Gontard and Wilhelmina Busch Scaharrer, two daughters of Adolphus Busch who had German husbands. Thanks to their marriages and their residences in Germany, both women were classified as enemies of the United States. Palmer was convinced that their brother, August, was somehow getting money to them from St. Louis. Busch sent Charles Nagel, a Busch attorney and former Secretary of Commerce and Labor under President Taft, to Washington to explain that since the start of the war in April 1917, the family had been investing a portion of the sisters' estate in United States Liberty Bonds.

Not to be denied some sort of action against the German-American brewing family, Palmer turned his attentions to Lilly Busch, Augustus' wife. Mrs. Busch had been vacationing in Germany with her son August and his family when the war broke out in 1914. August and his family returned to the United States but Lilly, who had turned seventy a few weeks before the conflict began, stayed behind. Like many people, she did not believe the war would last for long and she was also concerned about the safety of her married daughters in Germany. In addition, she had not been feeling well and was prone to seasickness, so she planned to make the trip home "under more favorable conditions."

Unfortunately, those conditions failed to develop and in late 1917, she was still in Europe and working for the Red Cross. She was far from the front lines but in enemy territory nonetheless, which Palmer believed provided evidence of her disloyalty. He informed the Busch family that he planned to seize her entire estate, including stocks, bonds, bank accounts, and real estate, on the grounds that her residence in Germany made her a traitor. He didn't care that she had lived in the United States for all but six months of her seventy-four years and was a natural born citizen, the daughter of immigrant parents. Charles Nagel managed to stop Palmer from seizing the estate outright, but only because Palmer conceded that Lilly's precise legal status was not clear. As a compromise, Nagel gave all of Lilly's property titles and deeds to the Union Trust Company of St. Louis, which agreed to hold them until the matter could be settled.

In early May, Palmer managed to seize the $40 million-dollar estate of George Ehret, founder of the Hell's Gate Brewery in New York. He took the brewery, Ehret's real estate holdings, his mansion at 94th Street and Park Avenue and his vast art collection. Like Lilly Busch, the eighty-three-year-old brewer had been caught in Germany when the war broke out. He had been an American citizen for forty years, but he was in poor health and had been unable to leave. None of that mattered to Palmer. He told reporters, "If Mr. Ehret should return to American and thus lose his enemy character, the Department of Justice would entertain any claim that he might make to have his property returned." It remained unspoken that while his claim would be entertained, there was no guarantee of fairness.

Wayne Wheeler saw all of this as a golden opportunity. With news of war in the papers each day, and with everything German being discredited, he knew it was time to act. He wrote to Palmer, "I am informed that there are a number of breweries in this country which are owned in part by alien enemies. It is reported to me that Annhauser [sic] Busch Company and some of the Milwaukee companies are largely controlled by alien Germans... Have you made any investigation? If not would you be willing to do so if we could give you any clue that would justify your taking such action?"

At the same time that Wheeler was attempting to use Palmer's actions for his own gain, Lilly Busch was on her way home to America. August, desperate to get his mother out of harm's way, persuaded Harry Hawes, a former Senator, Busch attorney and family friend, to travel across the Atlantic and accompany Lilly home. She managed to make her way out of Germany to neutral Switzerland, where she met Hawes in mid-January. He tried to convince her to stay there but Lilly was insistent on making the 6,000-mile journey back home to St. Louis. She rested in Switzerland for two months, tended by a physician, Hawes, her maid and Ruby Baumann, a St. Louis woman who had recently divorced her German army officer husband. When the doctor cleared her for travel in March 1918, the group departed for Spain, where they would board a ship bound for America.

The news that she was returning to America inspired a flurry of gossip back home. A New York newspaper, eager to discredit her claimed that she was "prominent in German court circles," that the Kaiser and the Crown Prince regularly visited her at her "castle on the Rhine" and that she had given a million dollars to a German military hospital. None of these claims contained even a shred of truth. A concerned – and clearly deluded – St. Louis citizen wrote to Attorney General Thomas Gregory and urged him to search Lilly and the rest of her party when they landed in the United States. The letter stated, "Mrs. Bush [sic] has relatives and son-in-laws in the German army and its [sic] best to be sure than sorry, and see that they dont [sic] slip one over on us by sending some secret code or other information to agents here."

Lilly knew nothing of the trouble back home. She could only concentrate on navigating through Europe, which had been ravaged by the war. She and her traveling companions were confronted with railroad strikes, closed borders, an air raid in Paris, several canceled sailings and U-boat scares. Finally, on June 17, 1918, the party reached Key West and set foot on American soil.

Four days before Lilly's arrival, unknown to her and to everyone else in the family, an official investigation had been launched into whether or not she was a German sympathizer and spy. The director of Naval Intelligence had ordered Lieutenant J. Vining Harris to "question, search and report destination" of the Busch party. Harris turned the job over to A.E. Gregory, who worked for the Justice Department. Gregory boarded the steamer when it arrived in port and arrested Lilly Busch, Harry Hawes, Mrs. Baumann and Lilly's

Mrs. Lilly Busch with her children in 1905.

maid and seized all of their luggage and papers. Out on the dock, August Busch, Mrs. Hawes, a collection of Busch friends and family, and a swarm of reporters waited for Lilly to appear. They stood for two hours before a reporter arrived with the news that Mitchell Palmer had seized all of Lilly's property. "The entire estate reverted to the government," he said and was now subject to disposition as Palmer saw fit.

Moments after August heard the news, his mother appeared at the gangway with a U.S. marshal guarding the entire party. Lilly burst into tears when she saw her son and her family. As she walked toward August, a Marine darted forward and restrained her. Lilly sobbed, "August, they won't let me see you tonight." Mother and son were allowed a brief embrace before the marshal led her into the nearby customs house. Eventually, the entire party, without their baggage, boarded cabs and were taken through downtown Key West to the Oversea Hotel on Fleming Street. Guards were stationed outside Lilly's door and a marshal's wife was placed in her room. The distraught Mrs. Busch went to bed.

The following morning, Gregory allowed August and Mrs. Hawes to visit with Lilly, but they were ordered to speak in English only. Later, after lunch, Gregory and Lieutenant Harris returned to the hotel and interrogated Lilly for two hours. What was said is unknown, but whatever it was, it failed to satisfy Gregory, who informed Harris that he intended to search "the person and effects" of Mrs. Busch, her maid, and Mrs. Baumann. A doctor and the marshal's wife escorted Lilly into her room, where a newspaper reported the doctor "laid the old lady on a bed and examined her private parts, making a very thorough examination of her vagina and womb." When he was finished with Lilly, he carried out the same search on Mrs. Baumann and the maid. Lilly spent the rest of what must have been the most humiliating day of her life in the company of a federal agent and the marshal's wife. She had the small consolation of being able to visit with her son.

The next morning, Lieutenant Harris returned to the hotel alone. He spoke with Lilly one last time and then spoke to the press an hour later. "No person in the world could doubt that woman's sincerity," he told reporters. He promised August Busch that he would recommend a public statement be made that "absolutely vindicated her" of any crime or improper activity. The guards were dismissed and an exhausted Lilly Busch was finally allowed to go home.

But Palmer was not finished with the brewers. Just days after Lilly Busch was exonerated in Key West, he found evidence that a group of prominent beer makers, including Gustav Pabst, Jacob Ruppert, Joseph Uhlein, and George Ehret, had loaned Arthur Brisbane the money to buy the *Washington Times*. Brisbane was one of America's most respected newspaper editors and was also an outspoken critic of Prohibition. Annie Lemp's husband, Alexander Konta, was named as one of Brisbane's investors but he denied any connection to the man.

At the same time, Palmer was arranging for the arrest of Edward R. Rumely, the owner of the *New York Evening Mail*, claiming that Rumely had bought the paper using money from German sources. A month later, Justice Department agents arrested Rumely on perjury charges. Palmer told reporters that German cash had paid for the purchase of the newspaper and that Kurt Reisinger, a grandson of Adolphus Busch, had also invested. He also claimed that Lilly Busch had been questioned in Key West in part because federal officials believed that she had supplied Rumely with money. She hadn't, and there was no evidence to even suggest that this was the case.

Working quickly, Palmer and Wayne Wheel connected these otherwise unconnected events – the brewer's loan to Brisbane and Rumely's use of German money to purchase an American newspaper – and claimed that American beer brewers were financing and organizing enemy propaganda during a time of war. By September 1918, Palmer and Wheeler had engineered Senate hearings to investigate the charges that German-American brewers were using newspapers and illegal campaign contributions to control the outcome of elections and spread German propaganda.

The hearings began on September 27. Over the course of several excruciating weeks, five senators grilled Brisbane, United States Brewing Association director Hugh Fox and three officers from the association. The hearings were a colossal waste of time. Arthur Brisbane easily dismissed the claims against him and managed to undermine Palmer and the entire purpose of the hearings. "From the day I owned the *Times*, I wrote as vigorously, as savagely and as earnestly against the German side and in favor of America as I have ever done on any subject in my life," he declared. He laughed at the brewer's alleged "German connections." "The only brewers I know are men born in America," he said.

The senate committee got even less from Hugh Fox, who was questioned for two days. He denied ever having a boycott against men or companies that supported Prohibition. He also denied that the Brewers' Association owned any newspapers and that he or the association ever received money from the German government or promoted German propaganda.

The senators came out of the hearings looking ridiculous. Not only had they not proved anything about anyone, they weren't even able to distinguish between the Brewers' Association, the National Association of Commerce and Labor and the German-American Alliance. The whole thing was a befuddled mess, but the average American would have only known this by actually sitting in on the hearings because the nation's newspapers had already tried the brewers and found them guilty. "Enemy Propaganda backed by Brewers," read one headline and only someone willing to read past this – and the article's first few inaccurate statements – would learn that there was no evidence linking anyone to anything. In fact, the so-called "evidence" consisted of a speech that was written by Charles Hexamer in 1915, two years before the United States entered the war. In the speech, Hexamer protested the sale of munitions to the Allies, as did millions of other Americans at the time, and urged America to stay out of the war. Annie Lemp Konta's book, A *Plea for Moderation: Based Upon Observations of an American Woman in a Belligerent Country*, echoed the same idea, which was a popular sentiment at the time. Neither Hexamer's speech, nor Annie's book, were evidence of treason or disloyalty to the United States, no matter how the anti-German zealots tried to twist things around.

But even without the hearings, the government was using the war as an excuse to close the brewers' doors. On September 6, President Wilson announced that in order to preserve supplies of grain and fuel, the breweries would be shut down at midnight on December 1. A few days later, the Food Administration ended all purchases of corn, rice and barley by breweries. They could use the stock they had on hand, and were welcome to any malt they could find, but once that was gone, they were simply out of business.

Many of the nation's beer makers held emergency meetings, wondering what could be done with their companies and properties. Many of them were wealthy enough that they could wait out the war and not have to worry about when they could began production again. They still refused to believe that a national Prohibition would end their business for good.

August Busch had no interest in waiting out anything. He had already converted his Busch-Sulzer Diesel Engine Company into a submarine engine manufacturing plant for the Navy. Now he offered his St. Louis brewery to the U.S. government for use as a munitions factory. He set out for Washington to make the deal and told reporters, "Give me a chance and I'll make the cartridge manufacturers look like pikers." When reporters asked him about Prohibition, Busch replied, "I am not now interested in the Prohibition question. I am only concerned now in doing what I can to help the government, and secondly, to take care of my employees in St. Louis."

Most of the other brewers scoffed at his plans, believing it was unlikely that the United States needed or wanted another munitions plant. Busch knew this and sadly shook his head. "The men who have done nothing but the work they are engaged in all their lives would make a poor fist at learning the munitions-making trade or any other. None of them is young and it is difficult to teach an old dog new tricks." Busch's attitude explains why his company survived Prohibition when many other brewers did not.

Ignoring his critics, Busch pushed ahead with his plans, determined to save the family company and cement his reputation as a loyal American. He ran a full-page advertisement in the St. Louis newspapers announcing that he would hand over the entire seventy-five city blocks and the $60 million worth of Anheuser-Busch facilities to federal officials if they wanted it for wartime use. He also used the ad to refute the "false reports and statements being circulated with reckless disregard for truth." Anheuser-Busch was an American company, founded by Americans and continuously owned and operated by Americans. He reminded readers that the company paid more than $3 million in taxes every year and employed nearly seven thousand men and women. The Busch family contributed a half-million dollars to the Red Cross and had purchased more than $3 million in Liberty Bonds. "Anheuser-Busch was founded on the solid rock of Americanism," Busch added, "and grew to be a great institution under the protection of American democracy."

Government officials decided against converting the brewery to a munitions factory, but did lease a large section of one Anheuser-Busch building for the storage of weapons and ammunition. The lease turned out be a short-term one when the war ended on November 11, 1918.

But nothing could be done to save the nation's breweries. While Wheeler and Palmer were plotting to destroy the brewers; while August Busch was working to save his family's reputation and company; while Senate committees were muddling through pointless investigations; while millions of American, German, French and English young men were dying in the trenches of Europe, one state legislature after another had ratified the Prohibition amendment. On January 16, 1919, Nebraska was the last to approve the law, making it the necessary thirty-sixth vote.

Prohibition would become law of the land at midnight on January 17, 1920.

11. "While Rome Burned...."
The Fall of the Lemp Empire

Like most American brewers of the time, Billy Lemp was stunned by the developments that led to the coming of Prohibition and the passage of the Volstead Act, which gave Prohibition its teeth by making it enforceable by law. Again, like so many others, Billy never really believed that beer could ever become illegal. Thanks to this, he was totally unprepared for the news that came in January 1919 that the sale, consumption and manufacture of alcohol would come to an end in one year.

Some brewers, notably Anheuser-Busch, began to immediately work on other projects, like ice cream, baker's yeast and soft drinks. Others, like the Lemp Brewery, faltered along for a time with no clear plans for the future. Finally, Billy decided to follow the lead of some of the other breweries and produce a beverage known as "near beer," which would duplicate the real thing in all aspects except for the alcohol content. Near beer proved somewhat popular at first, but once Prohibition was in full swing, those who continued to drink found it easy to obtain the real thing from their neighborhood bootlegger. Demand for near beer became non-existent and production largely came to a halt.

The Lemp Brewery's near beer never even lasted until the start of Prohibition. The company's non-alcoholic malt brew was called Cerva, and it was said to be quite good. While Cerva sold moderately well, revenues from it were never going to be enough to cover the overhead of the entire plant. Production of

Cerva was suspended in June 1919.

Soon after, Billy closed the doors of the Lemp factory for good.

The Lemps were not in need of money. All of the remaining family members were extravagantly wealthy independent of their brewery profits and they lacked any real incentive to try and keep the company going. Recent years had been tough for the brewing industry. With the backlash against German-American brewers caused by the war, and the propaganda spread by Prohibition advocates, sales had been low. Billy never saw the need to upgrade the brewery facilities and unlike his father, he was not interested in modern techniques that would have made the aging place more efficient. The end had likely been coming for some time before Prohibition, but the new law signed the brewery's death warrant.

The brewery was closed without notice. There were no farewell ceremonies and employees only learned of the factory's closing when they arrived for work one day to find the doors and gates chained and locked.

An era in St. Louis brewing history had come to an end.

"Anybody who says they can't find a drink ain't trying..." Prohibition Beer in St. Louis

When the Eighteenth Amendment to the Constitution abolishing the sale and distribution of alcohol took effect on January 17, 1920, many believed that it would cure America's social ill. Little did they know at the time, but it would actually do just the opposite. America's great thirst for the forbidden liquor bred corruption in every corner. Law enforcement officials became open to bribes because the majority of them did not agree with the law. Worse yet, Prohibition gave birth to the great days of organized crime. America's gangsters had previously concerned themselves with acts of violence, racketeering and prostitution but the huge profits that came to be made with the sale of illegal liquor built criminal empires.

Prohibition, made effective by the Volstead Act, lasted until 1933. It stopped the manufacture, transportation, importation and sale of alcoholic beverages – or at least it was supposed to. The making of small amounts of home-brewed beer and wine for personal consumption was permitted and so stores selling home-brewing equipment sprang up everywhere. Many of them did most of their business with bootleggers. Medicinal alcohol could be purchased at pharmacies with a doctor's prescription, a loophole that many doctors and pharmacists eagerly exploited, until the government took steps to close it. The only alcoholic beverage that could be legally sold was near beer, which had such a low alcohol content that most drinkers didn't consider it worth the trouble, especially when the real thing was available from the friendly local bootlegger.

Today, we can look back at the advocates of Prohibition and call them naïve and misguided. We can also say that many of the politicians who supported them were hypocrites who were primarily interested in garnering votes. However, the majority of the Prohibitionists sincerely believed their cause was just and that the movement would solve America's problems. They believed that people would have more spending money; crime rates would fall so drastically that police forces could be trimmed down to a bare minimum and jails and prisons could be closed down. They also believed that poverty would be abolished; corn and grain that had been "wasted" on making alcohol could be used to feed the hungry at home and overseas, and men who once staggered home from the saloon on a Saturday night would be up bright and early on Sunday morning to take their wives and children to church. It seems like wishful thinking to us now but to the Prohibitionists of the day, it was a bright vision for the future.

But of course Prohibition didn't stop anyone from drinking. In fact, it made drinking the "in thing" to do, simply because it was forbidden. Across the country, more than 200,000 "speakeasys" opened. These

Illegally brewed beer was seized and destroyed all over the country during the years of Prohibition.

drinking establishments were so named because many of them were located behind, above, or below legitimate businesses and patrons were urged to speak in hushed tones to avoid discovery. Huge bootlegging operations sprang into existence to supply the speakeasys and those who wanted to buy booze for home consumption. Disrespect for the law became the fashion as people who would never before have dreamed of doing anything illegal were now serving illicit liquor in their homes or drinking in the neighborhood speakeasy. As a famous saying of the time went, "Anybody who says they can't find a drink ain't trying."

By outlawing alcohol, the authorities made criminals out of millions of otherwise law-abiding citizens. They seriously undermined the respect people had for law and order and worst of all, they gave the criminal underworld the chance to make more money than they ever dreamed possible. All of the money that had been made by robbery, prostitution, loansharking, bookmaking, extortion and other criminal pursuits was nothing compared to the windfall that came from bootlegging. Organized crime that was syndicated on a national, corporate scale was born and it became so powerful that it has never been shut down.

Prohibition was widely considered to be doomed by 1928, but it hung on for another five years before being repealed in 1933. By then, it had taken its toll. The court systems had become clogged; jails and prisons were filled, often with people who had never been in trouble with the law before; trusted politicians, officials and police officers had been corrupted; and millions of dollars had been spent hiring new Prohibition agents, coast guard officers and cops. The occasional drunken violence associated with seedy bars was nothing compared to the wholesale bloodshed that erupted in city streets as bootleggers battled for control of the liquor trade.

Prohibition, instead of creating law and order, utterly corrupted it. Businesses were destroyed and lives were lost – all because someone decided it was a bad idea for a man to be able to have a beer.

Although the brewing industry was officially shut down with the coming of Prohibition in 1920, a gradual decline had already been underway for years. The problems began around 1912, when the anti-saloon ordnances and local prohibitions against alcohol began gaining popularity around the country. By 1917, thanks to pressure from the Anti-Saloon League and other such organizations, the government began wartime rationing of grain and fuel that could be used by the breweries. The industry never had time to recover from the war before it was faced with the Eighteenth Amendment.

Even so, brewing was still a major industry in St. Louis. More than nine thousand people were employed in the local breweries in the middle 1910s. Millions of dollars were being pumped into the city's economy and it was estimated that at least forty-five thousand people were at least partially dependent on the brewing industry, such as those in the barrel-making trade and the glass bottle works. Altogether, even in its declining years, beer making was still a $140 million annual industry in St. Louis. This was money that was effectively taken away by the coming of Prohibition. Joseph Hahn, secretary of Local 6 of the Brewers and Maltsters Union in St. Louis wrote, "I would judge that, in St. Louis, 4,000 are unemployed as a result of Prohibition. Figuring the wage of these men at $5 per day, or $20,000 per day, which is the purchasing power that has been destroyed, thereby causing unemployment in other industries, I think that we can safely say that another 5,000 men are on the streets in St. Louis because of Prohibition."

Many average brewery workers made it through the Prohibition years by taking up other occupations. By 1928, only about twelve hundred men remained in Local 6 of the Brewers and Maltsters Union, although few of them had steady employment. Those still working in the unions found compromise was necessary. In November 1924, one hundred and fifty men working in Anheuser-Busch's corn products department accepted wage cuts of $1.20 to $4.80 per week, which saved the company money. All the men were employed by one of five brewery workers' unions. August Busch, Jr., the plant's general superintendent, told a union committee that the wage contracts would not be renewed unless the salary reduction was accepted in the corn products department. A refusal meant that the plant would change to an open shop system, which opened the place up to non-union employees. The workers had little choice but to go along.

Only seven of the twenty-one breweries in St. Louis that operated during Prohibition were still manufacturing beverages in 1928. Not all of them had seen Prohibition as an obstacle that could not be overcome. Some wanted to ride it out and were confident (at least publicly) that the situation would not be permanent. Many secured licenses to make near beer, which was legal under the Volstead Act. Some also made soda or food products that were ultimately used in the home-brew process, like malt syrup and yeast.

Anheuser-Busch Ice Cream trucks

Among those was Anheuser-Busch, although August Busch claimed to be dismayed that his products were being put to illegal uses. "If you really want to know, we ended up as the biggest bootlegging supply house in the United States," August Busch, Jr. was later quoted as saying. "Every goddamn thing you can think of. Oh, the malt syrup cookies! You could no more eat the malt syrup cookies. They were so bitter. It damn near broke Daddy's heart."

Anheuser-Busch stopped brewing beer in October 1918. It sold off half of its one hundred and fifty buildings that were being unused, and turned to making glucose, corn sugar, corn oil, livestock feed, a

Anheuser-Busch began production of their popular Bevo soft drink during production, using the character of "Bevo the Fox" to market the line. The brewing house still exists on the factory's property today and stone images of Bevo decorate the exterior.

(Right) An Ad for Anheuser-Busch's malt syrup -- a very popular item for bootleggers.

frozen eggnog product, ice cream and a chocolate-covered ice cream bar called Smack, a forerunner of the Eskimo Pie. The company also converted its old wagon shop into a manufacturing plant for truck and motor coach bodies. They made a special refrigerated truck for hauling ice cream, built diesel engines for military submarines, operated a coal company and the Hotel Adolphus in Dallas, Texas, and ran a small gauge railway known as the St. Louis and O'Fallon line.

In 1926, Anheuser-Busch secured a permit to resume the manufacture of Malt-Nutrine, an alcoholic tonic for new mothers that had been originally produced by the brewery about thirty years before Prohibition. It also made a near beer called Bevo, carbonated coffee, tea drinks called Caffo and Buschtee, Busch Extra Dry Ginger Ale, and a beverage syrup known as Grape Bouquet. August Busch, Jr. later recalled his father calling him into his office shortly before Prohibition. "He looked out the window at the brewery and he said, 'You all can afford to ride this out, to retire, but in my book Prohibition is a challenge and we owe it to our employees to keep going.'" Busch said, "My brother and I swore that, come hell or high water, we would keep it going."

Anheuser-Busch was not the only brewery to hang on. In Washington, Missouri, another Busch brewery – founded in 1855 by John Busch, Adolphus' brother – also survived Prohibition. The John B. Busch Brewery sold the trademark rights to its cereal beverage, Buscho, to Anheuser-Busch and went into the ice cream, soda and potato chip business. It later became a distributor for Anheuser-Busch products.

The Fischbach Brewery in St. Charles had installed a new cold storage plant and a thirty-five ton ice machine shortly before the start of Prohibition. The equipment found a new use when the place was converted into the St. Charles Dairy in 1919, specializing in milk and twenty-five flavors of ice cream. The place became a great success. However, Jacob Fischbach, the brewery's founder, was fined $1,500 in 1925 when one hundred and eighty barrels of beer were found in the basement. The beer had been brewed before Prohibition and there was no record as to how many barrels had been sold off after the new law was

passed. Deputy U.S. Marshals dumped the beer into the sewer.

The Bluff City Brewery, across the Mississippi in Alton, Illinois, survived Prohibition by selling ice, bottled near beer and a popular brand of root beer. Another Alton brewer, Reck, closed down in 1919 after an unsuccessful attempt to start an ice business. The owner, Anton Reck, died a few years later, in 1922, and soon after, a group formed by some men from Joliet tried to buy the defunct brewery, allegedly for the purpose of making near beer, fruit syrups and soft drinks. When it turned out that the men were actually bootleggers who were attempting to start up the brewery again, the deal collapsed.

The shuttered Klausmann Brewery near South Broadway in St. Louis was being run by bootleggers in September 1930, when an explosion ripped through the place. Firemen found two stills (one of which had exploded) and eight 2,500-gallon mash vats inside the abandoned brewery. Traffic over the Jefferson Barracks streetcar line was delayed for forty-five minutes following the accident.

It should come as no surprise that more than a few breweries crossed the line into law breaking during Prohibition. Brewers with licenses to manufacture near beer began with real beer and then sent it through a machine that removed the alcohol. This led to a constant temptation to skip the latter part of the process and leave the alcohol intact. Not all breweries got involved in bootlegging, but quite a few of them did. For many of them, it was critical to their survival. In 1926, Major Walter A. Green, a former chief Prohibition investigator wrote: "Prohibition enforcement experts believe that 90 percent of all brewers must cheat part or all of the time, or go out of business. That is only opinion, to be sure, but it is indicative. Add to this anything you like for the incalculable but enormous amount of near-beer that is needled with alcohol, and you have a possible total which will upset any idea that there isn't much 'kick-beer' to be had. The drys, of course, soft-pedal on the number of criminally active breweries, but the number is very large, and the output is a satisfying flood to the thirsty."

For a short time after Prohibition began, about a half-dozen breweries in St. Louis continued to secretly make real beer on certain days, until prohibition agents put a stop to the practice. Most of the beer was distributed by Edward "Jellyroll" Hogan, a well-known St. Louis gangster. Hogan and his brother, James, ran a gang that first received public attention between 1921 and 1923 after a series of bloody shoot-outs with another notorious St. Louis mob, Egan's Rats. Jellyroll was one of six sons born to Police Officer Edward J. Hogan. Like many gangsters, Hogan became intimately involved in political affairs in the city and was even elected to the state legislature in 1916. He managed to survive the gang wars of the early 1920s and continued in politics. In 1941, Hogan was part of the Democratic effort to prevent St. Louis Republican and Governor-Elect Forrest C. Donnell from taking office by demanding a recount, but the effort failed. Hogan remained in politics for fifty years, serving five terms in the state house and four terms in the senate. He retired in 1960 and passed away three years later at the age of seventy-seven.

Edward "Jellyroll" Hogan in the 1920s

During Prohibition, Hogan was not just dodging bullets, he also had some brushes with the law. In April 1925, Hogan and brewer Joseph Griesedieck were indicted for conspiracy to violate the Volstead Act by shipping a train car filled with beer to Jefferson City. The charges were later dropped by Judge Charles B. Faris because both Hogan and Griesedieck had testified before a grand jury that was investigating beer protection rackets. Faris ruled that the interrogation of a witness by the grand jury barred the indictment of that person on any charge connected to the matter about which he had testified.

Officials at Anheuser-Busch were said to have spent thousands of dollars trying to make sure that no real beer was stolen from the brewery. In spite of this, brewery employees claimed that August, Jr. often took real beer from the plant for his personal use and that many employees were allowed to drink it on the job.

Temperance workers in St. Louis kept the authorities informed about the law-breaking breweries in town. In June 1921, Bessie M. Shupp, secretary of the local branch of the Anti-Saloon League and daughter of the league's Missouri superintendent, W. C. Shupp, wrote to Governor Arthur M. Hyde to tell him about several breweries in the city that were producing real beer. These included

The Obert Brewery was raided several times during Prohibition because they continued to brew real beer.

Eventually, the demand for alcohol brought about the repeal of Prohibition and the "noble experiment" came to an end at last.

the Louis Obert Brewery, Hyde Park Brewing Company and the Griesedieck Brothers. "Most every saloon here is now selling the products of one or more of these breweries," she added.

The Obert Brewery was raided twice in September 1921. On September 8, Prohibition agents raided the plant and confiscated a truck that was loaded with one hundred and seventy-eight bottles of real beer. A sign on the truck identified it as belonging to the "St. Louis Baker's Association – All Goods Delivered Promptly." After a complaint by W.C. Shupp, a second raid was carried out later in the month. This time, a truck loaded with ninety cases of real beer was seized in front of the brewery. Despite the raids, the Obert Brewery managed to somehow keep its manufacturing license and stayed in business until 1927, when financial failure closed it down for six years.

The Oberts were not the only ones skirting the law. A list of renegade breweries made newspaper reports during the Prohibition years, including Schoor-Kolkschneider in St. Louis, Old Appleton in rural

Missouri, Mascoutah Brewing Company in Illinois, Griesedieck-Western Brewery in Belleville, Missouri, and many others.

As the years passed, Prohibition became increasingly despised and was widely regarded as having been a failure in terms of eradicating the social ills of America. If anything, the law had made things worse. During the elections of 1932, one of the Democratic Party's campaign promises was to repeal Prohibition. After Franklin D. Roosevelt won the White House, the Democrats made good on their platform. They certainly had the public behind them since the "noble experiment," as Prohibition was often called, was now regarded as a total failure.

The Twenty-First Amendment to the Constitution, designed to undo the Volstead Act, was introduced on February 14, 1933, and ratified by the House of Representatives. The required three-fourths of the states voting in favor of repeal did not happen until December 5, 1933. But for the nation's brewers, repeal came early. The Cullen-Harrison bill was passed on March 22 and allowed for the production of real beer again. The brewers' needed a head start to get ready for "New Beer's Eve," set for midnight on April 7.

The terrible days of Prohibition had finally come to an end for the breweries of St. Louis, but for some of them, it was far too late. Prohibition had destroyed too many lives and businesses and had left the Lemp brewing empire in complete and total ruin.

The Death of Elsa Lemp

The arrival of Prohibition was the start another tragic series of years for the Lemp family. If the destruction of their legacy was not terrible enough, the early months of 1920 became even worse with the death of Elsa Lemp, the youngest child in the family.

Elsa, always a headstrong and independent woman, had seen more than her share of personal tragedy. After her father's suicide in 1904 and the death of her mother two years later, she had entered into a turbulent, violent and unhappy marriage that ended with a stillborn baby and a quiet divorce in 1919. Elsa spent the following year alone, traveling and visiting with family and friends. At some point, she reconciled with her former husband, Thomas Wright, the president of the More-Jones Brass and Metal Company. On March 8, 1920, they remarried in New York City and then returned to St. Louis and their home at 13 Hortense Place in the Central West End.

The fighting and unhappiness of the early days of their marriage seemed to be a thing of the past. The staff made no mention of anything out of the ordinary taking place in the house during the early days of March 1920, and yet, by the morning of March 20, Elsa Lemp Wright was dead.

The night of March 19 was a restless one for Elsa. She suffered from frequent bouts of indigestion and nausea and her ailments caused periods of severe depression. Today, her problems would likely be diagnosed as Irritable Bowel Syndrome, which is often brought on by stress. If Elsa was suffering from severe stress such a short time after her re-marriage to Wright, it's possible that she was having

Elsa's husband, Thomas Wright

second thoughts about the reconciliation. Whatever the cause of her suffering, she was awake for most of the night.

We only have her husband's version of events to account for what happened in their bedroom the following morning. When Wright awoke, Elsa told him that she was feeling better but she wanted to remain in bed. Wright agreed that this was the best thing to do and he went into the bathroom and turned on the water in the tub. He then returned to the bedroom for a change of underwear, retrieved it from the closet and went back into the bathroom. Moments after he closed the door, he heard a sharp cracking sound over the noise of the running water.

Thinking that it was Elsa trying to get his attention, Wright opened the door and called to his wife. When she didn't answer, he walked into the bedroom and found her on the bed. Her eyes were open and she seemed to be looking at him. When Wright got closer, he saw a revolver lying next to her.

One of the maids, Martha Westin, recalled what happened next. "At about 8:45, I heard Mr. Wright scream my name, that something terrible had happened... I saw Mr. Wright come running from his room. I went in there and found Mrs. Wright still alive, with her eyes partly open." Kate Reuckert, the upstairs maid, reported that Elsa "was laying [sic] on the bed, she wasn't struggling or anything; and she took one long breath and I took hold of her arm and tried to rub her. I thought there was life in her and with that Mr. Wright came in, and she took two long breaths after Mr. Wright came in." Elsa tried to speak but couldn't and a few moments later, she took a last shuddering breath and died. No note or letter was ever found and Wright could give no reason as to why she would have killed herself. He said he was not even aware that she owned a gun.

None of the servants witnessed the shooting and none of them said they heard a gunshot. If they ever suspected that Wright had anything to do with his wife's death, they never mentioned it to anyone in the hours and days that followed.

A telephone call was placed to Dr. M.B. Clopton, who was quickly summoned to the house, along with Samuel Fordyce, a family friend who – probably not coincidentally – was an attorney. Circuit Attorney Lawrence McDaniel said that he was notified about Elsa's death a few minutes after 9:00 a.m. and it was through his notification that the city coroner received information about what was already being called a suicide.

Strangely, the police were not contacted about Elsa's death for more than two hours. They might not have been contacted at all but for an accident that occurred as Edwin Lemp was rushing to his sister's house. Edwin had been having breakfast with Associate City Counselor William Killoren when he received a telephone call from Samuel Fordyce, urging him to come to his sister's house. Shaken by the news of his sister's death, Edwin asked Killoren to accompany him to Hortense Place. As they were driving there, Edwin inadvertently struck and injured Mrs. Lucille Hern at the intersection of Locust Street and Jefferson Avenue.

According to Killoren's report of the accident, which occurred about 11:00 a.m., Mrs. Hern was crossing Locust Street from north to south when a traffic officer signaled for east and west traffic to proceed through the intersection. Mrs. Hern became confused and ran back toward the north curb, stepping in front of Edwin's car. She was taken to the hospital with minor injuries.

When the police arrived at the accident scene, Killoren passed on the information to Chief Martin O'Brien that "something was wrong" at 13 Hortense Place. O'Brien passed on the message to the Newstead Avenue Police Station, which served the Central West End, and officers were dispatched to the Wright house. Wright became "highly agitated" under the scrutiny of the police investigation that followed. His only excuse for not contacting the authorities was that he was bewildered and didn't know what to do. He was questioned at the scene for more than two hours but was never taken into custody.

The police were willing to accept the verdict of suicide. But was it really? There was no real evidence to prove that Elsa took her own life. She did suffer from depression, brought on by her unhappy marriage and the death of her child, but according to family and friends, she did not seem suicidal. There had been a pistol found next to her in the bed, but the only witness to her "suicide" was her husband, who claimed to have heard a loud cracking sound, but said he did not see the gun being fired. The only person with knowledge of what happened in the bedroom was Thomas Wright, who did not contact the police after his wife was shot but called his attorney instead. Wright became agitated under police questioning. Was it because he was upset about Elsa's death – or because he had something to hide? In most murder investigations, the husband is the initial suspect but in this case, the police were quick to dismiss foul play and they agreed that Elsa had committed suicide. Was it because of the influence that the wealthy husband (and his influential friends) wielded in the city, or was there something left out of the police report that ruled out murder?

Those questions will likely never be answered, but of all of the deaths in the Lemp family, the alleged suicide of Elsa Lemp remains the most mysterious. There are members of the Lemp family who do not, to this day, believe that she committed suicide; they are still convinced that Thomas Wright had something to hide.

While the strange circumstances around Elsa's death suggest that there was more to the story than what was told, her brother Billy seemed to find little out of the ordinary about the tragedy. Billy hurried to the house when he heard the news, arriving around the same time as Edwin. When Billy was told what had happened, he only had one comment to make.

"That's the Lemp family for you," he said.

The Destruction of What His Father Had Built...

It was obvious to almost everyone that knew him that Billy had lost interest in brewing beer long before Prohibition reared its ugly head. No major improvements had been made to the Lemp Brewery since 1911 and while the states were in the process of ratifying the Eighteenth Amendment, the factory was slowly crumbling and becoming obsolete. But in spite of this, Billy never dreamed that the work of a lifetime would soon become illegal in the land that had embraced his family and allowed them to live the American dream. He was bitter, angry, and most of all he felt betrayed. Prohibition broke his spirit and with this death of his sister, the baby of the family who had always been everyone's favorite, Billy simply had nothing left.

"We have done nothing since Prohibition. I am tired of seeing all the weeds in the courtyard and the dust upon the windows," he said in the spring of 1920. "I am out of the brewery business for good. I am 54 years old and it is time to quit."

The family brewing empire, built by his father and his grandfather before him, had fallen. Now, as the brewery sat idle and neglected, Billy felt that he had no choice but to sell off everything. Beer was likely never coming back, he thought, and if it did, he just wasn't sure that he cared anymore.

Not all of the brewers in St. Louis felt the same way. Joseph "Papa Joe" Griesedieck believed the opposite of what Billy did. He was sure that someday, perhaps soon, the American people would realize that Prohibition would never

Joseph "Papa Joe" Griesedieck

work and it would be repealed. He was determined to keep his business going until that time, but things were looking grim. He was in trouble with his creditors and was looking for a solution to his financial woes. As a longtime friend of Billy's, Griesedieck understood his friend's unhappiness and came to him with the idea of buying the Falstaff logo that Billy's father had created and building a new brewing company around it.

(Left) The original Falstaff logo included the Lemp name.
(Right) Joe Griesedieck's new Falstaff logo.

Billy's first reaction was a negative one. The Lemp family had built a good name and reputation over the years and he couldn't conceive of it being taken over by someone else. Griesedieck was quick to explain that it was merely the name and logo of Falstaff, one of the Lemp's lines, that he was seeking, not the Lemp name itself. Billy was well aware of his friend's financial difficulties, brought on by Prohibition, and he eventually relented. The plan had to be approved by the directors of the William J. Lemp Brewing Company, but Billy managed to get that approval a short time later.

Griesedieck was able to get excellent terms from Bill for securing the famous Falstaff name and the shield logo that had been emblazoned with the Lemp name for so many years. The total price was only $25,000 and it was agreed that Griesedieck would pay $5,000 in cash and the balance within three months. The agreement was later amended, with the balance to be paid within nine months.

Griesedieck began trying to turn things around with the Falstaff name. He and his son, Alvin, organized and issued stock in a new company, Falstaff Corporation, with offices on Forest Park Boulevard. They soon began making a near beer with the Falstaff name in hopes of competing with the popular Anheuser-Busch Bevo brand. As it turned out, many of Falstaff's customers preferred their beer with the alcohol intact. Alvin Griesedieck later wrote, "Falstaff was one of the few 'near beers' that would successfully absorb alcohol when added in the bottle or keg. Needless to say, my visits with our distributors took me to many so-called 'spike joints', some entirely respectable, others no better or worse that some of our less reputable taverns of today. It was not the type of business that I would have particularly selected, but in those times, we could not afford to be choosy." Joseph Griesedieck had a few run-ins with the law during the years of Prohibition, when he was willing to do most anything to keep the doors open. To supplement the company, Falstaff also cured bacon and ham and sold it under the Falstaff label. The brewery also made a root beer and obtained a franchise to manufacture Canada Dry ginger ale.

The strategy of expanding the company during what should have been the worst time in its history worked and Falstaff marked a period of incredible growth and prosperity over the course of the next few years. "Papa Joe" died in 1938 and Alvin took over the company, opening breweries in new markets across the country. The company remained in St. Louis until 1975 but the Falstaff brand began to be phased out in the 1980s. A variety of problems plagued the company, including an expensive lawsuit, an unpopular change in formula and a number of aging and inefficient breweries, and by 1990, the Falstaff Brewing Corporation was defunct. The once-famous brand finally ceased production in 2005.

The Lemp Brewery, which was abandoned in 1919, was finally sold off in 1922.

Joseph Griesedieck turned his hopes and energy into a business that defied the odds for decades, but Billy Lemp no longer shared his friend's enthusiasm for the brewing business. He told his secretary and friend, Henry Vahlkamp, on several occasions that even if beer production ever resumed, the business would never be the same. He saw no point in hanging onto the aging hulk of a brewery that was down the street from the Lemp offices and decided to put it up for sale. In 1919, the brewery had been valued at $7 million, but three years later, when it came time to auction it off, it was worth only half that amount.

Billy hired the Joseph P. Day auctioneering company to handle the sale, which went to great lengths to advertise that fact that one of the world's great manufacturing plants would be sold, in parts or as a whole, to the highest bidder. The company prepared a detailed 12-page booklet that described the huge complex and praised it as a first-rate facility that could be adapted to many industrial uses. The booklet contained many photographs and detailed drawings of the brewery's eighteen buildings. A map was also included, which covered what were the plant's fourteen acres in 1922.

The brewery had been almost self-sufficient during its heyday, with full-time carpentry, masonry and painting shops. All of these were highlighted in the booklet, as well as the benefits of other structures, some containing more than one million square feet of space. Others boasted twenty-five foot ceilings and the proximity to railroad spurs and the Mississippi River.

The Lemp Brewery had stopped production in 1919, but the factory itself had been built to last forever with heavy stone foundations, solid brick walls, cast-iron columns and steel girders. Some of the buildings stood six stories high and modern electric elevators had been installed throughout the property, including in the eighteen gigantic grain storage bins. Even after sitting unused and nearly abandoned for several years, the brewery was still better equipped and more advanced than many that were still in use in St. Louis and across the Midwest.

The auction was held at 2:00 p.m. on Wednesday, June 28, 1922. On that day, the magnificent brewery was sold off in parts to five companies, with the bulk of it going to the International Shoe Company (whose name remains on one of the old brewery smokestacks today) for the disappointing sum of only $585,000. Even though he didn't need the money, Billy had planned to recoup at least twenty-five or thirty percent of the brewery's worth from the sale. He was stunned to receive such a paltry amount. "How would anybody feel to get eight cents on the dollar for a great plant like that?" Billy questioned. "They told us that when Prohibition came that we could make something out of our plants, but look what happened."

The months that followed the sale of the brewery were difficult ones for Billy. He had watched his family's company crumble before his eyes and with the sale of the famed Lemp logo and Falstaff name, followed by the auctioning off of the brewery; he had managed to destroy everything that his father and grandfather had worked so hard to build. Billy knew that he would never want for anything for the rest of his life and that his fortune would remain intact, but the responsibility that he felt for the brewery's loss weighed heavy on his shoulders. He became depressed and his friends and employees began to speak of his erratic behavior. He often complained of poor health and feeling nervous.

Then, in the late fall of 1922, Billy seemed to rally and began feeling better. He began making plans to rid himself of the last vestiges of the Lemp brewing business once and for all. He told friends that he intended to liquidate the corporation and sell off the corner saloon sites and the rest of the real estate associated with the brewery. After that, he would sell some of his other property holdings and just "take it easy for awhile." Billy decided to put *Alswel* on the market for $175,000, stating that he planned to take an extended trip to Europe with his wife.

Billy was still having days of illness during the holiday season of 1922, but he seemed better than he had been. His plans for shedding some of his business concerns had reinvigorated him and he began making preparations to be away from the office during his upcoming trip. His employees noticed Billy was smiling again as he walked into the office in the morning – which made what happened on December 29 both tragic and inexplicable.

12. "The Dutch Act"

By August 1920, Otto F. Stifel was a shell of his former self. The once easy-going man, who loved horse racing and baseball, was now a nervous wreck whose bizarre behavior included chain-smoking cigarettes and locking himself in his office, where he could be heard muttering to himself for hours. His son, Carl, and his brother-in-law, Edwin Conrades, considered sending him to a sanitarium to recuperate.

Beer had been Otto Stifel's life. He had trained in the brewer's art in Germany, the homeland of his immigrant parents, and in 1908 had founded Stifel's Union Brewery at Michigan and Gravois avenues on St. Louis' south side. The brewing business had been good to him. He was one of the organizers of the St. Louis Federal League Baseball Club and he owned a horse farm in Valley Park on the outskirts of St. Louis County. Stifel was well regarded. He had friends among the socialites, politicians and business leaders of the city and was also beloved by working class people, scores of whom he quietly helped over the years.

Otto F. Stifel

After his death, a close friend told a reporter for the *St. Louis Star,* "No person in distress ever appealed to Otto Stifel and failed to get food for his family and help in finding profitable employment for himself. He could not bear to see suffering of any kind without doing something to relieve the sufferer. On his daily arrival at the brewery office, usually at 10 a.m., he always found several old men, cripples and pensioners of his, many of them getting from him a daily allowance."

By 1920, though, those days were over. Prohibition had ruined the St. Louis brewing industry. Stifel closed his brewery, in which he had more than $1 million invested, and he put $500,000 into a margarine manufacturing plant, a business he knew nothing about. Within a short time, he was ruined. Broke and despondent, arguments began to occur with family members over missing funds. He appealed for assistance to several of his friends but many of them were in the same situation as Stifel. He had spent many years helping other people, but when he needed his kindness returned, there was no one to help him.

On August 17, Stifel wrote a series of suicide notes to the public and to his family. He left the notes in his bungalow at the farm in Valley Park before going to have supper with the farm's caretaker, Edward Paubel, and his wife. Paubel then drove him to Barrett's Station to see his old friend, E.C. Mahanay. Stifel's mood lightened when he saw Mahanay and several friends sitting on the porch of the general store. He instructed the storekeeper to give all the men a good cigar, then he paid for them and took one for himself. They discussed politics, business and friendship and Stifel asked Mahanay what he would do to a fellow in whom he had lost confidence. "I would tell him to go to hell," Mahanay said and Stifel laughed loudly in reply.

The next morning, after having breakfast with Mr. and Mrs. Paubel, Stifel took the early morning train back to St. Louis. Oddly, he returned to the farm just three hours later. He was described as being agitated and obviously upset. While alone in his bungalow, he picked up a revolver, placed it in his mouth and pulled the trigger. At noon, Edward Paubel entered the house to call his employer to dinner and found him dead on the floor. He was sixteen days short of his fifty-eighth birthday.

Stifel was not the only St. Louis brewer to take his own life in the early part of the twentieth century. Suicides by prominent local German-Americans, including several brewers, became so notorious that their deaths became known as carrying out the "Dutch Act." The phrase, which was a corruption of the word *Deutsch,* or German, was coined by members of the St. Louis Police Department who investigated the untimely deaths.

August A. Busch

Another suicidal brewer was Patrick Henry Nolan, the vice-president and general manager of the Mutual Brewing Company of St. Louis, which was founded in 1912. Largely owned by saloon owners in the area, the brewery was plagued by financial problems in late 1914. Nolan committed suicide at the brewery office the night before a scheduled appearance in bankruptcy court.

August A. Busch scrambled during the Prohibition years to keep the family business going and with the repeal in 1933, things looked promising for the company. However, it was ill health that drove Busch to suicide. After complaining of recurring chest pains on the morning of February 13, 1934, he shot himself with a revolver that he kept in the nightstand of his bedroom at Grant's Farm. He left behind an unsigned note that simply read, "Goodbye precious mama and adorable children."

Busch had followed a close friend to the grave, just a little more than eleven years after Billy Lemp ended his own life with a revolver.

When company secretary Henry Vahlkamp arrived at the brewery offices, located in the former Lemp family home, at 9:00 a.m. on December 29, 1922, he found Billy was already there. The two of them were joined shortly after by Olivia Berchek, a stenographer for the brewery and Billy's personal secretary.

Vahlkamp later recalled that Billy's face was flushed that morning and that when he entered his employer's office, Billy had an elbow on the desk and was resting his forehead on his hand. He asked Billy how he was feeling and the other man replied that he felt quite bad.

"I think you are looking better today that you did yesterday," Vahlkamp noted in an effort to cheer him up.

"You may think so," Billy said glumly, "but I am feeling worse."

Vahlkamp left and went to his own office on the second floor of the converted mansion.

Moments after this exchange, Miss Berchek telephoned Billy's wife, Ellie, about instructions for the day's mail and as she was speaking to her, Billy picked up the other line and spoke to his wife himself. The secretary recalled that he spoke very quietly and she did not hear what turned out to be his last words to his wife. After he finished the conversation, Bercheck asked him a question about some copying that she was doing from a blueprint. He first told her that what she had was fine and then he changed his mind and suggested that she go down to the basement and speak to the brewery's architect, Guy Norton.

While she was on her way downstairs, she heard a loud noise. Because there were men working in the basement, she thought nothing of it, assuming that someone had dropped something. But when she came back upstairs, she found Billy lying on the floor in a pool of blood. She told the police, "The porter heard the noise from down in the basement and came upstairs; he was the only one who realized it [the noise] was a shot."

The porter came into the office to find Billy lying on the floor with his with his feet under the desk. He called for help and men from the office across the hall came in as he was placing a pillow under Billy's head. Billy was gasping for air when his employees came rushing into the office.

Apparently, just after speaking to Miss Bercheck, Lemp had shot himself in the heart with a .38 caliber revolver. He had unbuttoned his vest and fired the gun through his shirt. Vahlkamp, who hurried into the office when he heard the news, arrived to find Billy barely alive. He sent for the police and the coroner's physician but by the time the doctor arrived, Billy was dead.

Officer John H. Schramm, one of the first policemen to arrive on the scene, told a reporter for the *St. Louis Star* that Billy had apparently dragged a heavy chair from its usual place in the office to a space about four feet between his desk and the west wall. Billy evidently sat down in the chair before shooting himself. He was discovered after he slid out of the chair lying on his back with his revolver at his side.

Officers found two bullet wounds in the left side of his chest, about a half-inch apart. Since there were two discharged shells in the gun's chamber, it was initially thought that a second shot might have been fired by accident as Billy's hand jerked. However, the inquest later determined that only one of the two shells had been recently fired, indicating that Billy left the other chamber empty as a precaution since he normally carried the gun in his pocket. Captain William Doyle of the Wyoming Street Police Station, the lead police investigator on the scene, searched Lemp's pockets and desk for a suicide note, but as with his father and possibly his sister before him, Billy left no indication as to why he had ended his life.

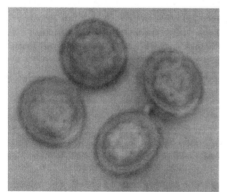
The cuff links that Billy was wearing on the day that he committed suicide.

When interviewed by the newspapers, Billy's close friend, August A. Busch, said he was confused by Billy's suicide. He noted that had recently decided to sell off many of his real estate assets, including his home, *Alswel,* and relax for a few months. A week before he shot himself, Billy had dined with Busch, who said that Billy seemed "cheerful" at the time and that he gave no indication that he was worrying about business or anything else. "He was a fine fellow," Busch added, "and it is hard to believe that he has taken his own life."

Billy's son, William Lemp III, however, was not as shocked as everyone else was. He rushed to the office when he heard what had happened and knelt down on the floor next to his father's body. "You knew I knew it," he sobbed. "I was afraid this was coming." He refused to explain his remarks to the police.

Ellie Lemp collapsed when she received the news of her husband's suicide. She did not go to the Lemp office that day and declined to accept visitors at the Chase Hotel, where the Lemps had been living since placing *Alswel* on the market.

When interviewed after the shooting, many of Billy's friends and employees mentioned Billy's erratic behavior, dating back many years. Their recollections painted a picture of a man with serious mood swings and often-violent behavior, which seemed to indicate that he suffered from manic-depressive episodes, or what we would consider today to be bipolar disorder. Such a condition, unknown to medicine at the time, would certainly explain the collapse of Billy's marriage, his sometimes-vicious temper and then the calm, orderly manner in which he would carry out his business. His moods often varied between times of happiness and periods of dark depression. Everyone assumed that his melancholy was caused by the death of his sister Elsa and the loss of the brewing business, but it's more likely that it was a chemical imbalance (possibly affecting several members of the family) that led to Billy's unusual behavior and eventual suicide.

In the weeks before his death, Billy had been admitted to the hospital three times, complaining of what he called "nervous chills." His secretary, Olivia Berchek, said, "....he was very morose... he was always peculiar about things, very precise and for the last three or four weeks he didn't seem to care. He didn't fight back at anything. He just let everything go, contrary to his former attitude toward things; and on Thursday afternoon, he said to me, 'I have had enough doctors, haven't I?' Later he said, 'Don't you think I have had enough trouble? I have had about enough.'"

Billy's funeral was held at the family mansion on December 31. The offices were used as the setting for the service for sentimental reasons, staff members said, having been used for the funerals of Billy's parents years before. He was interred in the family mausoleum at Bellefontaine Cemetery, in the crypt just above that of Elsa's.

Billy's bad financial luck followed him to the grave. *Alswel*, which had been built for $125,000 in 1914, was auctioned off in May 1925 for $118,500 to a Chicago real estate broker. All of the furnishings went with the house, as well as the one hundred and ninety-two acres that surrounded it. Billy's estate, valued at a little less than $1 million in 1923, was divided between his widow and his son. By the end of the 1920s, the Lemp company, once one of the largest breweries in the country and a worldwide purveyor of beer, was largely forgotten.

With the factory sold, Billy gone and his brothers and sisters involved in their own lives and endeavors, the days of the Lemp empire had come to an end at last. His two siblings remaining in St. Louis, Charles and Edwin, had left the family enterprise long before it had breathed its last. Charles worked in banking and finance and Edwin had entered a life in seclusion at his estate in Kirkwood in 1911. The fortune they had amassed was more than enough to keep the surviving members of the family comfortable through the Great Depression and beyond.

But the days of Lemp tragedy were not yet over.

13. "Out of the Ashes"
The Short-Lived Return of Lemp Beer

In 1933, Prohibition was officially repealed and almost immediately, beer was once again being brewed in St. Louis. The future was bright once more for many of the local companies, like Falstaff, which had received Federal Permit Number One, making it the first legally brewed real beer in America since 1919.

But dark days were still ahead for the Lemp family. The seemingly endless string of disasters that had plagued them since the death of Frederick Lemp continued, this time centered around Billy's son, William Lemp III, who had apparently inherited his father's bad luck.

William did not have an easy life, despite the fortune he had inherited from his father. He struggled as a young man, often apparently unable to overcome the lack of attention that he received from his father as a child. Always eager to please, time ran out for him when his father committed suicide when William was only twenty-two. He quickly ran through his inheritance and had problems with money for most of his life. His family helped as much as they could and his Uncle Charles even gave him a job at the Indemnity Company of America for a time, where William served as vice-president and treasurer of the firm. During this time of improved fortune, he and his wife, Agnes, purchased *Alswel,* his father's old home, in hopes of keeping it in the Lemp family. But the good times were short-lived.

By 1934, William was in trouble again. He and Agnes were having great difficulties hanging onto his father's house. Things got so bad that the Board of Finance of the Methodist Episcopal Church, which held the mortgage on *Alswel,* sued the Lemps in December for interest and principal that had been unpaid since May of that year. Eventually, the church had to foreclose on the estate, which was then valued at $200,000. Today, the house is in the hands of private owners, but it remains almost unchanged from when Billy lived there. The surrounding acres dwindled in size until 1987, when the last of them were sold as part of a residential subdivision known as Lemp Estates.

William's bad luck also bled over into his marriage. In February 1937, Agnes obtained a decree of maintenance against her husband that provided her with a small monthly stipend. She alleged that William had left her in March 1936 and that she had not given him any reason to do so. He had failed to support her since that time. She stated in the court records that her finances were so bad that she had to pawn some of her jewelry and that during the Christmas season she had been forced to take employment in a downtown department store. William and Agnes were divorced soon after the maintenance decree was filed.

In 1939, William thought he had the answer to all of his financial woes. With beer now firmly re-established in American culture after the dismal years of Prohibition, William came to believe that the time was right to revive the once-popular Lemp name and begin brewing beer again. To accomplish this, he entered into an agreement with Central Breweries, Inc. of East St. Louis, Illinois, giving them the license to use the Lemp name in connection with their beer. In return, the brewery would pay royalties on all beer brewed by them "under the corporate name including the name 'Lemp.'"

In October 1939, Central changed its name to the William J. Lemp Brewing Company and launched a massive advertising campaign to announce the return of the once-famous Lemp name. Full-page newspaper ads touted that the century-old formula was again being bottled. Official production of Lemp Extra Pale beer began on November 1, 1939.

At first, sales exceeded the expectations that anyone could have had for a beer that had been out of the public mind for more than two decades. The new venture seemed destined for great success and William believed that he could finally restore the luster of the Lemp empire --- but this was not meant to be. In less than a year, the company was in serious financial trouble. By September 1940, the William J. Lemp Brewing Company had managed to accumulate a massive amount of debt, including $120,000 in outstanding accounts and $34,000 advanced to the company by its officers and others. They also owed $8,300 in back taxes. Even worse, $108,000 in interest on second mortgage bonds came due that same month. The company's actual assets were recorded as $150,000, which included thirteen thousand barrels of beer that were on hand.

William Lemp, III who turned out to be as unlucky as his father when it came to life and love.

Trading in the company's stock was suspended on December 19, 1940 on the St. Louis Stock Exchange. The company was insolvent and the stockholders' interest had been wiped out. Early in 1941, the company was declared bankrupt. The revival of the once-powerful Lemp name had failed to live up to the promise of its early years. The defunct company was taken over in December by Ems Brewing Company, which terminated all contracts made with William Lemp III. By 1945, they had discontinued the use of the Lemp name in connection with their beer.

The Lemp empire had collapsed again, almost before it could struggle out of the ashes, and this time, it would never rise again.

Tragically, William died soon after the company did. He was walking down the street on March 12, 1943 when he suffered a brain aneurysm and collapsed on the sidewalk.

14. "In Case I am Found Dead, Blame it on No One But Me."

In 1929, Charles Lemp moved back into the family mansion. He never married and had lived in the mansion until 1911, when Billy decided to convert the house into office space. Charles had taken up residence at the exclusive St. Louis Racquet Club and was pleased when he was able to move back home again. Several years had been spent renovating the house and work was finally finished by 1929.

Thanks to his business interests, Charles had not been affected by the closing of the Lemp Brewery. In addition to his insurance company, he also owned a number of rental properties, had real estate investments and even owned a small electric railroad line for a time. He was active in St. Louis politics and was a powerful member of the local Democratic Party. None of his business or political responsibilities kept him from traveling and he journeyed around the world, often buying artwork and souvenirs that became the source of conversation to the visitors who came to the Lemp Mansion.

Charles in his later years

Charles had always been eccentric but his brother Edwin believed that his return to the family home, the scene of so much tragedy over the years, made his condition more pronounced. In fact, Edwin had urged his brother to let him sell the house after Billy's death but Charles wouldn't hear of it. The house has been his home for his entire life and he couldn't imagine living anywhere else. He eventually developed a number of strange habits and unusual quirks, many of which (including his mandatory 5:00 a.m. wake-up time) were also impressed upon guests who came to stay.

As time passed, he became even more eccentric, terrified of germs and illness. Visitors were never allowed to wear their shoes in the house and Charles refused to shake anyone's hand. He often showered five of six times each day and anything that he handled from outside of the house, including money, had to be washed before he touched it. Charles' strange behavior increased with age. He became more and more reclusive and eventually stopped letting visitors, even old friends and family members, come to call. He lived alone, assisted by his last two servants, Albert Bittner and his wife, Lena. Aside from the Bittners, his only companions were a parrot and his German Shepherd, Cerva, which had been named for the Lemps' ill-fated near beer. Late in life, he developed severe arthritis and was in constant pain.

In 1949, unable to stand the pain anymore, Charles finally ended his life, the fourth member of his family to do so, all using pistols and three of them under the same roof.

On the morning of May 10, Alfred Bittner left the servants' quarters in the attic and went to the kitchen to prepare breakfast for Charles as he normally did. He then placed the breakfast tray on the desk in the office next to Lemp's bedroom, as he had been doing for years. Bittner later recalled that the door to the bedroom was closed and he did not look inside. At about 8:00 a.m., Bittner returned to the office to remove the tray and found it to be untouched. Concerned, he opened the bedroom door to see if Charles was awake and discovered

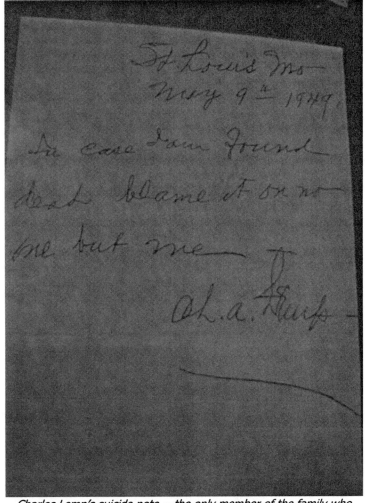

Charles Lemp's suicide note -- the only member of the family who took his own life and left a note behind, cryptic as it might have been.

that he was dead from a bullet wound to the head. Bittner called for his wife and she telephoned Charles' nephew, Richard Hawes (the husband of Marion Lemp, Frederick's daughter). Hawes, in turn, summoned the police to the house.

When family members and the police arrived, they found Charles lying in bed, wearing a white shirt and lightly holding a .38 caliber Army Colt revolver in his right hand, which was draped across his chest. He was the only one of the family who had left a suicide note behind. He had dated an unusual letter May 9 and had written, "In case I am found dead blame it on no one but me," and had signed it at the bottom.

Oddly, Charles had made detailed funeral arrangements for himself long before his death. He would not be interred at the family mausoleum at Bellefontaine Cemetery and while this might not be so unusual, the rest of his instructions were. In a letter that was received at a south St. Louis funeral home in 1941, Charles ordered that, upon his death, his body should be immediately taken to the Missouri Crematory. His ashes were then to be placed in a wicker box and buried on his farm. He also ordered that his body not be bathed, changed or clothed and that no services were to be held for him and no death notice published, no matter what any surviving members of his family might want. On May 11, 1949, Edwin Lemp picked up his brother's remains at the funeral home and took them to the farm to be buried. And while these instructions were certainly odd, they were not the most enduring mystery about this arrangement – after all of these years, there is no record of where Charles Lemp's farm was located or where his body was actually placed. To this day, it remains a mystery.

As eccentric as Charles may have been, he never lost his financial acumen. His investments did very well and he left behind a sizable fortune. His multi-million dollar estate included stocks and bonds in thirty-five corporations, more than $230,000 in cash and scores of real estate holdings. In his will, he made a specific bequest to Edwin of $47, 345. There appeared to be no rhyme or reason as to this exact amount, but one can only assume that Edwin understood. The two daughters of Geoffrey Konta, who was Annie Lemp Konta's son, Anne Marie Brewer and Phyllis Oliveri, received half of Charles' estate. The other half went to Marion Lemp Hawes, the daughter of his brother Frederick.

By the time of Charles' suicide in 1949, almost every member of the immediately family was gone. Annie had died in 1939 and Louis had passed away in 1931. Only Hilda and Edwin remained. When Hilda passed on in 1951, it left Edwin as the last survivor of a family that had seen more than its share of both triumph and tragedy.

Did Charles Lemp Shoot his Dog before he Killed Himself?

One of the strangest myths to surround the Lemp family is the lingering rumor that Charles Lemp shot his dog, a beloved German Shepherd named Cerva, before he took his own life in 1949. Fortunately, this was not the case. He did not shoot Cerva (or himself) in the basement of the house, as the stories have claimed. Charles used a pistol to shoot himself while lying in his bed in the second floor master suite of the house. Cerva was unharmed.

It remains a mystery as to how this story got started. Some have claimed that it appeared in a book that featured a chapter on the Lemps that was written in the early 1990s. Most likely, it has the same source as the legend of the "Monkey Boy" -- someone's wild imagination.

15. "Into the Woods"
Edwin Lemp's Retreat from the World

The Lemp family, once large and prosperous, had been almost utterly wiped out by the middle part of the twentieth century. While nieces and nephews still remained, the only surviving member of the immediate family was Edwin, who had long avoided the life that had turned so tragic for the rest of his family. He was a quiet, reclusive man who had walked away from the Lemp Brewery in 1913 and retired at the age of only thirty-three. His disillusionment with the rest of the world led him to abandon the social life of St. Louis and seek solitude in what were still the wild regions of western St. Louis County.

With a love of nature and the outdoors, Edwin often camped and hiked in the forests and along the bluffs of the Meramec River. During one of his trips in 1909, he camped on a high bluff near Kirkwood that overlooked the river. He became entranced with the spot and returned to it every weekend for the next two summers, exploring the countryside and entertaining his friends with camp dinners and outings. Convinced that he wanted to stay in the spot for the rest of his life, he purchased three thousand feet of land along the river and proceeded to build a magnificent home. It was a house that he had been building in his mind for some time, one that combining fine living with nature, and he named the estate *Cragwold* for the rough outcroppings of rock in the area.

Construction began on *Cragwold* in 1911 and was one of four estates (Billy Lemp's *Alswel* was another) built near the Meramec River by wealthy St. Louisians with ties to German-America brewing families. The estates were secluded enough to allow the owners to live in a rural setting but were conveniently close to St. Louis by way of the expanding commuter railroad services of the late 1800s.

Cragwold, which contained approximately eleven thousand square feet of living space, was hard to classify by strict architectural style. However, architects Harry Clymer and Francis Drischler embraced the ideals of the Arts and Crafts movement in designing the house, using natural building materials, references to historic building methods, and a close connection to the natural landscape. The design of the house and the character of its grounds reflected Edwin's love of nature and his fascination with exotic animals. *Cragwold* was designed around a large center atrium that was filled with tropical plants and several species of exotic birds. By the 1920s, the grounds became home to more animals and birds from many continents, including South America and Africa. Edwin was eventually licensed so that the estate could be operated as a Federal Game Farm. He bought, sold and traded with zoos all over the country, including the St. Louis Zoo, to which he was closely connected and made several endowments. He bred and raised exotic animals until the time of his death.

The Arts and Crafts elements of the house made it uniquely American. The movement encompassed several different styles that were closely related and influenced one another. The Prairie, Craftsman and Bungalow styles were all American styles that grew out of the Arts and Crafts movement, which was created as sort of a rebellion against the onset of the industrial revolution. People were looking for a way to

Edwin Lemp's Cragwold

reinstate simplicity back into architecture and to raise the quality of the product, which was made by hand, rather than by machine. By using local crafts and materials, it was felt this type of design created a harmony between the house and its natural setting.

With his love of nature, it was easy to see why Edwin was influenced by the Arts and Crafts movement as he explained what he wanted in the estate's design. The idea had been in his head for some time but it took Clymer and Drishcler, who had already built several Arts and Crafts bungalows in St. Louis, to put it onto paper. The resulting house embodied the main ideals of the Arts and Crafts movement with its use of local material, such as the local fieldstone that was used for exterior walls. It also incorporated bungalow elements, like exposed rafter tails, a low roof and the connection between the house and the gardens. Every room on the north, west and south sides of the house opened onto a wide terrace that provided a view of the river valley to the west. Edwin's passion for nature inspired the central atrium of the house, which became a scaled-down tropical rainforest.

In some degree, Edwin's love of nature proved that he was a child of the times. The late nineteenth and early twentieth century was marked by the birth of the American conservation movement. The roots of it lie in the writings and work of me like George Perkins Marsh and Henry David Thoreau, who presented arguments for preserving the American wilderness as early as the 1840s. Later, men such as Frederick Law Olmstead, John Burroughs, John Wesley Powell, John Muir and Theodore Roosevelt would further the conservation movement with their own writings. Olmstead not only designed New York's Central Park, he also did important work at Yosemite, Niagara Falls and the Adirondacks. Burroughs published a number of books that interested the public in conservation while Powell was the geologist who mapped the Grand

Canyon and the Rocky Mountains. Muir founded the Sierra Club and Theodore Roosevelt, as the twenty-sixth president of the United States, made conservation an important part of his domestic policy. In 1903, he established a federally protected wildlife refuge in Florida, the first of fifty-three that he would create as president. He also established national parks like Yellowstone and national monuments like the Grand Canyon in Arizona and the Natural Bridges in Utah.

Inside of the Cragwold *atrium*

Edwin was born in 1880 and grew up during the heyday of the American conservation movement. Not only was he well read and educated, but his love for nature drew him to the movement. He had been keeping canaries, parrots and exotic animals since he was a child and as an adult, with acres and acres of open land, he became known for his extensive animal collection. The estate became one of the earliest game farms in Missouri and was likely one of the earliest exotic animal preserves in the entire country. But this was not just the menagerie of an eccentric millionaire. Edwin was friendly with George Vierheller, the director of the St. Louis Zoon between 1922 and 1960. Edwin served on the Zoological Board of Control from the middle 1920s until 1945. During this time, he worked closely with Vierheller on plans to build a new Bird House and a new Antelope House. Many of the animals raised at *Cragwold* either started out at the zoo or ended up there. Edwin often purchased animals from the St. Louis Zoo when the herds needed to be thinned or he purchased animals from other zoos to breed and raised their offspring at his farm, a move that would benefit zoos across the country.

His collection began in the atrium, which originally contained only a few plants and a few parrots. Gradually, it turned into a lush jungle of tropical birds with trees and plants that grew all the way to the ceiling. He kept twenty-four varieties of parrots and just as many types of finches. Most of the parrots were kept in cages but the finches and other birds flew free. Among the collection were macaws, cockatoos, gray Java sparrows, Japanese Robins, a Russian Bullfinch, Amazon Parrots and a boisterous Macaw that would screech "Whiskey, doctor" at visitors and then make a chuckling sound. Edwin was particularly attached to this bird, which he had found in a New York pet shop.

A staff member in one of Edwin's farm trucks.

Edwin, later in life at Cragwold

When Edwin walked in, the bird had greeted him with a friendly, "How are you?" Edwin was so impressed that he bought it on the spot for $800. Another prized piece of his collection was a small Senegal parrot from Africa. It was the only such bird in captivity in the entire country.

Edwin also raised scores of other animals, including antelope, water buffalo, llamas, emus, Sacred Cattle from India, Siberian Yaks, buffalo, deer, antelope, Barbary sheep and many more. Twelve varieties of pheasants and sixty peacocks called the estate home and wandered near the scenic duck pond that contained, in addition to ducks, several types of cranes and aquatic birds.

While Edwin's love for animals and the outdoors may have defined his home and lifestyle, his interests were not confined to nature. Like the other members of his family, he had a taste for the finer things and his wealth allowed him to indulge in an extensive personal library, a collection of fine art and travel around the world. He was also a gourmet when it came to food and wine. While he was still working at the Lemp Brewery, he outfitted his office with a charcoal grill on which he created gourmet dinners for friends.

Edwin became known as not only a chef, but as a superb party planner. He was famous for his dinner parties and it became a treat to be one of his guests. Charles always issued invitations two weeks prior to the special evening. When one received one of his invitations, it was never turned down. Edwin would spend several days putting together the perfect guest list and once he made his selections final, he could never be persuaded to make changes or additions. He consulted on the menu with his German cook, and then Edwin carefully chose the correct china, dinner service and even the flowers for the centerpiece. Even well-traveled and experienced friends later commented that they had never attended such an exquisite dinner. Many of them campaigned for future invitations, but Edwin had his own method of choosing who attended, and on which night, and nothing that anyone said or did could sway him from his plans.

As amazing as Edwin's dinner parties were, he was equally acclaimed for what he called his "kitchen parties." These were dinners prepared for a handful of close friends. When once such evening was planned, Edwin gave the kitchen staff the night off, put on an apron himself and put together simple, but stunning, meals for his guests. The dinners were always served in the kitchen and often included scrambled eggs, steaks and a special baked potato, the recipe for which was a closely guarded secret. Every ingredient was fresh and of the highest quality, hand-picked from local farms. The meat was always locally butchered and with some recipes, he allowed it to marinate for weeks days before cooking and serving it.

Edwin had what was perhaps one of the first true gourmet kitchens in the region. It was outfitted with spices and ingredients from around the world, along with copper molds, special brushes and chef's tools, and heavy porcelain utensils and cook pots. Almost all of the cooking at *Cragwold* was done in porcelain because Edwin believed that metal cookware discolored food and took away its natural flavor. He rarely fried anything, preferring everything to be grilled, stewed, broiled or baked.

The kitchen was also equipped with a vast basement storage area, where Edwin kept cooking supplies and ingredients for months in advance. There were rows and rows of canned goods, imported caviar, anchovies, pickled mushrooms, brandied peaches, truffles and more. Condiments like mustard and pepper were ground by the cook. Edwin never let cost or distance stand in the way of the perfect meal and he thought nothing of sending away to New York, Milwaukee, London or Shanghai for a certain sauce or spice.

Edwin also had a passion for clothing. His formal, custom-made suits became his trademark. He enjoyed wearing a fine suit, even for ordinary occasions and always had a fresh carnation delivered each day to wear in his lapel. He was fortunate in that he could afford custom tailoring because there was little that he could buy off the rack. Like the rest of the men in his family, he was diminutive, standing only five feet, two inches tall. He spared no expense when it came to having clothing and shoes made. He purchased shirts by the dozen and used a converted bedroom and several walk-in closets to house his enormous wardrobe. His array of finery included more than two hundred coats and ninety pair of size six shoes and riding boots.

While Edwin loved to entertain, he also enjoyed the peace and tranquility of *Cragwold*, at least in the early years. On many mornings after breakfast Edwin took long, leisurely walks around the estate. He loved to read and play the piano and later, he had a swimming pool installed. Nestled among the garden trees, the pool was flanked by lily ponds and edged with spruce, cedar and papyrus grasses. He loved to bask in the sun after his afternoon swims.

The garden was also used for the small, intimate parties that he gave for his closest friends. The swimming pool was often filled with floating candles and gardenias, which filled the air with fragrance.

Several days each week, Edwin went into the city, where he kept an office on Seventh Street, near Olive. The office was not only a place to conduct business but was also a meeting place for his friends. Edwin often entertained there and at his suite at the Chase Hotel, which he used whenever he stayed overnight in St. Louis.

But Edwin mostly preferred to be at *Cragwold*, where he felt most at home. The estate was run with subtle care and precision. While it seemed to be a carefree, quiet place, Edwin preferred to have things done in certain ways. For example, at 6:00 p.m. each day, unless guests were expected, the gates to the estate were promptly locked. For many years, the household staff consisted of two butlers, a maid, and a houseman whose duty it was to feed, water and watch over the atrium birds. Two farmers were kept on staff to tend to Edwin's wildlife collection. The servants were quartered in cottages about one-quarter mile from the main house, hidden away in heavy woods and over a stone bridge. This gave the illusion each night that Edwin was totally alone on the estate, which he preferred during his younger years. Each night, in the quiet, he read in the library. He might curl up with a book and read all night if the notion appealed to him. His only companions in those days were his two German shepherds, Mike and Edith, who he called "Schatzi," the German word for sweetheart. The two dogs usually slept on his bed each night.

Edwin spent many years in solitude at *Cragwold* but only his nights were spent alone. His lavish parties and frequent dinners continued for decades. However, as he grew older, he became increasingly reclusive.

The last remaining piece from Edwin's art collection. Somehow, this photographic nude was not destroyed in the fire when John Bopp carried out his friend and employer's last wishes. The piece remains safely in the hands of family members today.

As friends passed away, he failed to make new ones. His entertaining became more and more infrequent and finally ceased altogether. He began avoiding people and yet, strangely, he was gripped with a growing fear of being left alone. The long nights spent in the house by himself became a thing of the past. He had managed to escape the family "curse," but as time passed, he grew more and more eccentric. He never spoke about his family or their tragic lives, but the events of the past must have preyed on him all the same. The fears that he developed led to him hiring a companion who would always stay with him at *Cragwold*.

His most loyal friend and companion was John Bopp, the caretaker of the estate for the last thirty years of Edwin's life. Bopp's loyalty to his employer was absolute and it is believed that he was never away from the estate for more than few days at a time during his entire tenure there. He never discussed any of Edwin's personal habits and remained faithful to him, even after his friend's death.

Edwin passed away quietly of natural causes at age ninety in 1970. The last order that John Bopp carried out for him must have been the most difficult. According to Edwin's wishes, he burned all of the paintings that Lemp had collected throughout his long life, as well as a number of priceless Lemp family papers and artifacts. These irreplaceable pieces of history vanished in the smoke of a blazing bonfire and like the glory days of the Lemp empire were lost forever.

16. "One of the Most Haunted Houses in America"

The Lemp Mansion was built in 1868 as a residence for Jacob Feickert, the father-in-law of William Lemp. As the Lemp Brewery grew and expanded, William built homes for his stepmother and for his wife's parents near the brewery and he began using the mansion as a residence and auxiliary brewing office. Although it was already an impressive place, William had the thirty-three-room home renovated into a showplace of the Gilded Age.

Always fascinated by new technology, William continued adding onto the house for the rest of his life. A radiator system was installed in 1884, five years after radiant heat was invented. The grand staircase was removed to install an open-air elevator. William's bathroom was dominated by a glass-enclosed, free-standing shower that William saw in an Italian hotel and had shipped back to St. Louis, where there was nothing like it at the time. At the rear of the house he installed three massive fireproof vaults where the Lemps stored their art collections. Each vault was fifteen feet wide, twenty-five feet deep, and thirteen feet high. Behind the parlor was an atrium filled with tropical plants and exotic birds. The house was remodeled again in 1904 and again in 1911, when it was turned into offices for the brewery. It underwent remodeling a third time in 1929, when Charles moved back home.

After Charles' suicide, the mansion was sold and turned into a boarding house. Shortly after that, it fell on hard times and began to deteriorate, along with the nearby neighborhood. In later years, stories began to emerge that residents of the boarding house often complained of hearing ghostly knocks and phantom footsteps in the house. As these tales spread, it became increasingly hard to find tenants to occupy the rooms and because of this, the former Lemp Mansion was rarely filled.

A strange account from the days following Charles' death was told to me by a woman who, as a young girl in 1949, decided to sneak into the house with some friends one day. The house was vacant at the time and the group managed to get in the front door. They started up the main staircase, climbing the steps to the first landing and preparing to go up the last flight of stairs to the upper level. Just as they

An early illustration of the Lemp Mansion

The Lemp Mansion in 1922 during Billy Lemp's funeral.

reached the landing, they looked up and saw a filmy apparition coming down the steps toward them. The woman described it as looking like an almost human-shaped puff of smoke. The group took one look at it and bolted. When she told this story for the first time in the late 1990s, the woman, who was quite elderly by that time, stated that she had never been back in the mansion since.

The house's decline continued until 1975, when Richard Pointer and his family purchased it. The Pointers began remodeling and renovating the place, working for many years to turn it into a combination restaurant and inn. But they were soon to find out that they were not alone in the house. The bulk of the remodeling was done in the 1970s and during this time, construction workers reported that ghostly events were occurring in the house. Almost all of them confessed that they believed the place was haunted and told of feeling as though they were being watched. They spoke of hearing unexplained sounds and complained of tools that vanished and then returned in different places from where they had been left.

At one point in the renovations, a painter was brought in to work on the ceilings. He stayed in the house overnight while he completed the job. One day, he ran downstairs to tell one of the Pointers that he had heard the sound of horses' hooves on the cobblestones outside his window. Pointer convinced the painter that he was mistaken; there were no horses and no cobblestones outside the house. In time, the man finished the ceilings and left, but the story stayed on Pointer's mind. Later that year, he noticed that some of the grass in the yard had turned brown. He dug it up and found that beneath the top level of soil was a layer of cobblestones. During the Lemps' residency in the house, that portion of the yard had been a drive leading to the carriage house.

Later in the restoration, another artist was brought in to restore the painted ceiling in one of the front dining rooms. It had been covered over with paper years before. While he was lying on his back on the scaffolding, the artist felt a sensation of what he believed was a "spirit" moving past him. It frightened him so badly that he left the house without his brushes and tools and refused to return and get them. A few months after this event, an elderly man came into the restaurant and told one of the staff members that he had once been a driver for the Lemp family. He explained that the ceiling in the dining room had been papered over because William Lemp hated the design that had been painted on it. The staff members, upon hearing this story, recalled the artist saying that he had gotten the distinct impression that the "spirit" he encountered had been angry. Was it perhaps because he was restoring the unwanted ceiling painting?

During the restorations, Pointer's son, Dick, lived alone in the house and became quite an expert on the ghostly manifestations. One night, he was lying in bed reading when he heard a door slam loudly in another part of the house. No one else was supposed to be there and he was sure that he had locked all of the doors. Fearing that someone might have broken in, he and his dog, a Doberman pinscher named Shadow, decided to take a look around. The dog was spooked by this time, and having also heard the sound, she had her ears turned up, listening for anything else. They searched the entire house and found no one there. Every door was locked, just as Pointer had left them. He reported that the same thing happened again about a month later; again, nothing was found.

After the restaurant opened, staff members began to report their own odd experiences. Glasses were seen to lift off the bar and fly through the air, sounds were often heard that had no explanation and some people even glimpsed apparitions that appeared and vanished at will. In addition, many customers and visitors to the house reported some pretty weird incidents. It was said that doors locked and unlocked on their own, the piano in the bar played by itself, voices and sounds came from nowhere and the ghost of a woman was seen occasionally. Some claimed that it was Lillian Handlan, Billy's ex-wife and the famed "Lavender Lady," even though she never actually lived in the house. Perhaps the indignities that she suffered at the hands of her former husband managed to draw her to his family's home after death.

Late one evening, Dick was bartending after most of the customers had departed. He noticed the water in a pitcher was swirling around of its own volition. He thought he was imagining it but all of the customers who remained that night swore they saw the same thing. Then, one night in August 1981, Dick and an employee were startled to hear the piano play a few notes by itself. There was no one around it at the time and in fact, no one else was in the entire building. The piano has continued to be the source of eerie occurrences as the years have passed. No matter where it has been placed in the house, whether in the main hallway upstairs or in one of the guest rooms, its keys have reportedly tinkled without the touch of human

Lemp Mansion dining room

hands.

And while the ghostly atmosphere of the place has admittedly attracted a number of curious patrons, it has also caused the Pointers to lose a number of valuable employees. One of them was a former waitress named Bonnie Strayhorn, who encountered an unusual customer while working one day. The restaurant had not yet opened for business when she saw a dark-haired man seated at one of the tables in the rear dining room. She was surprised that someone had come in so early, but she went over to ask if he would like a cup of coffee. He simply sat unmoving and did not answer. Bonnie frowned and glanced away for a moment. When she looked back moments later, the man was gone. She has continued to maintain that he could not have left the room in the brief seconds when she was not looking at him. After that incident, she left the Lemp Mansion and went to work in a non-haunted location.

The house has attracted ghost hunters from around the country. Many of them are lured by the publicity the house has received as a haunted location. The mansion has appeared in scores of magazines, newspaper articles, books and television shows over the years, first gaining national attention in November 1980 when *Life* magazine included it in an article entitled "Terrifying Tales of Nine Haunted Houses."

The first local notoriety gained by the mansion as a haunted place can be traced back to the 1970s, when it was investigated by the "Haunt Hunters." These two St. Louis men, Phil Goodwilling and Gordon Hoener, actively researched ghost stories and sightings in the area and during that period, they conducted a class on ghosts at St. Louis University. They promised their students that they would take them to a real haunted place and decided that the Lemp Mansion fit the bill. In October 1979, they brought the class to the house and invited along a local television crew to film the event.

Goodwilling and Hoener divided the students into groups of four and gave each group a writing planchette to try and contact the spirits. The devices, like the small rolling platforms that come with Ouija boards, were supposed to be used to spell out messages from the ghosts.

One of the groups asked: "Is there an unseen presence that wishes to communicate?"

"Yes," came the answer scrawled on a large piece of paper as the planchette, with its pencil tip, moved across the surface.

The students asked another question: "Will you identify yourself?"

The planchette scratched out a reply: "Charles Lemp."

Goodwilling later noted that the students who received this message were the most skeptical in the class. He also noted that no one in the room that night, with the exception of Dick Pointer, had any idea that Charles had committed suicide. At that time, the history of the house had not been widely publicized.

After the name was revealed, the spirit added that he had taken his own life. When asked why he did this, the spirit replied in three words: "Help, death, rest."

It might also be added that by the time this séance was over, the four students were no longer the most skeptical in the class.

In November, the Haunt Hunters returned to the house, bringing along a camera crew from the popular show of the era, *Real People*. Goodwilling and Hoener participated in a séance with two other persons, neither of whom had any knowledge about the past history of the mansion. They once again made contact with a spirit who identified himself as Charles Lemp. They asked a question: "Is there a message for someone in this house?"

The answer came: "Yes, yes, Edwin, money."

The group then asked if there was anything they could do to free the spirit from being trapped in the house. "Yes, yes," the ghost replied. Unfortunately, they were unsuccessful in finding out what they could do to help.

Goodwilling felt that if the spirit was actually Charles Lemp, then he might have stayed behind in the house because of his suicide. He might have had a message for his brother, Edwin Lemp, whom he tried to contact during the séance. He may have believed that Edwin was still alive and based on the conversation, was trying to pass along a message about money. Could this be what caused Charles Lemp's ghost to remain behind?

Most important perhaps, to the reader is the question of whether the Lemp Mansion still remains haunted today. Many will tell you that it does. The current owners accept this as an aspect of the house's unusual ambience. One of them, Paul Pointer, helps to maintain the place as a popular eating and lodging establishment. He says he accepts the ghosts as just another part of this unique mansion. "People come here expecting to experience weird things," he said, "and fortunately for us, they are rarely disappointed."

I first heard about the Lemp Mansion and its hauntings back in the early 1990s, when the first (wildly skewed) stories about the ghosts began to appear in what few ghost books were available in those days. At my first opportunity, I traveled to St. Louis to see the house and a couple of years later I spent the night there for the first time. Even then, it was an amazing house, although the bed and breakfast service was in its early stages. I stayed there on a scorching June night with a few friends and aside from a couple of struggling window units, there were no cooling system in the place. The house was stifling until about 2:00 a.m., when it finally started to cool down.

On the bright side, we had the entire place to ourselves and Paul Pointer gave us permission to roam anywhere we wanted to. We took him up on it and scoured the mansion from top to bottom in search of not only ghosts, but an entrance to the legendary caverns that were supposed to exist under the house. The book that I had read, which featured the Lemp Mansion, had been badly out of date and it stated that the caves were accessible from the mansion. Later, when I started researching the house for my own writings about the Lemp family, I would find out that the cave entrance in the basement had been closed for many years. I never gave up on the idea of getting into the cave, however, and eventually, my persistence paid off (as recounted in an earlier chapter of this book).

My first stay in the Lemp Mansion was largely uneventful, although there was one incident that occurred that I have never been able to explain. At some point, around 3:00 a.m., we heard someone on the main staircase that leads from the front foyer to the second floor. We were sitting in the hallway at the top of the stairs, talking quietly, when we heard what sounded like heavy footsteps. One of my friends got up and walked over to see if someone, perhaps one of the staff members, had returned to the mansion. She called the rest of us over when she noticed that although we could all still hear someone walking, there was no one on the staircase! All of us witnessed this eerie phenomenon, which continued for several minutes and went up and down the stairs several times.

While it was occurring, I went down the stairs to see if I could sense anyone going past me, or if there was a temperature change or some sort of movement. I never

Author Leslie Rule

felt a thing but there was no denying that we could hear someone walking. The footsteps continued for a few minutes and then stopped. We looked under the steps, up and down them and even tried measuring and jumping on them. We were unable to duplicate the sounds that we heard. It sounded exactly like someone wearing heavy boots pacing back and forth and if they were anything else I can't begin to imagine what it was.

In August 2003, I invited my friend Leslie Rule, a fellow ghost writer and the daughter of crime author Ann Rule, to come to Alton, Illinois, and speak at an event that I was hosting there. She had wanted to stay somewhere haunted while in the area and I helped her to make arrangements to stay at the Lemp Mansion for several nights. She was very excited at the prospect until she called to make reservations and was told by co-owner Patty Pointer that she would have the mansion all to herself during her stay. Leslie was not enthused about sleeping in a haunted house alone and she asked me if I knew of anyone who would consider staying with her. I suggested that she contact my friend Anita Dytuco and together, they planned an overnight at the mansion.

Anita and her twenty-two-year-old daughter, Amy, picked up Leslie at the airport and all of us met for dinner. Anita and Amy had stopped by the mansion before dinner, picked up the keys and turned on the lights in their rooms "as a test," Amy explained. Since the lights in the empty house had a reputation for turning themselves off and on, she wanted to see what would happen. When we went back to the house after dinner and found that some of the lights were no longer on, though, she nervously dismissed this as someone playing a joke on them.

I wouldn't find out how scared Amy was about staying in the house until after I talked to her and Anita a few days later. Leslie later told me that the young woman was very tentative about exploring the house with her and that it took some urging to get her into some of the creepier parts, like the dark and ominous attic. To make matters worse, their flashlight batteries unexpectedly went out while they were in the attic, unsettling Amy even further.

But perhaps Amy had a good reason to be unsettled. A number of women who have worked in the house and have stayed the night there have had encounters with a female spirit or have heard someone calling their names. Some believe this spirit may be that of Elsa Lemp, who, while she did not die in the house, spent a large part of her life here. They were her happiest times and perhaps she has returned there seeking peace after her death. Regardless of who this lovely spirit may be, many women have encountered her --- including Amy.

A few days after her nerve-wracking stay, Amy told me that she had been trying go to sleep next to her mother in the Lavender Suite on the second floor and was having trouble dozing off. After tossing and turning for a while, she turned over and was terrified to see a woman in a long dress standing next to the bed. The woman looked very real but there was no way that she could have gotten into the room through the locked door. Before Amy could do or say anything, the woman leaned toward her, placed a finger to her lips in a "shushing" motion, as if to tell Amy to be quiet and go to sleep. The woman then simply vanished! Needless to say, Amy did not sleep for the rest of the night.

The next overnight that I hosted at the Lemp Mansion was in May 2004. It was a few days after the May 10 anniversary of Charles Lemp's suicide and I was joined at the house by a number of investigators, as well as my friends Dave Goodwin, Darren Deist, Rex Murray and Amanda Schmitt. We all enjoyed working with the various groups as they began their investigations. At one point, a strange event occurred that I was lucky enough to witness for myself.

One of the standard things that we do at the Lemp Mansion is bring along a Ouija board and give people a chance to work with in the house. Without going into the pros and cons of using a Ouija board, the reader may have noticed from earlier in the chapter that such devices have been involved with investigations at the house since the "Haunt Hunters" days of the 1970s. I always bring along a board and make it available for people to use if they choose to. Just to make it interesting, I tracked down and purchased an antique board that was made in 1915. I figured that if we were going to use a Ouija board in the Lemp Mansion, we might as well use one that came from the era when the place was in its heyday.

On this night, I put the Ouija board on a small table in the unfinished portion of the attic (which has since been remodeled into guest rooms) and placed some chairs around it to make it easier to use. The attic was quite a mess at that time. There were pieces of wood and old doors stacked around, and the air was thick with years of dust and grime. Previous visitors to the attic had left items behind, including a number of small candles that apparently been set up for a séance of some sort. The candles had burned down to the wick, leaving small foil holders scattered all over the attic's main room.

Throughout the evening, the separate groups took turns using the board during the time they were assigned to that section of the house. Nothing out of the ordinary took place as the evening went by but people were intrigued with the idea of experimenting with the antique Ouija board.

Just after midnight, I went up to the attic where Rex, Amanda, Darren and Dave were trying out the board. I sat down in one of the chairs and watched as Darren and Amanda tried to coax messages from any spirits who might be hanging around. For the next twenty minutes or so, they had absolutely no luck. Their fingers were placed lightly on the planchette and they asked question after question, waiting to see if it moved but nothing happened ---- nothing at all.

Finally, after another five minutes or so of frustration, Darren let out a sigh and suggested that someone else might want to give the board a try. Almost as soon as he spoke, all of us present heard the sound of something sliding across the floor. No one had been standing near it but somehow, one of the little candleholders had moved across the floor under its own power. The candleholder slid about ten feet, from one side of the room to the other, passing directly beneath Darren's chair! The room was now so quiet that you could have heard the proverbial pin drop.

"What was that?" someone asked and we quickly deduced that it had

The Lemp Mansion attic before the recent renovations.

Infrared photos taken during the séance in the attic. The lower photo was taken just seconds after the first and shows the blurred image of a man standing behind the table. There was no one else in the room at the time.

been one of the candleholders but we were unable to figure out just how it had moved.

We spent the next hour or so waiting to see if anything else would happen, but nothing else occurred. I have never been able to come up with an explanation for how the candleholder moved, other than to say that perhaps it was one of the spirits in the house. Were they trying to make themselves known to us and couldn't do it in any other way?

Since that time, I have visited and stayed the night at the Lemp Mansion on many other occasions. On one visit, soon after the incident with the candleholder, I was photographing another session with the Ouija board in the attic. Three young men who had joined me that night were using the board, while the father of one of them one of them and I were standing in the doorway watching. As I photographed the group huddled around the Ouija board, I noticed something very odd on the viewing screen of my camera — there was a fourth person in the room, standing behind them. The photo showed a blur of movement as this person moved past the table. I immediately showed the photo to the man standing next to me and he agreed that no one else had been in the room.

During another evening, I was joined by my friend John Winterbauer, who handles many events for my ghost tour companies. Everyone in our group had left for the night around 4:30 a.m. and John and I were going through the house, straightening chairs and making sure that everything was in order. The restaurant staff always left the dining rooms set up for the next day when they left at night and occasionally, our guests will move chairs or table items during the investigations. We had just finished in the front dining room (Billy Lemp's former office) when we heard the sound of breaking glass in the atrium in the back of the house. Fearing that perhaps a glass had been left too close to the edge of a table and had fallen and broken on the tile floor, we went back to take a look. I turned on the lights and we both looked around but there was nothing to see – nothing moved, there was no broken glass, nothing at all. We had no idea where the sound could have come from but wherever a glass had shattered, it had not been in our world!

As Paul Pointer once said, those who come to this house are rarely disappointed and I would have to agree. While not all of my stays at this old house have been eventful ones, at least when it comes to ghosts, I have to admit that the vivid sense of history that I have experienced when I'm here more than makes up for the lack of anything supernatural. If you're a ghost hunter, or a history buff, then I encourage you to visit the mansion of the once-mighty Lemp family. Their empire may have crumbled long ago but there is much to see here among the ruins of yesteryear.

BIBLIOGRAPHY

& RECOMMENDED READING

Amsler, Kevin – *Final Resting Place: Lives & Deaths of Famous St. Louisians*; 1997
Anderson, Will – *The Beer Book*; 1973
Baron, Stanley Wade – *Brewed in America*; 1962
Bartley, Mary – *St. Louis Lost*; 1994
Clevenger, Martha R. – *Indescribably Grand*; 1996
Cochran, Thomas C. – *The Pabst Brewing Company*; 1948
Corbett, Katherine T. and Howard S. Miller – *St. Louis in the Gilded Age*; 1993
Courtaway, Robbi – *Wetter than the Mississippi: Prohibition in St. Louis and Beyond*; 2008
Dry, Camile N. – *Pictorial St. Louis: The Great Metropolis of the Mississippi Valley*; 1875
Gill, McCune – *The St. Louis Story*; 1952
Goodwilling, Phil and Gordon Hoener – *Haunt Hunters*; 1981
Griesedieck, Alvin – *The Falstaff Story*; 1951
Herbst, Henry, Don Roussin and Kevin Kious – *St. Louis Brews: 200 Years of Brewing in St. Louis*; 2009
Hernon, Peter and Terry Ganey – *Under the Influence*; 1991
Holland, Gerald – *The King of Beer* (*American Mercury* Magazine); 1929
Jarvis, Sharon – *Dark Zones*; 1992
Kirschten, Ernest – *Catfish and Crystal*; 1960
Loughlin, Caroline and Catherine Anderson – *Forest Park*; 1986
McNulty, Elizabeth – *St. Louis Then and Now*; 2000

Ogle, Maureen – *Ambitious Brew: The Story of American Beer*, 2006
Plavchan, Ronald Jan – *History of Anheuser-Busch*, 1976
Primm, James Neal- *Lion of the Valley: St. Louis, Missouri*, 1981
Riccio, Dolores and Joan Bingham – *Haunted Houses USA*, 1989
Rother, Hubert and Charlotte – *Lost Caves of St. Louis*, 1996
Samuel, Ray, Leonard Huber and Warren Ogden – *Tales of the Mississippi*, 1955
Taylor, Troy – *Haunted St. Louis*, 2002
---------------- – *Haunting of America*, 2009
Toft, Carolyn – *St. Louis Landmarks and Historic Districts*, 2002
Walker, Stephen – *Lemp: The Hauntings History*, 1988
Weaver, H. Dwight – *Missouri Caves in History and Legend*, 2008
Winter, William C. – *The Civil War in St. Louis*, 1994
Witherspoon, Margaret Johansen – *Remembering the St. Louis World's Fair*, 1973
Yenne, Bill – *Beers of North America*, 1986

Personal Interviews, Correspondence and Recollections

Magazines, Periodicals, etc.
American Brewer
Jopin (Missouri) News-Herald
Mirror
Missouri Gazette
Missouri Republican
National Register of Historic Places
Riverfront Times
St. Louis Globe-Democrat
St. Louis Post-Dispatch
St. Louis Republic
St. Louis Star
Western Brewer

Special Thanks to:
Jill Hand – Editor
Mike Schwab – Cover Design
Andrew Paulsen
Cheryl Sochotsky
Stephanie Malcom
Len Adams
Steve Mangin
John Winterbauer
Dave Goodwin
Darren Deist
The Pointer Family
Stephen Walker
Rachel Morris
Helayna Taylor

ABOUT THE AUTHOR

Troy Taylor is an occultist, crime buff, supernatural historian and the author of nearly 80 books on ghosts, hauntings, history, crime and the unexplained in America.

He is also the founder of the American Ghost Society and the owner of the American Hauntings Tour company.

Taylor shares a birthday with one of his favorite authors, F. Scott Fitzgerald, but instead of living in New York and Paris like Fitzgerald, Taylor grew up in Illinois. Raised on the prairies of the state, he developed an interest in "things that go bump in the night" at an early age and as a young man, began developing ghost tours and writing about hauntings and crime in Chicago and Central Illinois. His writings have now taken him all over the country and into some of the most far-flung corners of the world.

He began his first book in 1989, which delved into the history and hauntings of his hometown of Decatur, Illinois, and in 1994, it spawned the Haunted Decatur Tour -- and eventually led to the founding of his Illinois Hauntings Tours (with current tours in Alton, Chicago, Decatur, Lebanon, Springfield & Jacksonville) and the American Hauntings Tours, which travel all over the country in search of haunted places.

Along with writing about the unusual and hosting tours, Taylor has also presented on the subjects of ghosts, hauntings and crime for public and private groups. He has also appeared in scores of newspaper and magazine articles about these subjects and in hundreds of radio and television broadcasts about the supernatural. Taylor has appeared in a number of documentary films, several television series and in one feature film about the paranormal.

When not traveling to the far-flung reaches of the country, Troy resides in Chicago.

Information on Troy's books and tour companies can be found at www.americanhauntings.org

CPSIA information can be obtained at www.ICGtesting.com

235049LV00002B/41-42/P

9 781892 523730